MODERN EGYPT

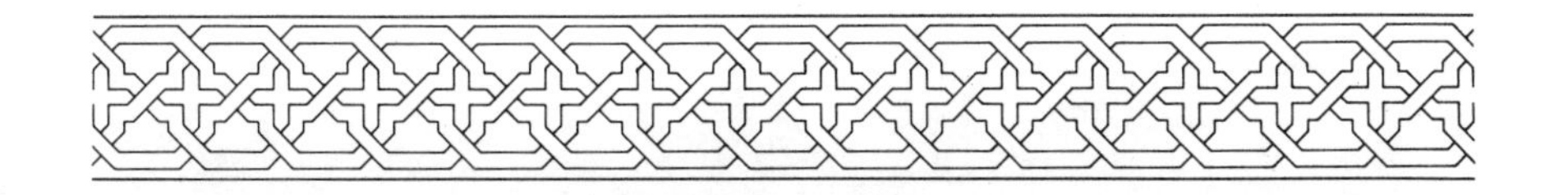

MODERN EGYPT

The Formation of a Nation-State

ARTHUR GOLDSCHMIDT, JR.

Westview Press / BOULDER, COLORADO

Hutchinson / LONDON MELBOURNE AUCKLAND JOHANNESBURG

Published in 1988 in the United States of America by Westview Press, Inc., 5500 Central Avenue, Boulder, Colorado 80301

Published in 1988 in Great Britain by Hutchinson Education, an imprint of Century Hutchinson Ltd, 62–65 Chandos Place, London WC2N 4NW

Century Hutchinson Australia Pty Ltd, PO Box 496, 16–22 Church Street, Hawthorn, Victoria 3122, Australia; Century Hutchinson New Zealand Limited, PO Box 40-086, Glenfield, Auckland 10, New Zealand; Century Hutchinson South Africa (Pty) Ltd, PO Box 337, Bergvlei, 2012 South Africa

Library of Congress Cataloging-in-Publication Data
Goldschmidt, Arthur, 1938–
Modern Egypt: the formation of a nation-state/Arthur Goldschmidt, Jr.
p. cm.
Bibliography: p.
Includes index.
ISBN 0-86531-182-X
ISBN 0-86531-183-8 (If published in PB)
1. Egypt—History—1798– . I. Title.
DT100.G65 1988
962—dc19

87-34551
CIP

British Library Cataloguing in Publication Data
Goldschmidt, Arthur, *1938–*
Modern Egypt: the formation of a nation state.
1. Egypt, history
I. Title
962
ISBN (UK) 0 09 175711 8

Printed and bound in the United States of America

The paper used in this publication meets the requirements of the American National Standard for Permanence of Paper for Printed Library Materials Z39.48-1984.

10 9 8 7 6 5 4 3 2 1

This book is dedicated to the memory of Kent Forster,
a member of the Department of History
at the Pennsylvania State University from 1940 to 1980,
department head for eleven of those years, and
a teacher, scholar, traveler, counselor, and friend

Contents

Preface ix

1 *Introduction* 1

2 *Napoleon and Mehmet Ali* 13

3 *The Rise of Western Influence* 23

4 *The British Occupation* 33

5 *Nationalist Resistance* 43

6 *Egypt's Ambiguous Independence* 55

7 *The Turning Point* 67

8 *The 1952 Revolution* 79

9 *The Revolution Matures* 95

10 *The Socialist Phase* 115

11 *The Opening and the Crossing* 137

12 *Since Sadat* 163

Glossary of Terms and Places 169
Biographical Dictionary 179
Bibliographic Essay 185
Index 195

Preface

Many people have attempted to write histories of modern Egypt, for the country seems to invite them. Of the twenty or more Arabic-speaking states, Egypt is the largest and the one with the most extensive recorded past. It has been a distinct political, economic, and cultural entity for a longer period of time than any other Middle Eastern state. Its independence struggle lasted longer and was more thoroughly chronicled than any other nationalist movement in the modern Arab world. Even though other histories of modern Egypt have been written in recent years, this one is addressed primarily to those readers not already conversant with the subject: to English-speaking university students, journalists, diplomats, travelers, new residents in the country, and others who may need a concise sketch of Egypt's evolution since its initial contacts with the West. This book will try to synthesize the findings of an intimidating array of scholarly books and articles that have appeared in recent years, in order to correct common misconceptions about Egypt's modern history. Although it is not footnoted, a lengthy bibliographic essay directs readers to further sources of information about the various subjects covered.

I would like to thank the following people for their guidance and advice: Carter Findley for being the first to ask me to write it; Lynne Rienner for agreeing, a long time ago, to let me write it for Westview Press; Kenneth Mayers for his research assistance and advice; Bahgat Korany and Afaf Lutfi al-Sayyid-Marsot for the extensive comments and criticisms that they wrote as publishers' readers; my senior seminar students in the spring semester of 1986 who read and critiqued the first draft of this book and, most of all, Christopher Manson, who reread it after the seminar was over; Magdy and Lydia Taha, Thomas Mayer, and my parents for also reading the manuscript and suggesting corrections; Holly Arrow and Jennifer Knerr of Westview Press for managing the project; Christine Arden for copyediting the work; Edythe Porpa for indexing it; and Don Kunze for preparing the maps. As authors must, I assume responsibility for any remaining errors of fact or interpretation.

I acknowledge also the support that I received from the Pennsylvania State University for a sabbatical leave and from the Council for the International Exchange of Scholars for a Fulbright Research Fellowship that I received in 1981–1982 to do the preliminary work on this book in Cairo. The Fulbright Commission's Cairo office and the history department of Cairo University helped me on the local scene. I also wish to acknowledge the benefit of the seminars of the American Research Center in Egypt and of the historians' "Nadwa" at Ayn Shams University for making me familiar with the research currently being conducted in modern Egyptian history.

This book is dedicated to the memory of a departed colleague, Kent Forster, who served as our department head for a long time, offered sound advice and encouragement to younger scholars, and (together with his wife, Jean) was a devoted friend to my wife and me and to many students and scholars coming from the Middle East. Kent visited Egypt only briefly, but he took a great interest in the country and in the Arab world generally. Without his help in advising me and securing for me a sabbatical leave when I was starting this project, this book could not have been written. I wish that he had lived to read it.

Arthur Goldschmidt, Jr.

CHAPTER ONE

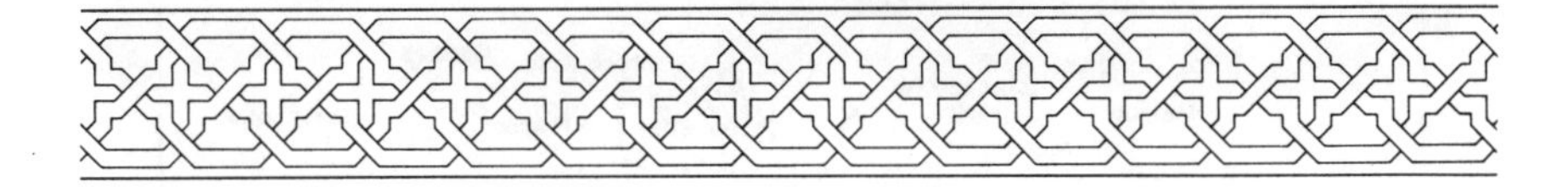

Introduction

Egypt means many things to many people. Few countries have more identities than Egypt. It is the land of the great River Nile; without its waters there would be no Egypt. It is a desert country; 97 percent of its land area is dry waste. Egypt is a Mediterranean country: more than half of its trade is with lands whose shores are washed by the same sea, and Egyptians share many of the folkways and customs of other peoples living on its shores. Its second largest city, Alexandria, has been a major Mediterranean port since it was founded by Alexander the Great, for whom it is named. Its third largest town, Port Said, lies at the junction of the Mediterranean and the Suez Canal. Egypt belongs also to the Red Sea; its ports at Suez and Qusayr connect with Arabia, Yemen, Ethiopia, and lands east. Situated in North Africa, Egypt is a bridge not only between the Arab West (*al-Maghrib*) and the Arab East (*al-Mashriq*) but also between pale Europeans and dark-skinned Africans. It is the most populous state in the Arab world and in that respect is second only to Turkey in the Middle East. Its capital, Cairo, is the largest city in the Arab world and is commonly regarded as its cultural and political center. By the same token, it is the largest city in Africa and has long served as the continent's chief commercial entrepôt.

Egypt, to most of its citizens, is a Muslim country, one of the first in Islamic history. It contains the millenary University of al-Azhar. It was Islam's greatest power center from the fall of the Abbasid caliphate until the rise of the Ottoman Empire. It has been the home or the refuge of many great Muslim thinkers from Imam al-Shafi'i to Ibn Khaldun to Muhammad Abduh. To some (and, long ago, most) Egyptians, it has been a Christian country, the refuge for the Holy Family, the land evangelized by St. Mark, the home of such church fathers as Arius and Athanasius, and the birthplace of monasticism. Before

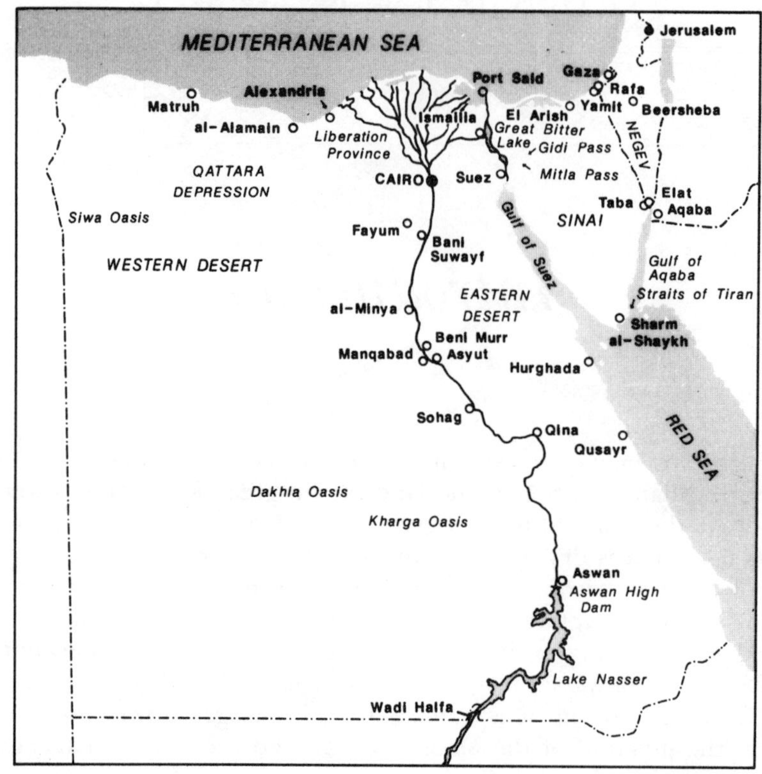

MAP 1. Modern Egypt

either Islam or Christianity existed, ancient Egypt helped give birth to Judaism, back when Abraham led his family and flocks into the land of Goshen, when Joseph counseled pharaohs, and when the infant Moses was found in the bulrushes. To tourists, and to generations of schoolchildren, Egypt is the archetypal ancient land of pharaohs, temples, pyramids, sphinxes, and obelisks.

To today's superpowers, Egypt is a strategic point in a deadly struggle for world mastery. A century ago, it was equally central in the rivalries and schemes of the European great powers. Napoleon Bonaparte called it "the world's most important country." From the seventh century to the nineteenth, Egypt was the linchpin of many Muslim dynastic states. Before that time, it was the granary for the Macedonian, Roman, and Byzantine empires. One must go back to the sixth century before the birth of Christ to find Egypt under the rule of Egyptians.

Since 1952, however, Egypt has definitely been ruled by Egyptians, though often in league with outside powers. Aside from the fluctuating influence of the United States and the USSR, Egypt's leaders have had to decide whether they were ruling an Arab, a Muslim, an African, a Nilotic, or a Mediterranean country. They have usually steered their policies by what they viewed as Egypt's best interests, but the issue of identity has remained a major one for politically articulate Egyptians. This book will treat that issue frequently.

Egypt is a many-faceted country. It may be viewed from many sides, or approached from many disciplinary angles. I have chosen history, not only because I have been trained as a historian but also because this perspective lets me adopt the viewpoints of a geographer, archaeologist, ethnologist, economist, political scientist, sociologist, and artist, as the need arises. My aim is to enable English-speaking students, journalists, new residents, and short-term visitors to understand what Egypt is, how it got to be that way, and where it is heading.

The Physical Environment

Egypt occupies the northeastern corner of the African continent, plus the Sinai Peninsula. Rainfall is scarce, except along the coast. Egypt depends almost entirely on the River Nile, which enters from the Sudan, passes through mountains of sandstone, tumbles down cataracts near Aswan, then rolls grandly along a wide river bed overlooked by limestone hills. After passing Cairo, it splits into several branches, creating the famous Delta, and empties into the Mediterranean Sea. No brooks or streams feed the river in Egypt. Much of the land is flat. The farther south one moves from the Mediterranean, the drier it becomes, and the more the temperature varies between summer and winter, or between day and night. Egypt's largest region is its Western, or Libyan, Desert. Except for scattered oases that support human habitation, it is an arid land typified by wind-blown sand, stony plains, and a few rugged mountains in the extreme southwest. The Eastern Desert is more mountainous and cut up by dry river beds that sometimes swell with water after heavy downpours. The Sinai Peninsula has rugged mountains in the south, large central plateaus, and a hilly Mediterranean coast. It, too, is sparsely inhabited.

Human Adaptation

If there had been no Nile, human habitation would have been limited to a narrow strip, in no case wider than 30 miles (48 kilometers), along the shores of the Mediterranean and Red seas. But even this great river could not have sustained human life, had the ancient

Egyptians not learned how to channel its annual flood, to store its waters for the dry season, and to plant their crops in its fertile alluvium. Most of the crops that we now associate with Egyptian agriculture were not native to the region; the ancients cultivated mainly emmer (a grain resembling wheat), barley, millet, dates, sycamore figs, grapes, and flax. They raised cattle akin to the African zebu, as well as donkeys, pigs, goats, and sheep. They harpooned fish from the Nile and snared waterfowl near its banks. Channeling, storing, and raising the Nile waters called for heavy and unremitting toil. Only a small elite of kings, nobles, priests, and warriors took part in that rich culture associated with ancient Egypt during the Archaic Period (3200–2680 B.C.) and under the Old Kingdom (2680–2258) and the Middle Kingdom (2150–1785).

Although the cliffs lining the Nile Valley caused the ancient Egyptians to view themselves as an isolated people, their land actually lay in the path of numerous routes used by traders and invaders. Around 1730 B.C. Egypt was conquered by West Asian horse nomads, the Hyksos, who became its first foreign rulers. After the Egyptians won back their independence and formed the New Kingdom (1580–1085), they became more militarized and imperialistic, extending their rule southward into Kush (now the Sudan) and eastward into Syria. Later, the Egyptians fell successively under the rule of Libyans from the west, Kushites from the south, and Assyrians and Persians from the east. Although Egyptian rulers managed each time to regain control of the land, Egypt could no longer isolate itself from its neighbors. Finally, when Alexander's Macedonians conquered Egypt in 332 B.C., the Egyptians ceased to be the masters in their own house. They did not, however, cease to be Egyptians.

An old Arab legend tells us that, when God created the peoples of the world, He let each of them choose some desirable attribute, but along with this endowment they would get a divine curse. The nomads of the Arabian Peninsula asked for freedom. "Very well," said the Lord, "I will give you vast deserts in which to roam with your flocks of goats and camels. No one will be able to rule over you. But with your freedom you will have poverty." Then He turned to the Syrians, who demanded brains, and said: "I will give you intelligence, nay, the brightest minds in all my creation. You will be the shrewdest merchants, the finest scholars, and the inventors of the greatest religions and philosophies. With your brains, though, you will have discord: You will be constantly at war with your neighbors, and among yourselves." Turning to the Egyptians, the Lord asked what they wanted. "We want never to go hungry," they replied. "All right," God said: "You will get the Nile. It will flood its banks regularly and water and fertilize your crops, so that you will have plenty to eat. But this will make you the envy of all other nations, and they will come into your country and rule over you. For this, you will always serve outsiders." And so, until oil was discovered in Arabia, the Arabs enjoyed freedom amid poverty, the Syrians were bright but contentious, and the Egyptians prospered under foreign domination.

Egyptians Under the Rule of Foreigners

Among the peoples of the ancient Near East, only the Egyptians have stayed where they were and remained what they were, although they have changed their language once and their religion twice. In a sense, they constitute the world's oldest nation. For most of their history, Egypt has been a state, but only in recent years has it been truly a nation-state, with a government claiming the allegiance of its subjects on the basis of a common identity. This is why I chose to call this book *Modern Egypt: The Formation of a Nation-State.*

From 332 B.C. until 1952 non-Egyptians governed the land while the Egyptians toiled to support them. Alexander's heirs, the Ptolemies, ruled until the time of Cleopatra (d. 30 B.C.), when Egypt fell under the control of the Romans. For almost seven centuries, Egypt remained a valued province of the Roman Empire and its successor state, Byzantium—so valued, in fact, that its peasants were forbidden to leave their land, because Egypt was a major source of Roman grain. A small Roman elite, concentrated mainly in Alexandria, lived comfortably, and many Egyptians, not to mention Jews, Greeks, and other peoples, strove to become like them. But most of the people remained peasant cultivators, differing little from their ancestors.

Christian Egypt

The Egyptians were among the first people to be exposed to Christianity. By the fourth century the country was predominantly Christian. During the Christological disputes of the fourth and fifth centuries, however, Egypt became estranged from the Orthodox church. The issue, somewhat abstruse to the modern mind, centered on the nature of Christ. It grew out of a disagreement between two Egyptian Christian thinkers: Arius, who believed in the primacy of Christ's human nature, and Athanasius, who stressed his divinity. At the Council of Nicaea (A.D. 325) the church fathers had agreed with Athanasius that Christ was the son of God, a person in the holy trinity. But was his nature human, divine, or some combination of both? Some Christians espoused what came to be called the Monophysite view, viewing Christ as wholly divine. Most Egyptian priests and their laity adopted this doctrine, as did many Christians farther east. At the Council of Chalcedon (A.D. 451), however, the majority of the bishops present denounced Monophysitism. Most Egyptian Christians rejected the Chalcedonian decision and came to feel estranged from the Orthodox church, centered in Constantinople, which continued to tax them to support a hierarchy of Greek Orthodox bishops and priests. In defiance, the Egyptians developed a parallel structure of their own, the Coptic Orthodox church. Today, most Christians have forgotten the doctrinal issues that once divided them, but the remaining Egyptian Copts have (with some exceptions) maintained their national identity by adhering to Coptic orthodoxy, distinct from other Orthodox, Catholic, or Protestant sects.

Egypt Under Arab Rule

As happened with other Monophysite Christians, the Copts' estrangement from Byzantine Orthodoxy aided the Arabs' rapid conquest of the Middle East in the seventh century. Historians do not agree as to whether the Copts really hailed the Muslim Arabs as liberators from their Byzantine masters, or whether they resisted them. The Arab armies, led by Amr (one of early Islam's greatest generals and statesmen), conquered the Nile Valley easily but faced stiff resistance in Alexandria, whose Byzantine governor could readily obtain reinforcements by sea. Historians do agree that the Muslim Arabs proved more tolerant than the Romans or the Byzantines had been. At first, they made little effort to convert Egypt's Copts to Islam. Indeed, the Arabs accepted payment of the *kharaj* (land tax) and the *jizyah* (head tax) at lower rates than the Byzantines had imposed earlier. Conversion to Islam was discouraged at first, precisely because the Arabs did not want to lose their revenues from the land and poll taxes. Egypt played a minor role in the first two centuries of Islamic history, but occasional revolts by Coptic peasants suggest that they did not always thrive under their new Muslim rulers.

The Establishment of Separate Muslim Dynasties

Egypt reemerged in the annals of political history in the late ninth century. By then, the power of the Abbasid caliphs of Baghdad was crumbling, due in part to the vastness of their domains but also to their importation of Turkish slave warriors, who had increasingly taken over the army and the administration from within. The Abbasids, renowned in the West in connection with Harun al-Rashid and the *Arabian Nights* (oddly enough, even though these tales were compiled in fifteenth-century Cairo, they were ascribed to ninth-century Baghdad), delegated more and more of their authority to local governors and commanders. One such governor was Ahmad Ibn Tulun, a Turkish soldier who had embraced Islam and was sent to Egypt. He seized control of Fustat, the garrison town from which Egypt was ruled, and stopped paying the tribute to Baghdad in 868. He and his family, called the Tulunids, ruled Egypt independently for about forty years. The Abbasid dynasty briefly regained control, then gave way to another ruling family, a relatively obscure dynasty called the Ikhshidids.

An interesting phase in medieval Egyptian history was the period from 969 to 1171, during which Egypt's Muslim rulers were Shi'is. Islam's sectarian divisions, though fewer and generally less intense than those of Christianity, are still quite complex. About 90 percent of all Muslims are Sunni, a word often mistranslated as "orthodox." Sunni Muslims are those who acknowledge the legitimacy of all the caliphs who ruled over the Islamic community after Muhammad's death in 632. Most of the rest are Shi'i; they believe that Muhammad's leadership of the Muslim community should have gone directly to Ali, his cousin and son-in-law. The Shi'is also maintain that Ali's descendants were Islam's rightful leaders, but they have split several times over which heir they recognized. One such split occurred when the sixth imam ("leader"), Ja'far, refused to appoint his eldest son, Isma'il, in favor of a younger one, due (some say) to Isma'il's alcoholism. Most Shi'is accepted Ja'far's designation; hence they are called Ja'faris (or, later on, "Twelvers" because they believe that their twelfth and final imam vanished but will return some day to restore righteousness on earth). But the dissident Isma'ilis won widespread support among the desert-dwelling tribes of Arabia and North Africa. One Isma'ili family, which called itself the Fatimids because of its claimed descent from Muhammad's daughter, Fatimah, seized control of Tunis in 909. The Isma'ilis were at this time campaigning throughout the Muslim world against the Abbasid caliphs' claim to authority. In particular, the Fatimids capitalized on the Abbasids' growing weakness and in 969 captured Egypt, followed by Syria and western Arabia.

Fatimid rule was a high point in Egypt's history. The Fatimids built near Fustat a new capital city, which they named *al-Qahirah* after the planet Mars (*al-Qahir* or "the Conqueror"); *Cairo* is its English equivalent. There they founded the mosque-university of al-Azhar as a training school for Shi'i propagandists. Although the Fatimids hoped to convert Sunni Muslims to Isma'ili Shi'ism, few Egyptians ever adopted their rather esoteric doctrines. The Fatimids' toleration for Jews and Christians helped to make Egypt an intellectual and commercial center for all peoples living in the Muslim world. Increasingly, though, Egyptians were converting from Christianity to Islam, owing probably to the advantages, social as well as economic and political, that accrued to them through conversion. But why did they convert to Sunni rather than Shi'i Islam? Apparently, the Fatimids were more eager to convert the Muslims in the Fertile Crescent, where the faltering Abbasids had fallen under the rule of a rival Shi'i dynasty, the Buyids, in 945. By the middle of the eleventh century, the real power within the Fatimid state was held by successive Armenians who had converted to Islam and then had risen to the position of *wazir*, Egypt's highest bureaucratic post.

The Crusades affected Egyptians more than any other people except those living in western Syria and Palestine, for Fatimid Egypt had become a major trading partner of the Italian city states of Genoa and Venice. The best known of the Crusader states, the Latin Kingdom of Jerusalem, invaded Egypt in 1167, hoping to take Cairo and to establish its rule over the Nile Valley and Delta. A Kurdish adventurer named Salah al-Din, in the process of repulsing the Crusaders, managed to become Egypt's *wazir*. Taking control in Cairo from the last Fatimid caliph in 1171, Salah al-Din restored Sunni Islam, and Egypt has remained Sunni to this day. Salah al-Din had come earlier to Egypt with his uncle at the behest of the ruler of Damascus, Nur al-Din, and upon the latter's death in 1174 he proceeded to take control of Syria. By controlling both Egypt and Syria, Salah al-Din managed to strengthen his army and surround the Latin Kingdom of Jerusalem. In 1187 he defeated the Crusaders and retook Jerusalem for Islam. Salah al-Din and his successors, the Ayyubid dynasty, enjoyed great prestige among Muslims for their victories over the Crusaders, who on several later occasions tried to invade Egypt. They failed. Much of the credit for stopping the Crusaders should be given to the Ayyubids' corps of slave soldiers, the Mamluks (the Arabic word for "owned men").

Mamluk Rule in Egypt

The Mamluks originated from the Turks of Central Asia and from various Christian groups in the Caucasus (who are usually referred to as Circassians). Brought in as boys or young men, they were converted to Islam, housed in barracks, placed under strict discipline, and trained in the arts of government and war, for which their familiarity with horseback riding gave them an advantage over other recruits. Freed from slavery once they reached maturity, these Mamluks carried great responsibilities and were rewarded with large land grants. Before long, they had became the power behind the Ayyubids of Egypt and Syria. Eventually, they seized control of both countries.

From 1250 until 1517 Egypt was ruled by the Mamluks, who successfully warded off attacks by the Mongols in 1260 and by Timur ("Tamerlane") around 1400. As they usually took control of the capital by force, not by heredity, we cannot speak of a "Mamluk dynasty." Egypt's historians commonly divide them into two groups: Bahri ("Nile River") and Burji ("tower-dwelling") Mamluks. The Bahri Mamluks, who reigned up to 1380, were mainly of Turkish extraction and are remembered for their beneficent rule, which did much to promote Egypt's agricultural, industrial, and commercial prosperity. Refined sugar and textiles are just two of the products that Egyptian merchants exported to Europe and to other parts of the Muslim world. The Burji Mamluks, on the other hand, are remembered for their rapacity and their debilitating quarrels, which led to the impoverishment of the country. This reputation, however, was not due solely to the Burji Mamluks' greed, for Egypt was ravaged by the Black Death in 1348 and revisited by the plague many times after that. Diminishing overland trade between the Mediterranean and the Red seas also cut the state's tariff revenues and further impoverished Egypt in the fifteenth century.

Farther north, starting in the early fourteenth century, a talented clan of Turkish border raiders was expanding its domain from western Asia Minor into southeastern Europe. Almost wiped out by Timur in 1402, this family managed to bounce back and to resume its conquests, taking Constantinople in 1453 and terminating the thousand year old Byzantine Empire. From that date, the lands of this family would be known as the Ottoman Empire. Up to the sixteenth century, though, the Ottomans ruled in what were mainly Christian lands. The leading Muslim empires were those of the Safavids in Iran and the Mamluks in Egypt and Syria. But under Sultan Selim I, the Ottoman armies, which had been trained to use firearms, defeated the Safavids and the Mamluks in rapid succession. As a result, Egypt became an Ottoman province in 1517. Cairo, which under the Mamluks had been Islam's greatest commercial and cultural center, turned into a backwater. Many of its artisans and scholars flocked to Constantinople (Istanbul) to seek the patronage of the Ottoman sultans. Even worse for Egypt was the diversion of Europe's main Asiatic trade route from the Mediterranean Sea to the Atlantic Ocean. This shift resulted from the successful voyages made by Portuguese ships around the Cape of Good Hope and from Columbus' "discovery" of the West Indies, leading to the spread of Spanish rule to the Caribbean and the Americas. The Ottomans did not want to prevent the Europeans from trading with their Egyptian and Syrian subjects or from crossing the Isthmus of Suez or the Fertile Crescent to reach lands farther east, for they had profited from the European commerce. It was the Europeans themselves who diverted the trade routes, slowly but inexorably impoverishing those lands that had formerly benefited from these routes.

Egyptian Relations with Europe

Egypt never stopped trading with the Europeans, especially the French. It continued to sell its spices and textiles, though in decreasing quantities, and in the late seventeenth century started transshipping coffee from the Yemen; but South American coffee gradually undercut the Arab product. As Egyptians bought larger quantities of manufactured woolen cloth and firearms from Europe in the eighteenth century, they began to run a trade deficit that was only partly made up by the sale of rice and wheat and the transshipment of Asian spices. One aspect of Egypt's commerce that continued to thrive was its trade with black Africans (especially Muslims) in gold, ivory, cloth, spices, and slaves.

The prevalence of tax-farming, a system under which Mamluks and ulama (Muslim scholars) paid the Ottoman government for the right to collect taxes on land and buildings, deprived peasants and artisans of the incentive to make any improvements on their properties. The system encouraged extortionate collection of whatever money or goods the tax-farmer could take from those defenseless peoples. At times when Mamluk quarrels necessitated large outlays on arms and fighting men, the price was usually paid by the tax-paying peasants, artisans, and merchants. Whole families fled from the settled lands and became nomads. By the end of the eighteenth century Egypt had become poorer, less populated, and more isolated from both Europe and lands east than it had been three centuries earlier. In popular histories, Egypt is portrayed as a neglected province of the Ottoman Empire that, while nominally under the control of a figurehead Ottoman governor, was actually misgoverned by rival Mamluk factions. Only Napoleon Bonaparte's occupation of Egypt in 1798 is credited with reversing this sad trend.

Changes in the Eighteenth Century

Recently, however, historians have been looking more closely at eighteenth-century Egypt. They now argue that France has claimed far too much credit for the awakening of modern Egypt and view this renaissance as having started somewhat earlier. In 1760 a Circassian Mamluk named Ali Bey "al-Kabir" took control of Cairo, hired an army of mercenaries (some of them Europeans) to supplement his Mamluk factions, raised taxes and set up a state monopoly on the grain trade to pay for the new troops, and deposed the Ottoman governor of Cairo. He then invaded Palestine and sent his brother-in-law and trusted lieutenant, Muhammad Abu al-Dhahab, to occupy Jiddah and Mecca. Ali Bey was overthrown by a rival Mamluk faction, which won Abu al-Dhahab to its side and put him in Ali's place. Abu al-Dhahab did not restore the Ottomans or the other Mamluk factions to power; rather, he strengthened Egypt's independent administration. During the eighteenth century ethnic Egyptians began to emerge as large landowners and local leaders in some of the provinces. The ulama continued to dispense justice and, where needed, to maintain local order. Meanwhile, an intellectual renaissance was starting at their university, al-Azhar, under the leadership of scholars like Hasan al-Attar and Abd al-Rahman al-Jabarti, about whom the coming chapter will have more to say.

Conclusion

The historical background provided by this chapter has depicted Egypt as a country invaded by tribal Hyksos horse soldiers, Libyans, Kushites, Assyrians, Persians, Alexander's Macedonians, Romans (and their Byzantine successors), Muslim Arabs, Turkish converts to Islam, North African Fatimids, Armenian converts, Kurds, Turkish and Circassian slaves, and the Ottoman Empire. Subsequent chapters will cover invasions by conquering European armies and humbler colonists. Yet the local Egyptian people managed to preserve and assert their distinct identity. It would be a mistake to view the emergence of modern Egypt as a mere reaction by its rulers and people to Napoleon's invasion or any other outside stimulus. On the contrary, Egypt's modernization was the outcome of political, social, and intellectual changes that were already starting to occur within the country. The interaction between foreign invaders and Egyptians created modern Egypt. The coming chapters will describe this interaction in greater detail.

CHAPTER TWO

Napoleon and Mehmet Ali

In the late eighteenth century Egypt was a poor, isolated, and neglected Ottoman province. It was not utterly stagnant, though. Even if Egypt had lost its central place in the international spice trade, many East Asian spices and some African gold still passed through Suez and Cairo. Egyptians continued to spin cotton, flax, and wool into thread and to weave fine textiles, but in smaller quantities than before. They still raised sugar, rice, and wheat for sale to Europe. However, the recurrent plague, famines caused by insufficient Nile floods, and civil disorders resulting from Mamluk rivalries and power struggles with Ottoman governors combined to make the country poorer. Unable to pay their taxes, some peasants were leaving their villages and turning into nomads. Between 1780 and 1798, some city-dwellers were reduced by starvation to eating dogs, cats, rats, manure, and in rare cases even their own children. The population, once as high as 10 million, had fallen to less than 4 million.

On the brighter side, the reigns of such Mamluks as Ali Bey (1760–1772) and Muhammad Bey Abu al-Dhahab (1772–1775) had proved that military and political power could be centralized and Egypt's resources could be mobilized, even though these leaders could not really detach the country from the Ottoman Empire. Intellectual and cultural life was reviving between 1760 and 1790, especially at al-Azhar University. One of its leading scholars was an immigrant from Yemen, Murtada al-Zabidi, whose *Taj al-'arus* did for Arabic what the *Oxford English Dictionary* does for the English language. There, too, Hasan al-Attar was beginning his long career as a theologian, philosopher, and logician. Abd al-Rahman al-Jabarti, a prolific biographer and historian, started writing his detailed account of contemporary events, now the major source for Egypt's political and social history in that era.

The French Invasion and Occupation

Meanwhile, the strongest European powers, Britain and France, fought a long series of bitter wars. Among the fiercest was the Seven Years' War (known in North America as the "French and Indian War"), leading to France's cession of Canada and India to Britain in 1763. France avenged its loss of Canada by aiding the British colonists during their Revolutionary War, but it still hoped to regain India. Egypt was already being discussed in France, during the reign of Louis XVI, as a stepping stone toward this goal.

The 1789 French Revolution only intensified the rivalry, as Britain joined the coalition of European monarchies seeking to overthrow the French First Republic and restore the Bourbon kings in Paris. By the late 1790s France was being governed by a quasi-dictatorial group, the Directory, which was at war with most of its neighbors. Some French extremists talked of invading England, deposing King George III and the House of Lords, and establishing a British republic. But it would not have been easy to defeat Britain's powerful navy, cross the English Channel, and take the islands. The Directory had placed its hopes on a dynamic young Corsican general, Napoleon Bonaparte, who in 1796–1797 had led France's republican army on a conquering swath across northern Italy and knocked Austria out of the hostile coalition. But what if Napoleon should try to seize power in Paris? Earlier, he had dispersed a republican militia with "a whiff of grapeshot," and the Directory feared that Napoleon could overthrow it as easily as he had helped it to power. Its answer was to equip Napoleon and his followers to strike at England by way of Egypt. True, England had almost no stake in Egypt at the time, but it would certainly fight to stop the French from crossing the Middle East and retaking India. Plainly stated, the first European attempt to occupy Egypt since the Crusades was dictated more by French domestic concerns than by international power politics. Any benefit to Egypt would be purely accidental.

Napoleon's expedition has won renown for having included 167 artists, scholars and scientists, who set out to explore and describe Egypt thoroughly. Their findings are recorded in a remarkable 23-volume work, *Description de l'Egypte,* which gave a detailed picture of the country and awakened Europe's interest in pharaonic Egypt. But the main aim of the expedition was conquest, not scholarship. Napoleon's armada, with some 30,000 troops, 13 large battleships, and 6 frigates, set out from Toulon in April 1798, captured Malta, evaded the swifter British fleet commanded by Admiral Horatio Nelson, and landed at Alexandria on 1 July. The resistance of sword-wielding Mamluks on horseback and a few irregular foot-soldiers bearing scythes proved ineffective.

The main challenges for the French expeditionary force were not military but logistical. Traversing the Delta meant crossing numerous canals and desert wastes, passing deserted villages, and enduring mosquitoes and dysentery—all under a hot Egyptian sun. Napoleon's troops would suffer more casualties from thirst and tropical diseases than from their enemies in battle. Lacking modern arms and discipline, the Mamluks were routed at Imbaba, near the Pyramids, and the French entered Cairo on 21 July.

Upon his arrival, Napoleon assured the Egyptians that he had not come to destroy Islam or to sever their country from the Ottoman Empire, but only to free them from Mamluk tyranny. Few believed these assurances, let alone his claims, based on his having defeated the pope and the Knights of Malta, that he was really a Muslim. When Nelson destroyed Napoleon's fleet in Abu Kir Bay on 1 August, the French were discredited; but the Egyptians lacked the means to resist, and it would take the British and the Ottomans months to get up an expedition to drive him out. Meanwhile, Napoleon set up a provisional governing council made up of ulama and descendants of Muhammad. This move only angered the Egyptians, who suspected the council would be used to raise taxes. After two months, a rebellion broke out, led by the merchant guilds and sufi brotherhoods, whose youth gangs dominated the Cairo streets. Firing down on the main mosques from the Citadel, the French proved that their rule would be as repressive as that of the Mamluks, only more ruthlessly efficient. The French soldiers' habits of public drinking, stealing private property, and accosting local women also offended local Muslims. French rule was already tarnished, in Egyptian eyes, by such acts as these.

Napoleon regarded Egypt as the first step toward his goal of taking India; soon he was leading his troops into Palestine. His failure to take the Ottoman fortress at Acre raised Egyptian hopes for a rescue from French rule, but in July 1799 Napoleon's troops easily repulsed an Ottoman landing at Abu Kir. Soon afterward he turned over his command of the Egyptian expedition to General Jean-Baptiste Kléber and sailed back to France, where he proceeded to overthrow the Directory and seize control of the country. Kléber reached an agreement with the Ottomans, the Convention of al-Arish, that would have restored Egypt to their control and allowed his troops to leave peacefully. The British government, however, ordered its fleet not to let the French pass until they surrendered and made a peace treaty with their enemies. By the time the British had reconsidered their position, fighting had resumed, the French had defeated the Ottoman army at Heliopolis, and Kléber had been assassinated by a Syrian youth.

The new French commander, General Jacques Abdallah Menou, had converted to Islam to marry an Egyptian. Less interested than Kléber in getting his troops out of Egypt, he restored the Egyptian council and drew up elaborate plans to encourage agriculture, commerce, and industry. These reforms would require higher taxes, and when Menou began to survey landholdings to increase their assessments, all social classes became alarmed. But relief was in sight. A joint Anglo-Ottoman force occupied the Nile Delta in March 1801 and defeated the French. Both the British and the Ottomans were eager to hasten France's military evacuation from Egypt (so, by then, were the French soldiers and scholars), but they disagreed on how to achieve it. Britain and the Ottoman Empire ended up signing separate peace treaties with France in 1802. The French troops departed, followed by the British, leaving behind an Ottoman army of occupation to restore order.

How much did the French occupation do for the emergence of modern Egypt? Although the work of the French scholars increased the West's knowledge of the country, it hardly influenced Egypt's intellectual elite. Napoleon's innovative governing council vanished once his army left. A few French soldiers remained to seek their fortunes in post-Napoleonic Egypt, just as some Mamluks and Egyptians accompanied Napoleon or his army back to France. At the same time, however, the British plan to help the Mamluks to resist any new French designs on Egypt also failed. Napoleon had strengthened the ulama. No longer would they defer to the Mamluk factions that had contended for mastery of Egypt before 1798. The Ottomans, then in the middle of a westernization program called the *Nizam-i-Jedid* ("New Order"), hoped to use their appointed governor to rule Egypt more directly than they had since the sixteenth century. They soon found, however, that they could not control the country. The French occupation had hastened political and social changes that had begun under Ali Bey and Abu al-Dhahab. Egypt would never go back.

The Rise of Mehmet Ali

But who would rule Egypt, if not the French, the British, the Mamluks, or the Ottomans? The traditional leaders of the Egyptian people were the ulama and the heads of the sufi orders, but they were unaccustomed to political responsibility and had split into many factions. Egyptians took it for granted that only foreigners were capable of governing their country. *Fi bilad Misr, khayrha li-ghayrha* ("In the land of Egypt, its good things belong to others") and *Ana basha winta basha, min yisu' il-himar?* ("If I were a lord and you were a lord, who would drive the donkey?") were two of the popular sayings that expressed this attitude. None would have expected Egypt to be taken over by a stocky Ottoman army officer, originally from the Macedonian port of Kavalla, the second-in-command of an Albanian regiment that came to Egypt in 1801. This man, called Muhammad 'Ali in Arabic and Mehmet Ali in Turkish, would become the founder of modern Egypt. His own background was probably Albanian, but he had been trained as an Ottoman officer. He spoke mainly Turkish, not Arabic. He did not learn to read and write until he was middle-aged. Yet Mehmet Ali succeeded where Napoleon had failed and accomplished more for Egypt than any of his better-educated descendants.

To anyone coming from the Balkans, the Nile Delta and Valley look like a paradise of verdant fields and flowing waters. Even if Egypt had suffered from a dismal succession of plagues, famines, low floods, Mamluk maladministration, and foreign military occupation, it had the potential to regain its ancient prosperity. But it needed a single powerful ruler, not a rabble of competitive warriors. By 1805 rivalries among the various Mamluk factions, abetted by the British, the French, and the Ottomans, had dissipated most of their strength and eliminated their leaders. Mehmet Ali proceeded to win the support of the ulama and guilds, discredit the Ottoman governor, and persuade the sultan to appoint him instead. From 1805 until 1848 he alone would be the Ottoman governor of Egypt.

It would not be historically accurate to claim that Mehmet Ali came to power with a plan to regenerate Egypt; his main aim was to consolidate his new position. In the early days of his rule, he constantly feared being deposed. If he collected taxes from the peasants at rates as extortionate as any Mamluk tax-farmer, it was because he wanted to enlarge his treasury, as a means of expanding his army and bodyguard. Eventually, the forces at his disposal would be large and strong enough to enable him to destroy the tax-farming system and to abolish many of Egypt's family and religious endowments, or *awqaf.* In their place, he established state control over the land, giving his government the power to determine what the peasants sowed, to supply their seed, tools, fertilizer, and irrigation water, and to set the prices it would pay for their produce. Later in his rule, when Egypt could afford to hire French engineers to supervise the construction of canals, dams, weirs, and barrages in a few favored areas of the Nile Valley and Delta, a new irrigation system came into being, enabling the peasants to raise three crops each year on lands where formerly they had grown only one. Cash crops, such as indigo, tobacco, sugar, and especially long-staple cotton, replaced those raised mainly for the peasants' subsistence. Gradually, Egypt (especially the Delta) regained its former agricultural prosperity. As a result, the peasants had to work harder. They also had a new incentive to increase their families, for they needed their children's labor in the fields. The population, which had been falling in the late eighteenth century, began to rise, gradually at first and then faster. Some say that it doubled during his reign. That is an exaggeration, but by 1880 it had certainly doubled since 1800.

Expanding cash-crop production could have benefited no one without corresponding developments in transportation and distribution. Mehmet Ali's reign saw the growth of a network of barge canals, river ports, and cart roads, together with grain weighing and storage facilities, cotton gins, sugar refineries, and other capital improvments. Egypt also became the first non-Western state to attempt an industrial revolution, introducing modern factories for the manufacture of soap, paper, cotton textiles, warships, and armaments. But it did not seem likely to work. Peasants had to be conscripted to work in the factories (the wages, when paid at all, were extremely low), most of the engineers and managers were foreign, and none of the industries would prove to be profitable to the Egyptian government. But as time passed, the factory became a fixture in the lives of many Egyptians. And with the factories came new educational institutions: schools of engineering, medicine, midwifery, languages and administration, and even arts and crafts.

All these westernizing reforms evolved gradually. Mehmet Ali had not started with a plan to develop Egypt. Rather, his main concern was to avoid being overthrown, as so many previous Ottoman governors had been. His appetite for revenues—preferably money, but anything of value that could be taken from Egypt's taxpayers—was insatiable. He needed money to pay out as tribute to the Ottoman sultan, bribes to keep bedouin Arabs from obstructing trade, and salaries for his civilian officials and military officers. Money enabled him to buy the newest ships and guns (or the wood and iron from which they would be built locally), to hire the ablest foreign technicians and teachers, and to still the objections of the ulama. Having used some Mamluk factions to help rid him of the others and to subdue the Arab tribes that had controlled Upper Egypt for a generation, he began to wipe them out entirely. No longer could the Mamluks replenish their ranks by importing new slaves from Central Asia or the Caucasus Mountains; they had either to become a hereditary caste or to die out altogether. He hastened their demise by inviting many of them in 1811 to a banquet at his fortified residence, the Cairo Citadel, where he had them massacred by his own men.

Egypt as a Military Power

Mehmet Ali made Egypt a military power second to none in the Middle East. His armies subdued the Wahhabi rebels in Arabia, restoring the holy cities of Mecca and Medina to Ottoman control in 1812 and sacking the Wahhabi capital, Dar'iyah, in 1818. Two years later they went on to capture the Upper Nile, seeking to control the ivory, gold, and slaves that Egypt had long imported from what is now the Sudan. In 1825, when the Greeks seemed to be winning their war for independence from the Ottoman Empire, his eldest son, Ibrahim, headed an Egyptian rescue mission. But the European powers sank the Turco-Egyptian fleet, giving victory to the Greeks, and the Ottoman sultan forgot his promise to reward his Egyptian viceroy with Syria and Crete. Mehmet Ali proceeded to send Ibrahim, accompanied by a large army, into Syria in 1831, and, by the end of the following year, his government's control extended from the Hijaz to central Anatolia. Had they not received Russia's timely military backing, the Ottomans could have lost their whole empire to Mehmet Ali and Ibrahim.

Egypt's army now numbered more than 100,000 men. The Albanians who a generation earlier had accompanied Mehmet Ali to Egypt were gone. They had been replaced by mercenary officers from Syria, Morocco, Tripoli, Bosnia, and Arabia, as well as from France and other European countries. Sudanese slaves had been tried out in the lower ranks, but most failed to withstand the rigors of Egypt's climate and endemic diseases. By the late 1820s Egyptian peasants were being drafted into Mehmet Ali's army. It was a bold move, disparaged by the foreign officers and resisted by the peasants, whose labor was sorely needed in the fields. Many peasants mutilated their bodies in the hope of being spared from the draft, and villagers held funerals for the youths who got taken. But the arming of some of those ethnic Egyptians ultimately allowed them—or their descendants—to play a larger part in Egypt's national life.

Mehmet Ali's weakness proved to be his relationship with the British. In 1807, soon after he had become Egypt's governor, they occupied Alexandria for a few weeks. Although their intent was to forestall a second French invasion, for the Napoleonic wars had resumed, Mehmet Ali thought that they were planning to help the Mamluks overthrow him, and the occupation left him suspicious of British motives. Actually, Britain, being mainly concerned with guarding its routes to India, did not yet have a coherent Middle Eastern policy. Passage from the Red Sea to the Mediterranean across Egypt or Sinai was dangerous and expensive, so the British were trying at this time to establish ties with the sultan of Oman and the various Arab amirs and shaykhs along the Gulf. They favored strengthening the Ottoman Empire over dividing it with Russia, but until Sultan Mahmud II murdered his rebellious janissary soldiers in 1826, they did not feel sure that it could survive. As for Egypt, Britain was willing to back anyone who could establish control—including Mehmet Ali, once he had wiped out the Mamluks. It is interesting to note that the second-in-command of the Hijaz campaign (1811–1818) was a Scottish soldier of fortune named Thomas Keith. The preponderance of French officers and technicians (many of them followers of the French utopian socialist, Claude Henri Saint-Simon) did not alarm the British in the 1820s, for their government was far more suspicious of Tsar Alexander's "Holy Alliance" and the conservatism of Austria's Metternich. The British did, however, join French and Russian forces in aiding the Greeks against the Ottoman Empire. It was only after the July 1830 Revolution, which brought Louis Philippe to power, that Britain resumed its old antagonism toward France. Britain's hostility was due more to suspected French designs on newly independent Belgium than to France's already close ties with Mehmet Ali.

British Opposition

Soon, however, the British came to suspect Mehmet Ali's French-backed Levant campaign of 1831–1833. Britain's foreign secretary, Lord Palmerston, opposed Mehmet Ali for several reasons: (1) An Egyptian empire could block British plans to develop a passage to India using the Euphrates River; (2) if Mehmet Ali overthrew Sultan Mahmud and took over the Ottoman Empire, he could upset the balance of power in Europe; (3) his successes could strengthen France to the detriment of Britain, which had only recently gone to great lengths to defeat Napoleon; and (4) his industries, if they proved successful, could take away markets for British manufactures, a primary concern of the capitalist middle class. But what resulted in 1833 from Ibrahim's conquest of Syria and his consequent advance into Anatolia was that Sultan Mahmud turned for help to Russia. In a treaty signed at Unkiar-Iskelesi, the Ottoman Empire made the Russians the guarantors of its territorial integrity, giving them (so the British believed) the right to send their warships through the Bosporus and the Dardanelles into the Mediterranean. Not wanting Russia to become the dominant state in Eastern Europe, Palmerston now had to find a way to roll back both the Franco-Egyptian and the Russian threats to the balance of power. In 1838 his government signed a commercial pact with the Ottoman Empire, one that seemed to strengthen the sultan against both Russia and France. But, in fact, the treaty resulted in making Britain the Ottomans' greatest trading partner for the rest of the nineteenth century. By limiting protective duties on manufactured goods imported into Ottoman territories, it also enabled cheap British manufactures to undercut the local handicrafts, thereby weakening and destroying industries—and trade guilds—wherever the treaty was applied, including, after 1841, Egypt.

In 1839 Sultan Mahmud II resolved to roll back the gains scored by Ibrahim earlier in the decade, but the Egyptian forces proved to be stronger. His army defeated, Mahmud died, whereupon his fleet sailed to Alexandria and defected to Egypt. But the Ottoman Empire did not fall. One of the earliest Turkish westernizers, Mustafa Reshid, took charge in Istanbul and in November 1839 had Mahmud's successor issue a reform declaration, the Noble Rescript of the Rose Chamber. This proclamation, which promised an end to tax-farming and other governmental injustices, persuaded London that the Ottoman Empire was worth saving. Acting in conjunction with all the European powers but France, which still backed Mehmet Ali and Ibrahim, the British issued an ultimatum to the Egyptian army to pull back. When it was ignored, they bombarded Acre and threatened to occupy Syria. After protracted negotiations, Mehmet Ali agreed to take his troops out of Syria in return for Ottoman recognition, backed by the European powers, of his right to pass the governorship of Egypt on to his heirs. This agreement, known as the London Convention of 1841, became the basis for Egypt's juridical status (which lasted up to 1914) as a privileged, autonomous province of the Ottoman Empire.

The Accomplishments of Mehmet Ali

Egypt was now an independent state in all but name. It had its own bureaucracy and army (although the size of the latter was limited). Its government could pursue its policies with only limited reference to the wishes of the Ottoman sultan. One serious loss for Egypt was the application of that 1838 Anglo-Ottoman commercial treaty, for no longer could Egypt protect its infant industries from competing foreign manufactures. But these businesses had not proved profitable, and by 1837 Mehmet Ali was already retrenching as a result of falling cotton prices. Further chagrined at being deprived of Syria, however, he lost interest after 1841 in his factories, schools, and estates, and began turning control over to his surviving sons and to his most trusted aides. This change in Mehmet Ali's commitment to Egypt, once the British had intervened to clip his wings, may lead us to question whether he deserves to be hailed as the founder of modern Egypt. Clearly, Mehmet Ali saw Egypt and its inhabitants as the means by which he could gain and keep power. He was the founder of the modern Egyptian state; he was not the first Egyptian nationalist.

Let one oft-told anecdote sum up his political philosophy. Among the youths he sent to Europe for their education were a few whom their French supervisor had selected to study what we now call public administration. Upon returning to Cairo, one of them was interviewed by Mehmet Ali. "What did you study in Europe?" asked the viceroy. "Civil administration." "And what is that?" The student replied: "It is the study of how to govern men's affairs." "What!" exclaimed Mehmet Ali, "You are not entering the administration. It is I who govern. Go to the Citadel and translate gunnery manuals!" And so the student was locked up to render French textbooks into Turkish and Arabic, for military technology—not civil administration—was what the viceroy felt the West had to offer.

In conclusion, Mehmet Ali's achievement lies in what survived his final years of demoralization. Egypt's new bureaucratic and military institutions, severed from those of the Ottoman Empire, gave his heirs room to maneuver and a freedom recognized by the European powers—with only vestigial restraints from Istanbul. Egyptians, Ottomans, and Westerners all became accustomed to seeing Egypt as an autonomous, virtually independent, state. Although many of Mehmet Ali's schools closed down or shrank in enrollment during the last years of his reign, Egypt now had a corps of technically trained bureaucrats and army officers, many of whom were committed to westernizing reform and to Egyptian autonomy. They would go on to serve his successors, Abbas, Sa'id, and Isma'il. The foundations of modern Egypt were well and truly laid.

CHAPTER THREE

The Rise of Western Influence

Europe's economic and cultural ascendancy over Egypt, given the conditions prevalent in the nineteenth century, was unavoidable. But its political and military control could have been delayed or mitigated if the Ottoman Empire had been stronger and, more important still, if Mehmet Ali's heirs had been as wise as he. Mehmet Ali may have been illiterate, but he had an uncanny ability to read the minds of people and nations. He refused to borrow money from European bankers to finance his westernizing reforms. He blocked numerous schemes to cut a canal from the Mediterranean to the Red Sea, fearing that it would someday prove as dangerous to Egypt as possession of the Bosporus and the Dardanelles had become for his Ottoman overlords. The British had already demonstrated that they would thwart any French attempt to control a key route to India. He was sure that Britain would eventually seize this proposed maritime canal across the Isthmus of Suez.

Mehmet Ali's Successors

Mehmet Ali's intended heir was his eldest son, Ibrahim, who had so successfully led the Egyptian army against the Wahhabis in Arabia, the Greeks in the Morea, and the Ottomans in Syria. Regrettably, he died suddenly in November 1848. Europeans attributed his death to the combined exertions of testing a racing horse, downing two bottles of iced champagne, and going to bed with a new concubine—a lot of work for a man near sixty. The real cause was tuberculosis, resulting from a chill he had contracted while campaigning, in summer uniform, in the snows of Anatolia. As Mehmet Ali was senile by this time and Ibrahim had been governing on his behalf, a new regent was needed. Under the customary rules of Muslim dynasties, the eldest male member of the family succeeded, making the new regent a grandson, Abbas Hilmi I, who took control officially when Mehmet Ali died soon afterward. Abbas has a dismal reputation among Europeans because he allegedly hated Christians and tried to undo Mehmet Ali's reforms. To be fair to Abbas, he continued the policy of divesting the state lands, factories, and schools that his grandfather had created but had allowed to deteriorate after 1841. Having been treated by Mehmet Ali and Ibrahim as a black sheep, Abbas, upon reaching office, dismissed their officials and advisers and reversed their pro-French policies.

New Routes to the East

One interesting consequence was that in 1850 Abbas gave to the British a concession to build Egypt's first rail line, linking Alexandria to Cairo. Since 1836 a British stagecoach line, paralleled by a line of semaphores, had joined Cairo to Suez. Now they would soon be supplanted by a railroad and a telegraph line. India seemed to be growing ever nearer to Europe. More and more people and goods were moving between Europe and India, but the best available method of transport was still the sailing ship, which took four months to round the Cape of Good Hope. The steamship, still rare on the high seas, could reduce the trip to three. Egypt's first railroad shortened it to about six weeks from London to Bombay, with transfers to a train at Alexandria, a stagecoach in Cairo, and another ship at Suez. Understandably, travelers and traders were among those most interested in a canal across the Isthmus of Suez. Earlier, the Directory had commissioned Napoleon's expedition to conduct a feasibility study. Some of Saint-Simon's utopian disciples had tried to win Mehmet Ali's support for the idea. A British officer of the Peninsular and Oriental Shipping Line had drafted a detailed canal project in 1841. By the early 1850s the obstacles were more political than technical.

In 1854 Abbas died—or was murdered by his palace guard. Mehmet Ali's eldest surviving son, Sa'id, became the new viceroy of Egypt. Sa'id had been educated by European teachers and strongly favored his father's policies of westernization from above. One of Sa'id's oldest friends was Ferdinand de Lesseps, a former diplomat, whom he had known twenty years earlier as France's consul in Alexandria. A devoted father, Mehmet Ali had strictly supervised his sons' physical training. Even as a boy, Sa'id had been overweight, a condition that Mehmet Ali made him overcome by climbing ships' masts and running around the palace while adhering to a spartan diet. Sa'id used to flee to the French consulate, where de Lesseps won his devotion by feeding him bowls of macaroni! When Sa'id came to power, de Lesseps, who had been obliged by his opposition to the Second Empire to resign from the diplomatic corps, hastened to Egypt. Soon he persuaded Sa'id, as a dear friend, to let him set up a company, chartered in Egypt, to cut a maritime canal from the Mediterranean to the Red Sea across the Isthmus of Suez. The company would be financed by the sale of shares to investors from every nation, including the Egyptian government, which would furnish the laborers needed to dig the canal. It would be managed by a board of directors, whose chairman would be named by Egypt's viceroy. In glowing terms, de Lesseps depicted the advantages that the Suez Canal would bring to European business, Egypt, Muslim pilgrims, and of course to Sa'id, whose name would be immortalized by the world's gratitude for having sponsored this stupendous engineering marvel.

Some modern writers portray de Lesseps as a knave and Sa'id as a fool. The truth is more complex. Sa'id's motives remain obscure. He certainly did want the glory of having patronized the canal and probably the barrier that it would put between his lands and those of his Ottoman suzerain. As a large landowner, he may have hoped to facilitate the foreign sale of cash crops such as sugar, rice, and long-staple cotton. De Lesseps sincerely believed in the canal; his material reward would be slight. But the Ottoman sultan, then preoccupied with the Crimean War, in which both France and Britain were helping his army to fight Russia, refused to give his consent. The British government, too, saw no benefit in a canal built by a French national, even if their countries happened then to be allied, for it recalled the times when Napoleon and Mehmet Ali had threatened to seize control of the main routes to India. In addition, a British subject had built the rail link between Alexandria and Cairo, a competing venture. Although British investors wanted to buy stock in de Lesseps' company, they were dissuaded from doing so by the opposition of Prime Minister Palmerston, Parliament, and the press. As a result, the company was unable to raise the 200 million francs (worth about US$40 million in 1860) needed to fund the construction. The work would require at least 20,000 laborers each year. The workers were to be conscripted by the Egyptian government from a population of 5 million, even though slavery and forced labor had been (in theory) outlawed by an Ottoman decree in 1841. A special canal would have to be cut from the Nile to carry water to the work site, just as food, equipment, and supplies would have to be transported into this bleak desert environment. The logistics were formidable. De Lesseps was neither an engineer nor a manager. But he was an inspiring leader, willing to flout conventional wisdom, Egyptian interests, and Ottoman laws, if doing so would get the canal built. When his company's shares failed to sell, he persuaded Sa'id to buy more of them. When he needed to buy or sell lands along the canal site, Sa'id helped. Sa'id, otherwise remembered as a friend of the Egyptian peasants, bewailed their forced departure from their fields and families; but somehow he always managed to conscript them, until the British pressured him to desist. Most of the canal was dug before the company had amassed the necessary capital (without the Ottoman sultan's permission) and before the labor supply dried up. When conscription stopped, the Egyptian government paid a handsome indemnity (the result of an arbitration proceeding headed by the French emperor, Napoleon III), enabling the company to purchase dredging machines that dug faster than the peasants. During the time when they were doing the work, many peasants had died of malnutrition, disease, and overwork. Some Egyptians maintain that the peasants (not the company) were expected to bring their own food, water, and tools, and that the peasant conscripts were often reduced to digging the canal with their bare hands. Other writers claim, however, that de Lesseps took pains to ameliorate working conditions and to pay the Egyptians promptly.

As the construction of the Suez Canal was an immense public works project, perhaps the greatest since Roman times, it is tempting to describe it at length; but other changes were taking place within Egypt during Sa'id's reign. The process of dismantling Mehmet Ali's monopolies on industry and farmland had continued under Abbas and was completed under Sa'id. In 1858 a new Ottoman Land Law, applicable also to Egypt, permitted individuals, whether subjects or foreigners, freely to buy and own land or other property within the Empire. Ethnic Egyptians, as well as descendants of Turkish or Circassian Mamluks, bought land and created new estates. Some were even becoming state officials and army officers, for Sa'id often took the sons of village headmen for training in his military and naval academies. This was Sa'id's means of controlling the village headmen, but it helped some of their sons to move into positions of power later on. One of the interesting trends in modern Egyptian history has been the gradual movement of ethnic Egyptians toward stage center: Nationalist leaders such as Ahmad Urabi and Sa'd Zaghlul, high-ranking administrators such as Isma'il Siddiq, Muslim reformers such as Muhammad Abduh, and intellectuals such as Ahmad Lutfi al-Sayyid all stemmed from Egyptian peasant backgrounds.

The Influx of Europeans

Europeans, too, became more prominent in the time of Sa'id, who encouraged them to settle in Alexandria and Cairo. Many performed great services for Egypt as entrepreneurs, engineers, and educators. But with them came a demimonde of stock speculators, swindlers, and vice peddlers, who were protected by the Capitulations. Treaties originally intended by the sultan to make it easier to do business with European Christians settling in the Ottoman Empire, these Capitulations exempted Westerners from the jurisdiction of local laws or the obligation to pay any taxes unless their governments had agreed to them. Greeks and Italians, often fleeing poverty in their own countries, were the most numerous abusers of the Capitulations, but every Western country took advantage of them. Native minorities, especially groups like the Armenians and the Jews, often took jobs as local consuls, interpreters, or attachés for European or U.S. diplomatic missions, gaining foreign nationality and hence legal and fiscal immunity as part of the bargain. Egypt's Muslims may have benefited from the canals, railways, paved streets, piped water, gas lights, and modern schools and factories that European enterprise brought, at least to Alexandria and Cairo. But they did not welcome the concomitant disruption of their lives, the exaltation of minorities, or the rising prices for houses and farmland.

Sa'id's reign was short. Near its end an ominous step would set a new trend. He was constantly being pressured by European settlers and investors (backed by their consuls) for various claims against the Egyptian government, and, although Egypt's fertile land usually yielded enough taxes to make state revenues match or exceed expenditures, he decided to borrow money from European bankers. When Isma'il succeeded him in 1863, Egypt had a foreign debt of about 6 million pounds sterling (US$30 million). As the son of Ibrahim and hence the grandson of Mehmet Ali, Isma'il seemed a promising ruler. He had received part of his education in the West and spoke fluent French. He had built up his private estates into model farms. And, in a talk to the European consuls following his accession, he had pledged himself not to increase the Egyptian national debt. He did not keep this promise.

Khedive Isma'il

The early years of Isma'il's reign were a boom period in Egypt. Civil war was raging in the United States, and the naval blockade imposed by the Union against the Confederacy prevented the cotton crop from reaching the textile mills of Lancashire. British spinners and weavers, facing financial ruin, were prepared to pay premium prices for cotton from other sources. Only a few countries were capable of raising cotton on a large scale. Of these, only Egypt could produce large quantities of the most highly prized, long-staple cotton used in the finest textiles. By 1863 any kind of cotton Egypt could grow was being sold to Europe at immense prices, and the country's economy was thriving. Bankers and other money-lenders flocked to Isma'il, trying to lure him into various public and private investments.

Historians disagree on how wisely Isma'il spent his revenues. All praise his investment in public schools, bridges, canals, railroads, cotton gins, sugar refineries, telegraph lines, and harbors. Some of his funds financed the Egyptian army and navy, the exploration of the Upper Nile, and the conquest of vast areas of East Africa. Scholars may rejoice that Isma'il's munificence helped pay for the Egyptian Museum, the National Library, and the Geographical Society. Isma'il also laid out what has become downtown Cairo, from the Ezbekia Gardens to the Nile, hired France's best-known landscape gardener to beautify the shoreline and the main avenues of the city, erected the Opera House, and commissioned the composition of *Aida.* He made the 1869 inauguration of the Suez Canal the occasion for a huge celebration, attended by the royalty, the aristocracy, and the artistic and intellectual leaders of Europe. These expenditures helped to make Egypt more autonomous and, in the eyes of nineteenth-century Europeans, more "civilized."

Some of Isma'il's expenditures earn little praise, however. Egypt's autonomy from the Ottoman Empire required other disbursements, in the form of bribes to Turkish politicians and increased tribute, to enable Isma'il to take the title of khedive (a Persian word corresponding, roughly, to "prince"), to make his son the successor to the khedivate instead of Prince Abd al-Halim (the last surviving son of Mehmet Ali), and to float foreign loans without first getting Ottoman permission. Large sums went to build palaces and yachts, to support his cronies, to buy Paris gowns for his wives, and to bribe influential journalists. The debt Egypt owed to foreigners skyrocketed and, once the American Civil War had ended and the South had resumed selling cotton to

Europe, the Egyptian cotton boom ceased, tax revenues fell, and the terms demanded by foreign bankers for loans became more stringent.

The Financial Crisis

By the mid-1870s, Khedive Isma'il was desperately seeking new sources of revenue. All that he could use as collateral was mortgaged. He offered to forgive Egyptian landowners one-half of their taxes in perpetuity if they paid six years' land tax in advance. In 1875 he reluctantly sold his government's shares of the Suez Canal Company to Britain for 4 million pounds, an ominous step toward British control. A British parliamentary commission investigated Egypt's finances and issued a report warning that the government was nearing bankruptcy. To allay the fears of Egypt's foreign bondholders, the khedive authorized in 1876 the creation of a debt commission made up of representatives of Britain, France, Italy, and Austria. When a new budget crisis arose, as a result of a low Nile and high military outlays required by Egypt's involvement in the Russo-Turkish War of 1877, he allowed Britain and France to set up their so-called Dual Financial Control over Egyptian state revenues and expenditures.

With the establishment of the Dual Control in August 1878, Isma'il brought an English and a French minister into his cabinet, with Nubar, an Armenian, as its premier. He pledged henceforth to rule through his ministers, putting an end to the khedivial despotism that had characterized Egyptian government since the rise of Mehmet Ali. In this announcement, he also made the oft-quoted remark: "My country is no longer in Africa; we are now a part of Europe."

Before discussing the Dual Control or the "European cabinet," let us examine this remark in the context of Egyptian conditions. The changes that had occurred in the country during the preceding half-century were no doubt extraordinary. When Napoleon landed in Alexandria, Egypt had no roads that could accommodate wheeled vehicles. During the time that Edward Lane, the British Orientalist, lived in Cairo in the 1830s to write his *Manners and Customs of the Modern Egyptians,* he still felt obliged to wear Muslim clothing, and all Egyptians still took their meals seated cross-legged on cushions and eating with their right hands. By 1878, Alexandria, Cairo, and the new towns along the Suez Canal—Port Said and Ismailia—had wide, straight streets, on which Europeans and westernized Egyptians raced their horse-drawn carriages. With the addition of railroad stations, hotels, restaurants, and department stores, these cities came to resemble Marseilles or New Orleans, if not Paris or New York.

They had gas lights and piped water. Telegraph lines were already in place, and the first telephones would be installed in 1881, long before most North American small towns would get them. Egypt's cities were indeed becoming part of Europe.

You may reply that these were superficial changes, beneficial to a small upper class at most. True, most Egyptians were still peasants living in abject poverty, illiterate, burdened by hard labor and high taxes, and unaffected (except inasmuch as they were paying for it) by the Europeanized lifestyle of the khedivial palace and city-dwelling elite. But the elite culture was Egypt's cutting edge. More profoundly, new ideas and institutions were evolving among the intellectuals. Al-Azhar University remained as committed as ever to the traditional Islamic sciences, but some teachers and students were breaking away. The most famous apostle of Muslim unity, Jamal al-Din "al- Afghani," came to Cairo in 1871. When the ulama barred him from lecturing at al-Azhar, he rented rooms in the nearby Khan al-Khalili bazaar and received many young Egyptians who were distressed at the state of their country. He inspired such Azharites as Muhammad Abduh to work for a reformed Islam and such writers as Adib Ishaq (a Syrian Christian) and Ya'qub Sannu' (an Egyptian Jew) to found political newspapers. Using the burgeoning Masonic lodges for cover, young Egyptian malcontents conspired to form the first revolutionary societies.

Khedive Isma'il inadvertently helped to create Egyptian nationalism by financing the earliest daily newspapers, setting up government schools, convoking the first representative assembly in 1866 in order to raise more taxes from the rural landowners, and establishing the Mixed Courts (to try civil cases involving foreign residents in Egypt) in 1876. The rudimentary journals, schools, parliaments, and law courts combined to nurture a new class of educated Egyptians whose occupations demanded an articulate response to what was happening in their country. Some of them would join forces with the army officers to form Egypt's first nationalist movement.

The educated Egyptians were particularly disturbed by the British and French intervention in their country's government, via the Dual Control. The British and French debt commissioners were trying to trim the Egyptian state expenditures. They placed Isma'il and his relatives on a stringent civil list and slashed disbursements on public works, education, and the military. These economies caused long delays in paying the salaries of the officers and soldiers, many of whom were reduced to dire poverty as a result of arrears in pay. An announcement in February 1879 that 1,600 of Egypt's 2,600 officers would temporarily be retired at half-pay led to a noisy street demonstration, during which some Egyptians seized the carriage of the finance minister (the

English member of Isma'il's "European cabinet") and manhandled several high-ranking officials. Isma'il soon appeared on the scene and ordered the demonstrators to return to their barracks, but he also dismissed the Dual Control and appointed a caretaker cabinet under the leadership of his son, Tawfiq. Led by one of Isma'il's most westernized ministers, Sharif, a group of Egyptians started to draw up a constitution that would have given real power to an elected assembly. Isma'il then rescinded the pay cuts and put Sharif in charge of a cabinet that, at least in the eyes of later generations, had nationalist leanings.

The Beginnings of Egyptian Nationalism

The European powers did not ignore these developments. Having watched Isma'il's debts rise to 93 million Egyptian pounds (an astronomical sum in 1879), they doubted that an independent government could or would raise the tax revenues needed to repay its European creditors. If any country could claim the "right" to send in its troops and take over the Egyptian government, it was France, which had done the most to westernize Egypt under Mehmet Ali and Isma'il. But Britain, just as it had tried to block France's efforts to build the Suez Canal, also opposed a unilateral French occupation and control over Egypt, the major stepping stone to India. Besides, Britain saw France as having been weakened politically by its loss to Germany in 1870–1871. It really wanted the Ottoman government to take charge. It remained an axiom of British Middle East policy to sustain the Ottoman Empire as a buffer against the expansion of any rival European power. In fact, one year earlier, British naval vessels had entered the Dardanelles to stop the Russians, who had won in the Balkans, from imposing a harsh peace treaty on Istanbul. What happened in Egypt in 1879 was that the European powers, led at the time by Germany, formally protested against Isma'il's efforts to change Egypt's financial agreements and then pressured the Ottoman sultan to depose him from the khedivate and to appoint Prince Tawfiq in his place.

Conclusion

The financial crisis discredited khedivial absolutism as a basis for Egypt's government. The system initiated by Mehmet Ali and developed by Sa'id and Isma'il both centralized Egypt's government and created a bureaucracy and an army with a fair degree of technical competence. It had started to involve ethnic Egyptians in addition to the foreign

Muslims who traditionally had dominated the central administration. It gave Egypt a modest degree of autonomy and westernization. But it also made the economy far too dependent on Western investors, causing social and political unrest in the country. Later on, Egyptian nationalists would regret that some form of parliamentary democracy did not replace khedivial absolutism, but indigenous political leadership was still scarce and weak, whereas the power and the ambitions of the Europeans were strong. The British and French governments were willing to bully Egypt's khedive on behalf of their own (mainly capitalist) constituents. The hopes and fears of the Europeans who had settled in Egypt, or who had purchased its government's bonds, or who feared for the security of the Suez Canal, all combined to influence the Egyptian policies of Britain and France. The national interests and desires of Egypt's popular leaders, as we shall see in the next chapter, did not.

CHAPTER FOUR

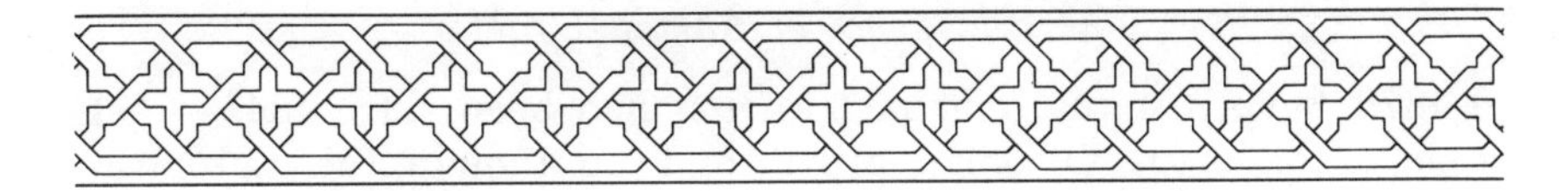

The British Occupation

On 25 June 1879 two telegrams reached the khedivial palace in Alexandria, one addressed to "Isma'il, ex-Khedive of Egypt," the other to "H. H. Khedive Tawfiq." In this way the Ottoman government made it known that it had deposed Isma'il in favor of his 27-year-old son. Two days later Isma'il sailed away on his khedivial yacht into a gilded exile in Naples. He never saw Egypt again.

Khedive Tawfiq's Dilemma

The new khedive, Tawfiq, has a mixed reputation among the historians of modern Egypt. He would eventually collaborate with the foreign powers seeking to control his country, perhaps because he had no alternative. Before his succession, he had been seen as a patriot, less flamboyant than his father, sympathetic to Sharif's constitution, and involved in a secret society formed by Jamal al-Din "al-Afghani." Once he had taken over, however, he could see that he stood between two fires: European military might and Muslim-Egyptian nationalist resistance. Both could encroach on his powers. Tawfiq chose the Europeans as the safer side. He appointed a new cabinet, headed by the autocratic Riyad Pasha, and restored the powers of the Dual Financial Control; but he did not readmit the British or French Controllers to his cabinet. The government expelled such agitators as Jamal al-Din and Ya'qub Sannu' from Egypt and closed the most radical newspapers. Khedive Tawfiq probably feared that spreading nationalism, whether military or civilian, might stir up new riots. A popular revolt could overthrow him, or draw in the Europeans to restore order. By using their influence to depose his father, the European powers had reduced the khedivate to a pawn in a larger political game. Egypt's ruling family would never recover its independence.

The Emergence of Ahmad Urabi

In 1879 Egypt's status remained what it had been since 1841—that of an autonomous Ottoman province. Even though the European ambassadors were now more influential and the Debt Commission would take more than half the government revenues in 1880 to start reducing its huge debt to foreign creditors, Egypt had no colonial governor and no foreign army of occupation. The problem was that the financial stringencies hurt nearly every Egyptian; they led to government cutbacks for the army, schools, public works, and even essential maintenance. The Egyptians felt that they bore an unfair share of the cuts, while the Turks, Circassians, and other foreigners in Egypt went practically unscathed. Most people could do nothing more than grumble, but the army officers had the power and organization to protest more effectively.

The role of the army in Egypt's political history has been surprisingly small. Until it successfully overthrew King Faruq in 1952, the army intervened in the government only once—during the 1879–1882 period, in what we commonly call the Urabi Revolution. The essential grievance of the Egyptian officers was that, having been taken into the army under Mehmet Ali and his successors, their advancement was blocked by Isma'il and now, under Tawfiq's austerity budget, they were being pensioned off or assigned to undesirable posts. The Turkish and Circassian officers, meanwhile, suffered less. The enlisted ranks, by this time overwhelmingly Egyptian and Sudanese, shared these grievances. In January 1881 a deputation of Egyptian officers, led by Colonel Ahmad Urabi, visited Riyad and also sent a petition to Khedive Tawfiq. When the war minister, Uthman Rifqi, called them to his office, planning to have them arrested and court-martialed, the officers arranged to have their men storm the War Ministry building and rescue them. When even Tawfiq's palace guard, hitherto presumed loyal to him, defected to the mutinous officers, he and Riyad gave in and replaced Rifqi with Mahmud Sami al-Barudi, who supported their demands. Barudi was revered by the Egyptian people as an officer, patriot, and poet; once he had begun to improve the lot of the officers and soldiers, Colonel Urabi was encouraged to make new demands.

The Egyptian officers still suspected that Khedive Tawfiq or Riyad were plotting against them with the European commissioners or the Turkish and Circassian officers, especially when Barudi lost his position as war minister and several regiments were transferred out of Cairo in September 1881. Now Urabi organized a huge demonstration in front of Abdin Palace, the official khedivial residence in the capital.

Legend has it that Tawfiq, accompanied by the British controller, confronted Urabi, with his 2,500 armed Egyptians arrayed about Abdin, boasting: "I am the khedive of this country and will do as I please." To this Urabi replied: "We are not slaves and will never from this day on be inherited." These words may never have been spoken, but they reflect both the spirit of the khedivial house (with its British patron) and that of the Egyptian officers, who, one generation removed from their peasant origins, were groping toward national dignity. At any rate, Tawfiq did heed the officers' demands: the dismissal of the Riyad cabinet, the strengthening of the existing representative assembly, and the enlargement of the Egyptian army. Lacking any force with which to counter Urabi's men, Khedive Tawfiq accepted his demands. Sharif was invited to replace Riyad, a group of legal scholars was convened to draft a new Egyptian constitution, and Sharif's government promptly called back all the retired officers and increased the size of the army.

The Egyptian people—landlords and peasants, professionals and government clerks, Christians and Muslims—hailed Urabi as the nation's savior. Enthusiastic demonstrations broke out wherever he went. The new constitution was proclaimed in November, elections were held, and the khedive opened Egypt's first representative body with legislative powers. But the Europeans feared for their safety, if they were living in Egypt, or for their bonds, if they had invested in its economy. Britain joined France in issuing a joint note that threatened to intervene to support the khedive, but, far from intimidating the Egyptian nationalists, this step only further emboldened them. They insisted that their new parliament must have the right to vote on the 1882 Egyptian budget—a prerogative claimed by the Dual Control, which was trying to keep the confidence of Egypt's creditors. Now some moderates, among them Sharif (who promptly resigned as prime minister), broke away from the nationalists, but Mahmud Sami al-Barudi took over as premier and Urabi became war minister. Both had vowed to defend Egypt's interests above those of the European bondholders. They suppressed a plot by some of the Turco-Circassian officers, discussed deposing Tawfiq and declaring a republic, and stirred up popular demonstrations against British and French meddling in Egypt.

European Intervention

What Urabi failed to do was to gauge the determination of the Europeans, especially the British, to safeguard their Egyptian interests:

the security of the Suez Canal, the repayment of the Egyptian government debts, and the safety of European residents in Egypt. The French wanted a joint military occupation with the British, and both powers sent warships to the eastern Mediterranean. The British expected the Ottoman government to intervene. But the Turkish stance was ambiguous: Publicly they reassured the Europeans, while privately they encouraged Urabi to resist them. After all, Russia had seized most of the Balkan lands in 1877 and had kept a portion of eastern Anatolia in the 1878 peace settlement that ended the Russo-Turkish War. Under the terms of that treaty, Britain had been allowed to occupy Cyprus and Austria had taken Bosnia. Then France occupied Tunisia in 1881. By this time, Muslims everywhere strongly opposed any further European expansion at Ottoman expense. But this strident opposition shook Britain's confidence that the Ottomans could control Egypt. Its government was headed by Sir William Gladstone, a Liberal who in 1876 had denounced Ottoman rule in Europe, yet now was loath to send British troops to Egypt.

A conference of European powers met in Constantinople during the summer of 1882, but its deliberations were inconclusive and irrelevant. In early June, riots broke out in Alexandria. Although the Egyptian government tried to stop them and to arrest the instigators (indeed, even though 3,000 Egyptians and only 50 Europeans were killed or wounded), the riots frightened many foreigners into taking refuge on the British and French battleships anchored offshore. The commander of the British fleet wanted a pretext to fire on Alexandria. When the Egyptian army refused to dismantle its coastal fortifications, the British ships (secretly encouraged by Khedive Tawfiq) bombarded them. Instead of aiding the British, the French fleet sailed away. In Paris a new government had taken over, one that refused to commit itself to a military occupation of Egypt. When fire broke out in Alexandria, British forces went in to restore order.

The Failure of the Urabi Revolution

Khedive Tawfiq, summering in Alexandria, publicly threw in his lot with the British, but in Cairo the Egyptian cabinet declared war on Britain. The British fleet entered the Suez Canal and landed at Ismailia, violating the canal's neutrality, but neither the company nor the Egyptian government had made plans to fortify the new waterway. Ferdinand de Lesseps had vowed that "his" canal would remain neutral, and Urabi (foolishly, as it turned out) trusted him. The British expeditionary force met the Egyptian army on 13 September at Tel-el-Kebir and won decisively, occupying Cairo the following day. Egyptian nationalism seemed to fade like a mirage. Urabi surrendered and was arrested and tried (along with many of his fellow nationalists) for treason. Although he was convicted, his death sentence was commuted to exile in Ceylon. Khedive Tawfiq, whose behavior strikes modern Egyptians as having been even more treasonous, was propped back on his throne. A more moderate (meaning pro-British) government took the place of the nationalist one.

The first Egyptian nationalist movement may have been popular, but it was too diffuse in its membership and too unfocused in its goals. Everyone could agree that Isma'il had put the country too far into debt and that the measures taken by the European commissioners to reassure Egypt's creditors were intolerable. But here the nationalists parted company. Some were revolutionaries, prepared to depose the khedive, even willing to join with Muslims elsewhere to resist Western power. Some were landowners of Egyptian extraction, anxious to keep privileges only recently gained through the westernizing reforms of Mehmet Ali and Isma'il. They tended to work with Egyptian army officers, who feared losing their limited power to their Turkish and Circassian rivals. Some belonged to the new class of civil servants, teachers, and journalists that was forming a rudimentary educated elite interested in national rights and duties. We shall hear more of them later.

The British Occupation

Gladstone's government, which earlier had expressed platonic sympathy for Urabi's aims and had opposed him mainly to prevent the French from seizing control of Egypt, now had to decide what to do with the British troops that had occupied the country. The Liberals did not want a long-term occupation—indeed, few Britons did—because they did not want to antagonize the French or inflame Muslim sensibilities. The British army was small and might later be needed elsewhere. They promised that they would stay just long enough to restore order in Egypt. But that was the problem. If restoring order meant giving power back to the khedive and suppressing the nationalist movement, the British had done these things within a few weeks. But if it meant solving the country's financial problems, which had caused the disorders in the first place, the British would have to stay for a long time, until the economy was reorganized.

The outbreak of an anti-Egyptian rebellion in the Sudan, led by the famous mahdi, Muhammad Ahmad, also complicated Britain's evacuation plans. A British force, sent to relieve the Egyptian garrison at Khartum, was ambushed in the desert. The subsequent attempt by the brilliant (but eccentric) General Charles Gordon to effect an Egyptian withdrawal from the Sudan in 1884–1885 also failed. Gordon and his troops (plus thousands of Egyptians) were killed by the mahdist rebels. British public opinion now demanded that their army remain in Egypt until it could avenge Gordon's death.

Even while the British were still planning to get out of Egypt, they were taking steps that would prolong their stay. Some writers have argued that their insistence on giving Urabi and his fellow nationalists a fair trial had undercut the khedivial government. Now discredited and weak in Egyptian eyes, it could survive only if the British stayed. In November 1882 the British abolished the Dual Control and appointed a financial adviser—British, of course—who was empowered to attend Egyptian cabinet meetings. A commission headed by Lord Dufferin came to study Egypt's government and issued a report calling for numerous reforms, which would take a long time to be carried out. Only some ever were. Egypt's economy was so weak that the government feared it would probably be unable, for several years to come, to raise enough money in taxes to pay what it owed to its creditors. More than half the state revenues had to go to the Debt Commission, and all other government expenditures had to be pared to the bone. Even so, the irrigation system, which had been neglected ever since the beginning of Egypt's budget crisis, needed to be repaired if the country was to survive. The Egyptian government also owed indemnities to those Europeans whose property had been destroyed during the Alexandria riots and was obliged to pay even the costs of the British occupation! The Egyptian army was dissolved and reorganized with fewer men and a small corps of European officers. The bureaucracy, too, was cut back. Many schools were shut down or reduced in size. All such measures became a necessary part of Egypt's race against bankruptcy.

The race was almost lost. Aside from the spreading rebellion in the Sudan mentioned earlier, the Egyptian government in 1883 had to deal with a severe cholera epidemic. Poverty, too, had caused many peasants to leave their villages and to turn to brigandage, leading to an upsurge of rural crime. The Egyptian Debt Commission was supposed to serve as a watchdog on the government's expenditures. But now that British troops had occupied Egypt, the representatives of the other European powers, especially France, acted more like the proverbial dog in the manger. Jealous of Britain's position in Egypt, they hoped that it would have to admit failure and pull out its troops.

In that year, 1883, the British government sent a new diplomatic representative, Sir Evelyn Baring, later called Lord Cromer (I will use the latter name, by which he is better known). Bearing the title of Her Majesty's Agent and Consul General in Cairo, for Egypt was still, legally, an Ottoman province, Cromer stayed in office for twenty-four years, gradually becoming the country's de facto governor.

At the outset, both Cromer and his home government expected their military occupation to be short lived. They had no long-term plans to modernize Egypt; they simply proposed to put the country's government and finances in order and, then, to leave. Temporary measures seemed to be needed. Cromer concentrated his efforts on fiscal reform and irrigation. He believed that lowering taxes and demands for forced labor, combined with better management of the Nile waters, would make the peasants more productive. The British financial adviser tried, therefore, to find ways to abolish the imposts that bore most heavily on peasants, such as the taxes on sheep and goats, grain-weighing, and salt. Within five years, the government was able to abolish forced labor, except for the requirement to guard the Nile during the flood season. Although money for large-scale construction projects was not available during the first years of the military occupation, British irrigation engineers brought in from India managed to repair the existing dams. A good example was the Delta barrage. Built under Mehmet Ali, it had been laid on weak foundations, had never properly directed the Nile flow, and had been abandoned by Sa'id as a white elephant. By means of various makeshift devices (including weighted cushions and mattresses from the khedivial harem), British engineers managed to stanch the leaking foundations and enable the barrage to back up the annual flood. With other emergency repairs to the Nile's dams and canals, the British achieved a dramatic rise in agricultural production at little public expense. Higher output yielded more tax revenues for the government, hastening the abolition of nuisance taxes and lowering the rates on the imposts that remained. After five years, the British felt that they had won the race against bankruptcy.

Many of Egypt's other problems remained unsolved, however. As mentioned earlier, the mahdi's rebellion in the Sudan spread, and the British could neither defeat nor make peace with the mahdi; so from 1885 to 1896 the Sudan, which had been won by Egyptian forces under Mehmet Ali and his successors, was lost. Even Upper Egypt was threatened with pro-mahdi insurrections during the 1880s. The first Egyptian government under the British occupation, headed by Sharif, resigned in protest over Britain's decision to give up the Sudan.

The next, led by Nubar, quit because of an ill-fated British effort to reorganize the interior ministry, the department responsible for maintaining public order. The British put off police reorganization for a while, but rural crime reached such alarming proportions that the government resorted to extrajudicial "commissions of brigandage" to arrest and punish suspected criminals. On the eve of the British occupation, the Egyptian government devised a new system of secular courts, the "National Tribunals," which began operation in 1883, following laws and procedures taken mainly from France's Napoleonic Law Code. Its jurisdiction was limited to Egyptian subjects, as distinct from the Mixed Courts that handled civil and commercial cases involving foreign nationals in Egypt. The British would rather have adapted the simpler legal structures that they had set up in India, but, not expecting to stay long in Egypt, they put off changing the legal system until the 1890s. By this time, Egypt had a growing corps of judges and lawyers trained by the French, so the British never could institute the legal reforms that they would have liked.

The British were so sure that their occupation would not last that they actually devised a withdrawal plan, by which their forces would be allowed to reenter Egypt for a three-year period in case a new revolution broke out. Although they thought they had gained the consent of the Ottoman government, French and Russian diplomats convinced the sultan that the British would use this right of reentry to make their occupation permanent and to cut Egypt off from Ottoman control. Their withdrawal plan was therefore never carried out. The British kept promising to go, but they stayed.

Khedive Tawfiq knew that he owed his throne to the British. As long as he remained alive, Cromer managed to govern Egypt from behind the scenes. A few dozen capable and dedicated British advisers quietly patched up the parts of the government in the greatest need of repair, while Egyptian ministers seemed to be in charge. The fiction was maintained that Egypt was a privileged, autonomous province of the Ottoman Empire, with the khedive serving as viceroy. He and his ministers, together with the British financial adviser, constituted the cabinet. Cromer expected to be consulted privately about the khedive's choice of ministers, and they in turn were expected to heed British advice as long as the occupation lasted, but the formal arrangements were honored. Egypt even had two representative bodies, the Legislative Council and the General Assembly (set up as a result of the Dufferin Commission's recommendations). Neither one was independent of the executive, though, and their legislative powers were almost nonexistent.

The Crises in Anglo-Khedivial Relations

Khedive Tawfiq died suddenly in January 1892, and the crises that followed would remove the veil from Britain's protectorate. Tawfiq's son, Abbas Hilmi II, was a high-spirited 17-year-old, studying at an Austrian military academy at the time of his father's unexpected death. At a time when the Ottoman government was strengthening control over its peripheral provinces and threatening to reassert its claim to the Sinai peninsula, both the Egyptian cabinet and the British wanted to avoid setting up a regency that might invite Ottoman intervention. By using the Muslim calendar (which encompassed 12 lunar months, or 354 days) instead of the Gregorian one, Abbas was reckoned to be 18 and hence ready to assume formal power. He and Cromer worked together to resist not only an Ottoman attempt to obtain the Sinai but also French and Russian efforts to sway him in choosing the members of his staff. Before long, however, the two men clashed.

Their dispute was partly generational, for Cromer seems to have harbored paternal feelings for this promising lad, while the young khedive naturally wanted to assert his personal independence. But their differences were also political. Abbas wanted to choose his own ministers; on his choices Cromer had to be "consulted," by which he really meant "obeyed." The first crisis arose in January 1893, when the pro-British prime minister, Mustafa Fahmi, believed to be very ill, offered his resignation. Without asking Cromer, the khedive appointed a nationalist in his place. Cromer reacted strongly. He called on the British government (headed, ironically, by Gladstone, who was still opposed to a long occupation) to send him additional troops and to issue a letter expressing the expectation that his advice would be followed as long as the occupation lasted. Abbas and Cromer compromised by appointing the veteran politician, Mustafa Riyad. Neither the khedive nor the consul was satisfied. A year later, the khedive, while inspecting Egypt's southern border defenses (then at Aswan), publicly criticized some British-led units of the Egyptian army. Sir Herbert Kitchener, newly appointed as its commander, took umbrage at Abbas' criticism and requested permission to resign. The khedive tried to patch up the quarrel before it got out of hand, but word of the incident reached Cromer, who accused a nationalist deputy minister of war of instigating it. If Egypt's army became infected with anti-British sentiment, a new Urabist movement might threaten the peace. Cromer told Riyad that the khedive must issue a statement expressing his complete satisfaction with all units of the army. Abbas obeyed but remained embittered. After that, everyone knew that the Egyptian ministers, and above all the khedive, had to obey the orders of the British, especially Lord Cromer.

Summary and Conclusion

The main reason the British occupied Egypt was the Suez Canal, which they had found would speed the movement of troops and goods between Europe and India. This discovery had been underscored by Britain's decision in 1875 to buy Egypt's shares in the Suez Canal. Britain simply could not allow any other power, or combination of states, to control either the canal or the country through which it had been cut. The British government and people also had a substantial interest in Egypt's finances. If the Egyptian government could not repay its debts, British subjects would be among the first to suffer (they dismissed the similar concern of French citizens). The British feared that a nationalist government, voicing the wishes of the Egyptian landlords and peasant taxpayers, might repudiate these obligations. A nationalist regime, which might heed an appeal to Islamic solidarity, could also turn against non-Muslim minorities and foreigners (who were conspicuously among the most wealthy and influential inhabitants of Egypt's main cities) and endanger public security. The British had occupied the country to keep the French from doing so first. They squelched the nationalist leaders easily, and most of their followers were soon silenced. They promised to leave promptly, but an early evacuation proved difficult because of the revolution in the Sudan, the financial crisis, and the obstructionism being waged by the other interested powers. The occupation became a veiled protectorate, the veil then fell off, and the Egyptians found that they had acquired yet another foreign master.

CHAPTER FIVE

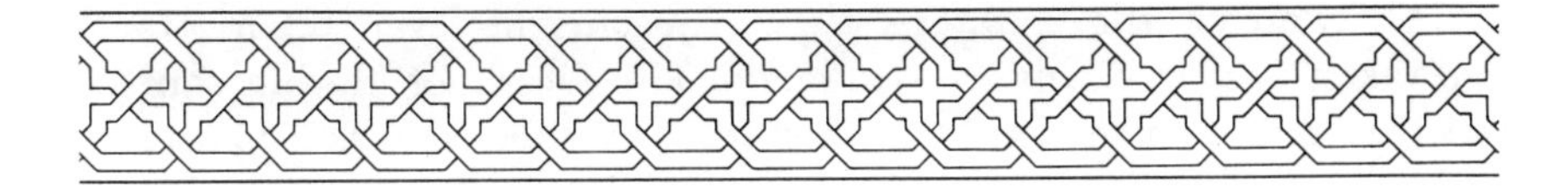

Nationalist Resistance

Britain's military occupation of Egypt in 1882, purportedly temporary, had no standing in international law, no formal recognition from the other European powers, and no formal acknowledgment from Egypt's internationally recognized suzerain, the Ottoman Empire. The British government promised many times after 1882 to withdraw its troops, but it never actually did so, for their presence supported not only the restoration and maintenance of order but also the strategic needs of the British Empire. Surprisingly, though, the number of British troops did not exceed 5,000, and the people of Egypt—from Khedive Tawfiq down to the peasants—accepted their presence. Although Tawfiq may have felt flashes of resentment against the occupying army (as he admitted to his intimates), he knew better than to resist openly. He realized that he would probably have been deposed—or worse—by Urabi's supporters. Although the French and the Ottoman governments opposed the British, practically all Egyptians followed Tawfiq's lead. It was only after Abbas Hilmi II succeeded him in 1892 that nationalist resistance reappeared.

The Idea of Nationalism

Traditional Islam has no room for nationalism. For observant Muslims, the Islamic community has always been the true focus of their loyalty. They abhor nationalism as a Western import that would divide them, yet they also believe that true Muslims will not long obey any ruler who does not enforce the Shari'ah, which encompasses the rules and laws of Islam. Centuries earlier, Islam's legal experts had advised Muslims who fell under non-Muslim rule to resist or, if resistance were impossible, to flee to a Muslim-ruled land. Few Egyptians did so after

1882. The westernizing reforms had already diluted the influence of the Shari'ah on the country's laws. Non-Muslims even before 1882 had taken part in Egypt's government. The facade of Muslim control was maintained in the early Cromer years as effectively as it had been under Mehmet Ali and Isma'il.

We can view the Egyptian nationalist groups that have grown up since 1892 in two ways: as affirmations of the originally Western idea that Egypt is a nation-state deserving the primary loyalty of its citizens, or as movements of resistance by Egyptians, largely though not wholly Muslim, against non-Muslim rule. The movement that began in the 1890s was of the first kind. Its founders belonged to an elite that had been educated abroad, in local schools set up by Europeans, or in Egyptian government schools, many of whose teachers were European. Most of them were lawyers, journalists, or teachers. They regarded Egypt as a nation, the world's oldest, waking up after centuries of sleep. They acknowledged the benefits of westernization, to themselves and to their country. They wanted Egypt to become a parliamentary democracy, with a constitutional monarch. The rights of citizenship should be enjoyed by all people who loved and lived in Egypt, whether they were Muslim, Christian, or Jewish, or indeed whether they were descended from ethnic Egyptians, from immigrants from other parts of the Muslim world, or from Europe. In fact, one of these nationalists, himself a Christian, coined the motto *Libres chez nous, hospitaliers pour tous.* This may be loosely translated as "Free in our home, hospitable to all who come." They refuted all foreign charges of xenophobia or religious fanaticism. Their first and main demand was for the British troops to leave Egypt.

The National Party

But this nationalist movement was not purely spontaneous; nor was it free from governmental influence. It began as a secret society, led in fact by the young Khedive Abbas under the influence of various Europeans in his palace staff. Their common bond was not so much love of Egypt as hatred of Lord Cromer. The man now regarded as the movement's founder, Mustafa Kamil, was initially a spokesman for Abbas. Both men were 18 years old in 1892 and probably remembered little about Egypt before the British occupation. They did, however, share an understandable resentment against Cromer's interference, buttressed by a growing number of British advisers in Egyptian government ministries as well as by the army of occupation. They were also able to seek support from the French in Egypt and from parties or factions in Europe that opposed the British occupation.

Mustafa Kamil, himself a student at the Khedivial Law School, was a leader among his peers in 1892. He was already editing a monthly magazine, *al-Madrasah* ("the School"), Egypt's first student journal. In January 1893 he led a protest march to the office of *al-Muqattam*, a pro-British daily newspaper, to support Khedive Abbas, who was then struggling with Cromer over the right to name his own ministers. Soon afterward, Mustafa transferred from the Khedivial to the French Law School, which taught the Napoleonic Code (the main basis of Egypt's Native Penal Code) to would-be Egyptian lawyers. That summer he went to Paris, ostensibly to pass his first-year finals there, but also to make contacts for the khedive and to demonstrate Egyptian loyalty to the Ottoman Empire by holding a banquet to honor the sultan's accession day. Even in less inflationary times, few students could have hosted a banquet in Paris without financial aid. For Mustafa, this aid came from the khedive. Later, funds would also come from the sultan.

Mustafa Kamil would devote the rest of his life to securing the British evacuation from Egypt. The Egyptian people were unarmed, unorganized, and, owing to Urabi's defeat in 1882, intimidated by Britain's power. He did not, therefore, view revolution as an effective means to end the British occupation. Conditioned by his legal training to think in terms of rights and obligations, he believed that independence would be secured through persuasion. He hoped that he could persuade the British directly. In 1896 he even wrote Gladstone a letter, to which the elder statesman, now retired, replied, saying that he thought the time had long since come for the British to leave Egypt. Most British officials had by then accepted an indefinite occupation, though, and saw no need to heed Mustafa Kamil or even Khedive Abbas. The French showed more sympathy, mainly because their own imperial interests in Africa would benefit from a British evacuation. Mustafa did find a French patron, Juliette Adam, the editor of an influential monthly, *La nouvelle revue*, who espoused Egyptian nationalism in its pages. At first he even hoped that the German and Austrian governments might join France and Russia in demanding that Britain fulfill its promises to leave Egypt. There was also the Ottoman Empire, Egypt's legitimate suzerain. Sultan Abdulhamid (r. 1876–1909) not only resented the British occupation but also pressed his claim to the Islamic caliphate in an effort to retain Egyptian loyalty. Mustafa courted his support (financial as well as moral) and exploited it when it enhanced his appeal to Muslim Egyptians.

As mentioned earlier, Egyptian nationalism could be regarded as a Muslim resistance movement against the rule of a non-Muslim power. Sultan Abdulhamid's claim to the caliphate was an element in a wider movement, popular at that time among Muslims under non-Muslim rule, called pan-Islam. This was the doctrine that urged Muslims to unite under the leadership of an Islamic ruler. In the 1890s the only one who could have united even Sunni Muslims was the Ottoman sultan-caliph. Egyptians, 90 percent of whom were Muslim, were susceptible to pan-Islamic appeals, as were the Indian Muslims, and the British worried about any such movement that could weaken their empire. The French, with Muslim subjects in Algeria, Tunisia, and Senegal, feared pan-Islam. So, too, did the Russians, who had conquered vast areas of the Caucasus Mountains and Central Asia. But Ottoman weakness, evident from the 1877 Russo-Turkish War, tended to blunt the movement's attractiveness. The sultan welcomed expressions of loyalty from young Egyptian nationalists and was willing to support them, but he lacked the power to confront Britain militarily. Only later, when Germany signed a formal alliance with the Ottomans at the outset of World War I, was such a confrontation possible.

Appeals to foreigners do not make a strong nationalist movement. If the Egyptians had secured their freedom from British rule through the actions of the continental European powers (or through the intervention of the Ottoman sultan), they would have become dependent on whomever "liberated" them. Only by mobilizing themselves could the Egyptians become nationalists. At first, Khedive Abbas looked to a man other than Mustafa Kamil to arouse Egyptian opinion. This was the editor of *al-Mu'ayyad,* Shaykh Ali Yusuf. It may be hard for younger readers nowadays to realize that daily newspapers were once the focal point of politics in both Western and non-Western countries. In Egypt, Urabi's defeat had briefly stunted the growth of political journalism, but even under Khedive Tawfiq the press had been reviving. In his time, the most respected newspapers were *al-Ahram,* founded in 1875 and still going strong today, and *al-Muqattam,* which began in 1889. Both were owned and edited by Syrian Christians, but *al-Ahram* was pro-French (its founders were Greek Catholics educated in French mission schools), whereas *al-Muqattam* (whose founders were graduates of the Syrian Protestant College run by U.S. missionaries in Beirut) supported the British, partly in reaction against *al-Ahram.* Shaykh Ali Yusuf, a poet and an Azharite with high ambitions but almost no money, began publishing *al-Mu'ayyad* in 1889, subsidized by a group of Egyptian Muslims headed by Riyad, partly to counterbalance *al-Muqattam.* In Egyptian politics, as in physics, for every action there is an equal and opposite reaction. When Abbas became khedive, *al-Mu'ayyad* emerged as his palace organ and the mouthpiece for Muslim Egyptian opinion. As long as Egyptian opposition to British rule was linked to Khedive Abbas, it had no need for its own nationalist newspaper.

By 1900, though, the Egyptian army, commanded mainly by British officers, had reconquered the Sudan, the French had given up hope of gaining power in the Nile Valley, and Khedive Abbas was starting to cultivate ties with the British. It is interesting that one of his close English friends was the prince of Wales, soon to become Edward VII after sixty years of being Queen Victoria's heir apparent. The prince once complained that Cromer tended to lecture him as if he were the khedive, and the two men undoubtedly shared a feeling of being long kept away from the power they felt entitled to exercise. As the khedive drew closer to the British, Mustafa Kamil and his followers started to pursue an independent policy. They could no longer count on getting published in *al-Mu'ayyad,* so they founded an explicitly nationalist daily, *al-Liwa'* ("The Banner"). Now Mustafa started writing about the people's political rights, constitutional government, and the expansion of public education, even as he continued to attack the British occupation. Abbas no longer wanted to oust the British, if he would then have to share his hard-won powers with a parliament. He grew tired of spending his money on the nationalists, who often backed Ottoman or pan-Islamic causes. Finally he broke with them, or they with him, in 1904, soon after France, in its *entente cordiale* with Britain, agreed not to demand a terminal date for its occupation of Egypt.

The story of the break is interesting. During his summer vacation in France, Abbas met privately with Mustafa Kamil and some of his followers. They began talking about Shaykh Ali Yusuf, who was trying to marry the daughter of Egypt's highest-ranking Muslim dignitary, the Shaykh al-Sadat. The Shari'ah Court voided the marriage, stating that Ali Yusuf belonged to a lower social class than his bride. The Khedive had backed Yusuf, who was, after all, his main spokesman. Mustafa criticized his actions as flouting Egyptian public opinion. "What is this public opinion, old fellow?" Abbas retorted. "If I put on a hat [a Muslim expression that meant conversion to Christianity] and walked through the streets of Cairo, no one would dare to say anything against me. Don't tell me what to do. I know my duty." Mustafa, for whom public opinion meant everything, left in anger and swore that he would break all ties with the khedive. His friends tried to patch up the quarrel, but as soon as they had returned to Egypt, Mustafa Kamil published in *al-Ahram,* as well as *al-Liwa',* his decision to work independent of the Palace.

What grievances did these nationalists have? Most European observers thought that Cromer had saved Egypt from bankruptcy. British engineers had revamped and expanded Nile irrigation, thereby giving the Delta and increasing portions of the Nile Valley enough water to grow three crops a year instead of one. Nuisance taxes had been abolished and other imposts lowered, increasing the discretionary income of the Egyptian people. No longer were peasants flogged with a rhinoceros hide or sent away from their families and fields to perform forced labor in other parts of Egypt. Slavery, outlawed (on paper) since Isma'il's time, now ceased to exist. Government corruption almost vanished. Once the financial crisis was over, Europeans resumed investing in Egypt. As a result of European entrepreneurship, Cairo and Alexandria acquired most of the amenities of Western cities: gas, electricity, street lights, piped drinking water, tram lines, and telephones. Many Westerners came to Egypt as tourists, and some as permanent residents, protected under the Capitulations from local laws and taxes. Egypt in the first decade of the twentieth century was more prosperous than it had been since early Mamluk times.

The nationalist objection was that the Egyptian people were not advancing toward self-rule but, rather, were being treated as tools serving British imperial interests. They could grow cotton to sell to the textile mills of Lancashire and they could buy their clothing from the same British firms, but they could not set up their own factories to spin thread, weave cloth, and fashion garments. The British scrimped on education long after the financial crisis had passed, never spending more than 3 percent of the Egyptian government budget on the schools. Parents paid higher tuition fees to send their children to public elementary and secondary schools than were charged by many private (including missionary) schools. Moreover, English was gradually replacing French as the main language of instruction, and for a long time the British opposed the use of Arabic, even in the elementary schools, claiming that it was unsuited to the teaching of the natural sciences and other modern subjects. The Egyptian ministers (most of whom were actually of Turkish or Circassian descent) were rubber stamps for their British advisers. The longer the British troops remained, the more numerous were the British advisers in the Egyptian government and army. The British had intended to turn power over to Egyptians gradually, but instead the higher posts went increasingly to their own men. The British advisers, officials, and officers were men of high caliber, but they tended to become more insular as their numbers increased and especially once their wives and children came out to live with them in Egypt. Salary bonuses could induce the men to learn Arabic, in order to deal better with Egyptians on and off the job, but their wives could hardly adjust to the cloistered harem life of Muslim Egypt. The British had their own social clubs, from which Egyptians were excluded even as guests, and mingling became the exception, not the rule. Even though Mustafa Kamil and his followers probably did not care to mingle with the British, the widening social gulf between the two sides increased feelings of mutual incomprehension and hostility.

Once he broke with the khedive, Mustafa Kamil became even more involved in Ottoman causes. He strengthened his ties with Sultan Abdulhamid and used pan-Islam as a means of gaining support from the Egyptian people. A key incident was the 1906 Taba Affair—the same Taba over which Egypt and Israel would contend in the 1980s. The British had long treated the Sinai as part of Egypt, as a buffer zone between the Ottoman Empire and the Suez Canal. When the Ottoman government tightened its hold on its remaining provinces, including southern Syria and the Hijaz, the British and the Turks eyed each other's moves warily. When Abbas had become khedive in 1892, Egypt turned over the garrisons that Mehmet Ali had established on the eastern shores of the Gulf of Aqaba; at the same time, Abbas resisted (with British backing) the Ottoman demand for the Egyptian forts on the western side of the Gulf. In 1906 Ottoman troops built a new fort at Taba, west of the line that the Egyptian government regarded as its border with their empire. The British sent warships into the eastern Mediterranean and threatened a show of force against the Ottoman Empire, which eventually agreed to demarcate a formal border. That frontier has since come to be known as the "international line," giving most of the Sinai Peninsula to Egypt. Egypt's nationalists—indeed, most Egyptians—backed the Ottoman claim against that of their own government. This stance may seem unpatriotic, but not if we consider that it was Britain whose interests were served by the claiming of Sinai for Egypt. But some Egyptians did attack the nationalists for preferring pan-Islamic causes to Egyptian ones. The Taba Affair was one (but not the only) instance of a recurrent struggle in this century between the territorial nationalist and supranationalist orientations of politically articulate Egyptians.

The Taba Affair helped cause an incident that did even more to strengthen the nationalist movement. A small group of British officers in uniform entered the Delta village of Dinshaway to shoot pigeons, a sport that offended many peasants who kept the birds as barnyard animals, particularly for their manure. A threshing floor caught on fire, and the villagers, thinking that the shooting was the cause, rushed at the officers with wooden staves and tried to disarm them. An officer's gun went off, a woman fell wounded (fatally, it appeared), and four other villagers were peppered with shot. The officers panicked. Two of them fled, but one of them died of sunstroke as he was running back to his camp. His comrade, finding him in the arms of a peasant who was trying in vain to revive him, assumed that the peasant had killed him and proceeded to beat him to death. The British authorities, upon hearing of the incident, took it to be a premeditated attack (inspired by the nationalist press) on their officers in uniform, and decided to teach the villagers a lesson. They set up a special court, not part of the native penal system, and tried fifty-two of the Dinshaway villagers before a panel of five judges, of whom only two were Egyptian. Four of the defendants were sentenced to hanging and some of the others to flogging or to jail terms. The hanging and flogging sentences were carried out in the presence of the Dinshaway villagers.

This barbarous act, due perhaps to panic in the wake of the Taba Affair, galvanized widespread anger against the British occupation of Egypt. Although British and European liberals were the first to protest, anger spread among all classes of Egyptian society. Many Egyptians, Christians as well as Muslims, flocked to Mustafa Kamil's standard. The widespread revulsion against the Dinshaway sentences led to demands for reform in the British administration and probably hastened Cromer's retirement in 1907. For the first time since the Urabi Revolution, large numbers of Egyptians became politically active. The khedive made peace with Mustafa. The two men agreed to set up English and French editions of *al-Liwa'* and to turn what had been a secret society into the National party, open to all Egyptians who wanted the British troops to leave their country. Another group of Egyptians, mainly landowners and intellectuals opposed to Mustafa's pro-Ottoman and pan-Islamic position during the Taba Affair, founded a newspaper named *al-Jaridah* and a rival party, *hizb al-ummah* ("party of the nation"). Many future political and literary leaders, among them Sa'd Zaghlul and Ahmad Lutfi al-Sayyid, joined the latter party. Because the National party claimed to speak for the people, Khedive Abbas and Ali Yusuf proceeded to form one directly under Palace control, the Constitutional Reform party, which revolved around *al-Mu'ayyad*.

How did Britain react to this proliferation of Egyptian political parties? The Liberals had swept into power in January 1906, but even their left wing was not so critical of British rule in Egypt as to call for total withdrawal. They did, however, want to make a greater effort to prepare Egyptians for eventual independence. Cromer's replacement, Sir Eldon Gorst, was a subtler man with extensive experience in Egypt as well as in the Foreign Office. He was quite willing to put more

Egyptians into responsible posts and to increase slightly the powers of the Legislative Council and the General Assembly. He had no desire to meet either National party leaders or those of the Ummah party, but he promptly began to win Khedive Abbas to his side. The loss of Palace support hurt the Nationalists, but they set up their formal party organization and elected Mustafa Kamil president for life. Two months later he died, probably of tuberculosis (but some said of poison). He was only 33 years old.

The death of Mustafa Kamil occasioned modern Egypt's first mass funeral demonstration, as civil servants walked off their jobs and students cut their classes to march behind his bier. Indeed, this demonstration showed the British clearly how popular the National party had become. But the death of its leader crippled the party, for a dispute arose over the succession. The Nationalists' choice, Muhammad Farid, was a decent and dignified man but neither a spellbinding orator nor a shrewd manipulator. He had been one of Mustafa Kamil's earliest backers. A man of independent means, he could not so easily be controlled by the offer (or denial) of cash subsidies from the khedive or the sultan. But the Nationalists split along several lines: Some wanted closer ties with the khedive, while others denounced his entente with the British; some favored pan-Islam and strong Ottoman ties, while others wanted to attract or retain the support of Egypt's non-Muslims; and some wanted to win Egypt's independence by fomenting an armed insurrection, while others believed in nonviolent persuasion.

The party continued to grow for two years, setting up branches in the provincial towns and a clubhouse in Cairo. Mustafa Kamil had founded a private school for boys; now the Nationalists established night schools for workers and consumer cooperatives. Farid supported labor unions—and even the first strike organized by Egyptian workers. But the most celebrated Nationalist was Abd al-Aziz Jawish, an Azharite shaykh who, appointed by Farid as the editor of *al-Liwa'*, wrote fiery editorials condemning the Dinshaway executions (which united the Egyptian people) and attacking the Copts (which divided them). Moderates and non-Muslims quit the Nationalist party, and its direction became increasingly radical and pan-Islamic. The 1908 Young Turk Revolution, which restored the 1876 Ottoman constitution, raised Nationalist hopes. Farid hastened to Istanbul to seek the support of the new regime, but the Young Turk leaders proved to be pro-British (they would change later). The Nationalists fared better at organizing the Egyptian students in Europe, and for several years Egyptian congresses were held in European cities, where they were attended by foreign politicians, journalists, and scholars. The congresses gained some support for Egyptian nationalism among socialist, pacifist, and fringe groups; they had no influence on British policy.

British Suppression of the Nationalists

The Egyptian government and its British advisers did worry about the party's influence on young people. In 1909 the cabinet revived an old law requiring all newspapers to be licensed, but anti-British papers found that they could evade it by appointing as editors or owners people claiming foreign nationality (and hence protection under the Capitulations), thereby weakening the law temporarily. The government, needing additional money to finance irrigation works, offered the Suez Canal Company a forty-year extension of its concession (i.e., from 1968 to 2008) for 4 million Egyptian pounds (then worth about US$20 million). The Nationalists vehemently opposed this deal, but so did most articulate Egyptians. Gorst advised the cabinet to submit the issue to the General Assembly, which voted it down almost unanimously. But before the vote was taken, Egypt's prime minister, Butros Ghali (grandfather of the current minister of state for foreign affairs, who has the same name), was shot by a young Nationalist. Subsequent investigation showed that the assassin belonged to a secret society that was forming revolutionary cells throughout Egypt to kill (or at least to intimidate) Egyptians collaborating with the British. This discovery led to a spate of new laws regulating the press, student political activities, and public meetings. Gorst stopped trying to give power to more Egyptians, then left office, stricken fatally with cancer. His successor was Lord Kitchener, the man who had quarreled with Khedive Abbas in 1894 and had led the reconquest of the Sudan in 1898. Kitchener took a much tougher stand against dissidents. The Nationalist leaders now faced severe limitations, prison terms, or exile. The faint-hearted quit the party; Muhammad Farid and Shaykh Jawish both sought freedom in Istanbul to go on waging their struggle.

Kitchener was a strong leader, popular in Britain and sincerely eager to improve Egyptian conditions, especially for the peasants. Egypt acquired its first agricultural cooperative banks and, indeed, its Ministry of Agriculture under Kitchener. The cabinet passed a law that prohibited lenders from taking a peasant's last 5 feddans (approximately 5.2 acres) as security for a loan. Although some contemporary observers viewed this act as a symbol of Kitchener's compassion for the Egyptian peasants, its practical effect was to make it well nigh impossible for the poorest ones to borrow enough money to make capital improvements. Kitchener disdained party politics, but he did let the Egyptians elect delegates to a new and more powerful representative body, the Legislative Assembly, in 1914. Sa'd Zaghlul was elected vice-president of the organization and began to emerge as a major opposition leader. Ummah party supporters played a large part in the Assembly, while the khedive found himself in relative isolation. Kitchener, who was giving serious thought to removing Abbas from office, was delighted at this result of his policies.

World War I

The outbreak of World War I caused the British to tighten their hold on Egypt and the Sudan. Once the Ottoman Empire had formally entered the war on the German side, the British severed Egypt's vestigial Turkish ties and declared a protectorate over the country. Khedive Abbas was deposed and an uncle, Husayn Kamil, took his place with the title of sultan. Nationalists still in Egypt were put under house arrest, the Legislative Assembly was adjourned indefinitely, and political life went into suspension. The prime minister, Husayn Rushdi, stayed in office on the understanding that the British protectorate would last only until the end of the war. Increasingly, however, the British ran Egypt like a crown colony. Hundreds of Britons were brought in to staff the Egyptian civil service, while thousands of British Empire troops—many of them Australians and New Zealanders—occupied Cairo, Alexandria, and the Suez Canal zone. Prices skyrocketed. Many Egyptians were conscripted to serve as auxiliaries in the several Allied armies that were using the country as their base of operations against the Turks; others had to contribute money, animals, or farm equipment to the war effort. As a result, the British lost much good will.

Overt opposition to British rule was banned within Egypt. Nationalists in exile kept up their campaign, taking advantage of wartime opportunities to get financial and moral support from the deposed khedive, the Ottoman government, and the Germans. Shaykh Jawish helped write the Ottoman Sultan's proclamation of jihad (Muslim struggle) against the Allies and later, in Berlin, edited *Die islamische Welt,* a pan-Islamic monthly. Muhammad Farid organized student groups, attended pacifist and socialist congresses, and reminded German and Ottoman officials of the Egyptian Nationalist demands for British evacuation and constitutional government. Some of their followers wanted to smuggle arms and organize a guerrilla movement in Egypt, and a few did make contacts with Sanusi rebels against the Italians in eastern Libya, but there was no revolution during the war.

Immediately following the armistice, however, conditions changed. The pent-up wartime grievances of the Egyptian people exploded in a nationwide revolution, involving Copts as well as Muslims, women as well as men, and all classes of Egypt's society. Demanding the complete independence of Egypt, the revolutionary movement, led by Sa'd Zaghlul, disrupted its government and finally caused the British to give up their protectorate. But this nationwide revolution, in which the National party had no public role, ushered in a new phase in the emergence of modern Egypt as a nation-state. Its story will be reserved for the following chapter.

CHAPTER SIX

Egypt's Ambiguous Independence

The end of World War I brought no peace to the world. Conflicts continued in some countries, and people rebelled in many others, but the outbreak of the revolution in Egypt surprised both the British and the Egyptians themselves. The expanded presence of British Empire troops and the increased demand for Egypt's agricultural products had brought wartime prosperity to some landlords and peasants. The high caliber of Egypt's prewar administration had led many foreigners to suppose that the Egyptians welcomed British protection. Indeed, the Egyptian people, except for the Nationalists in exile, had shown few signs of restiveness or pro-Turkish sentiment during the war. Concerned about making peace with Germany and its allies, the British in 1918 never thought of ending their protectorate over Egypt.

The Egyptian Delegation (Wafd)

But the Egyptians thought of nothing else. At most, they could tolerate the British protectorate only as a wartime measure. During the final months of the war, when the Allies were winning and could ponder when and where to hold a peace conference, Egyptians began to discuss sending a delegation (Arabic: *wafd*) that would express their demands to the world. Historians disagree over who first proposed to send an Egyptian Wafd to the postwar peace conference. But we do know that the prime minister, Husayn Rushdi, and Sultan Fu'ad (who had succeeded his brother in 1917) both favored greater autonomy from the British and that some of the old-line Nationalists were considering a popular revolution. However, the plan to organize a formal delegation was probably put forth by some of the old Ummah party members, particularly Abd al-Aziz Fahmi, Muhammad Mahmud, and the man whose name is now forever tied to the Egyptian Wafd and the 1919 Revolution, Sa'd Zaghlul.

Sa'd Zaghlul had an interesting and varied past. The son of a moderately wealthy village headman, he received his early education in mosque schools and at al-Azhar, where he had come under the influence of two of the nineteenth century's great Muslim reformers, Jamal al-Din "al-Afghani" and Muhammad Abduh. In the turbulent months leading up to the Urabi Revolution, Sa'd had helped Abduh edit the government newspaper and thus became deeply involved in the revolutionary events of 1882. Just after the British took over, he was arrested for belonging to a terrorist society. After being saved from execution, he adopted a safer course of action, going to France to study law. Upon completing his degree and returning to Egypt, he became a lawyer and then a judge in the national court system. His upward mobility was hastened by the patronage of an influential member of the khedivial family, Princess Nazli, and by his marriage to the daughter of Prime Minister Mustafa Fahmi. Both of these prominent figures were friendly with the British, and Sa'd became a favorite of Lord Cromer, who advised Khedive Abbas to name him education minister in 1906. During his farewell address in 1907, Cromer singled out Sa'd: "He possesses all the qualities necessary to serve his country. He is honest, he is capable, he has the courage of his convictions, he has been abused by many of the less worthy of his own countrymen. These are high qualifications. He should go far."

Sa'd Zaghlul did go far, but not in the direction that Cromer had in mind. Under Gorst, Sa'd, like many Ummah party members and sympathizers, became disillusioned with British rule. Although he became justice minister in 1910, he left the cabinet two years later because of differences with the other ministers (and probably also Khedive Abbas and Lord Kitchener). When Kitchener allowed the Egyptians to set up the Legislative Assembly and to hold elections, Sa'd ran and was elected by two separate constituencies. His legislative colleagues elected him vice-president of the Assembly in January 1914, and he became its leading critic of the government during its few months in session. When the war started, the Assembly was suspended and never reconvened, but it served as the associational basis for Sa'd Zaghlul and the other founders of the Egyptian delegation to the postwar peace conference. During the fall of 1918 the group met frequently to discuss their plans. As soon as the armistice was signed, they requested an appointment with the British high commissioner, Sir Reginald Wingate.

Two days later, Sa'd and a couple of his friends called on Wingate and formally asked for permission to talk with officials in the British Foreign Office about Egypt's demand for independence. Wingate gave no answer, but he did cable the foreign secretary, Lord [Arthur] Balfour, who eventually replied that his officials were too busy with preparations for the forthcoming Paris Peace Conference to talk with Sa'd Zaghlul or even with Prime Minister Rushdi. This rebuff angered the Egyptians, who noted that Arabs, Jews, and Armenians were asked to address the Peace Conference but that they were not. To refute allegations that Sa'd's Wafd did not truly represent the people, supporters throughout Egypt circulated petitions, and about 100,000 signers authorized the Wafd to speak for them. This act of circulating petitions made the Wafd assume a more formal organization, just as signing them made Egyptians feel more involved in the independence struggle. When even Rushdi was denied access to the Foreign Office, he resigned as prime minister. Likewise rebuffed was Wingate's recommendation, based on his intimate knowledge of Egyptian conditions, to invite both Husayn Rushdi and Sa'd Zaghlul to London. In fact, Wingate was recalled to London for consultation, a signal that he would probably be eased out of his position by a government that did not care to heed his advice.

As no Egyptian was willing to take charge of Egypt's government, unrest spread throughout the country. The British tried to nip it in the bud by exiling Sa'd Zaghlul and three of his Wafd colleagues to Malta. This measure infuriated the Egyptian people. Secondary-school students went out on strike, followed by government employees, judges, and lawyers. Before long, Egyptians were blowing up railroad tracks, cutting telegraph wires, and burning down buildings. Eight British soldiers were murdered in a railroad car. Street demonstrations, a few of them violent, became a daily occurrence. For the first time in their history, Egyptian women took part in these demonstrations. Coptic priests mounted the *minbar*s of mosques and Muslim *khatib*s stood in the pulpits of churches to preach the nearly forgotten lessons of national solidarity. The British were able to quell the violence by taking tougher police measures and by sending to Egypt a new high commissioner, General Edmund Allenby, who possessed great prestige because of his wartime role in the conquest of Palestine.

Allenby promptly called on all people to submit their proposals for steps to restore tranquillity and also released the detainees on Malta, freeing them to go to the Paris Peace Conference. It is one of the tragic ironies of Egyptian history that, on the very day when Sa'd

Zaghlul's Wafd reached Paris, the U.S. delegation to the peace conference issued a statement recognizing Britain's protectorate over Egypt. The Egyptians had hoped that President Woodrow Wilson would champion their claim to self-determination. Instead, they found that no one in Paris cared—not even the Americans. Demonstrations resumed in Egypt, and Allenby was hard-pressed to find any Egyptian willing to head a government, for fear of being assassinated.

Fruitless Independence Negotiations

Meanwhile, the British government announced that it would send to Egypt a mission, headed by a former Egyptian official, Lord Milner, to examine the causes of the disorders and to report "on the form of Constitution, which, *under the Protectorate,* will be best calculated to promote its peace and prosperity, the progressive development of self-governing institutions, and the protection of foreign interests." But politically articulate Egyptians had never wanted the protectorate, did not want to discuss its continuation, and now considered their spokesmen to be the Wafd in Paris. The Milner mission took eight months to reach Egypt and, once there, was boycotted by every Egyptian not in the palace or the cabinet. Sa'd Zaghlul negotiated informally with the Milner mission in London in 1920 and, together with the mission, drew up a memorandum that would have recognized Egypt's formal independence with an Anglo-Egyptian treaty, a continued British military presence, and British financial and judicial advisers. Zaghlul did not endorse this memorandum; rather, he insisted on referring it to the Egyptian people. Inasmuch as Milner's proposals fell far short of the complete independence that the demonstrators had called for, the Egyptian cabinet (anticipating the popular reaction) rejected them.

By 1921 it was clear that the British government would have to give up its protectorate. Now representatives of the two sides would have to agree on what Anglo-Egyptian relationship should take its place. Allenby obtained his government's authorization to tell Sultan Fu'ad that it would negotiate the question with an official Egyptian delegation. Fu'ad proceeded to appoint a new government, headed by Adli Yakan, a rival of Sa'd Zaghlul, who now returned from Paris to a tumultuous welcome in Egypt. Believing that he alone could negotiate with the British, Sa'd stirred up new demonstrations against Adli, who promptly formed an Egyptian delegation from which Sa'd and his followers were excluded. Adli's negotiations with Lord [George] Curzon (who had become the foreign secretary) went on for several months but collapsed when Britain insisted on keeping a garrison in Egypt. Adli could not compete with the Wafd's loyalty to Sa'd and the Egyptian people's vocal demands for complete independence. In Cairo, meanwhile, General Allenby concocted a compromise by which a non-Wafdist named Abd al-Khaliq Tharwat would succeed Adli as prime minister, Britain would recognize Egypt's independence, and Egypt would draft a constitution. The British exiled Sa'd again, this time for almost two years, thereby precipitating new strikes, riots, and demonstrations, for Sa'd had become, to most Egyptians, a symbol of their national dignity. The British cabinet wanted to dig in and keep the protectorate until the popular agitation ceased, but Allenby traveled to London and made a persuasive case for declaring Egypt's independence.

The Era of the Four Reserved Points

On 28 February 1922, the date of Allenby's return to Cairo, the British government issued a formal statement terminating its protectorate and declaring Egypt to be an independent sovereign state. But four points were reserved to Britain's discretion until it could reach an agreement with Egypt, namely:

1. security of British Empire communications in Egypt,
2. Egypt's defense against foreign aggression or interference,
3. protection of foreign interests and minorities in Egypt, and
4. the [status of the] Sudan.

The British thus greatly narrowed their area of concern, from reforming Egypt administratively and financially to guarding their strategic interests. The Egyptians had obtained not the Wafd's demand for complete independence but, rather, the partial autonomy that Milner had offered to Zaghlul in 1920 and Curzon to Adli in 1921. In the years to come, the Egyptians would continue to demand more independence, the British would concede as little as possible, and Egypt's real political and economic needs would be ignored by both sides.

Even if Egypt now enjoyed a vague sort of formal political independence, the country remained almost wholly dependent on foreigners. The Egyptian armed forces would have been too small and ill-equipped to defend Egypt and the Sudan without British assistance. Most of the high-ranking officers were British; the Muslim ones were still mainly of Turkish and Circassian descent. So indeed were most high-ranking officials of the Egyptian government. Nearly all public utilities, manufacturing firms, transportation companies, hotels, banks, and insurance companies were owned and managed by foreigners. No Egyptian sat on the administrative board of the Suez Canal Company. Egypt was home to some 200,000 foreign residents, who were still exempted from local laws and taxes by the Capitulations.

Although irksome limits on Egypt's independence remained, some signs of a new spirit appeared during and after the 1919 Revolution. An Egyptian named Tal'at Harb founded a giant financial institution called Bank Misr, which set up and financed an Egyptian-owned textile factory and paved the way for Egypt's economic independence. But what about cultural independence? Although Egypt's first secular university had been established in 1908, it was languishing for lack of state support by 1919, the foundation year of the American University in Cairo, which purchased its original buildings. But in 1925 the national university, of which Fu'ad had been the first president, was reorganized and established on its own campus in Giza. Moreover, Egypt was becoming the leader of popular Arab culture; in 1919 the first recording studio opened in Cairo, and during the 1920s several film companies began producing silent movies. Arabic newspapers and magazines proliferated rapidly, and more books were published in Cairo than in all other Arab capitals combined. Jacques Berque, in his influential history of the country, speaks of "the generation of 1919"—the group of thinkers and leaders who emerged after World War I to expand Egypt's intellectual horizons. Examples include Taha Husayn, who applied Western techniques of historical analysis to early Arabic poetry; Mahmud Mukhtar, Egypt's first great Muslim sculptor; Muhammad Husayn Haykal, who published a novel glorifying village life and a modernist interpretation of the life of Muhammad; Salama Musa, who advocated democratic socialism; and Huda Sha'rawi, who led Egyptian women in renouncing the veil and female seclusion.

Cultural advances were important, but the political struggles mattered most to educated Egyptians. The document that expressed their highest hopes was the 1923 constitution. It was written, after Britain's declaration of Egypt's independence, by a group of Egyptian legal scholars who drew heavily on the Belgian constitution as their model. The Wafd, leaderless while Sa'd Zaghlul was in exile, had nothing to do with it, and Sultan (now King) Fu'ad resented it, even though it empowered him to appoint prime ministers and to dissolve parliament. But Allenby, who kept the title of high commissioner until Britain and Egypt could agree on a treaty, favored it. The Egyptian government accepted the new constitution in April 1923, and at last the British agreed to end martial law in Egypt. Sa'd and his companions, as well as various Nationalists exiled since 1914, were allowed to return in time to compete in the first election for Egypt's new parliament. The Wafd, still viewing itself as the spokesman for the Egyptian people, reorganized itself as a political party, and its candidates won 179 of the 211 seats in the Chamber of Deputies. King Fu'ad therefore called on the Wafd party to form the first government, appointing Sa'd as the prime minister.

The Egyptians and the British both hoped that 1924 would be the year in which they resolved their political differences. Only Sa'd could negotiate a settlement that would be acceptable to most of the Egyptian people. Britain, meanwhile, had just elected its first Labor party government, which was thought to be less doctrinaire on British imperial matters than the Liberals or the Conservatives. Not even the Laborites, though, could give up strategic assets like the Suez Canal, and the Wafdists, for their part, could not stay in power on popular enthusiasm alone. From the Egyptian side, Sa'd faced two threats: Fu'ad, who detested the 1923 constitution and a parliament not firmly under his control; and the terrorist secret societies, holdovers from the 1919 Revolution, which believed that only force could drive the British out. In November 1924 terrorists assassinated the commander-in-chief of the Egyptian army, Sir Lee Stack, in the streets of Cairo. Allenby was outraged and publicly handed a stiff ultimatum to Sa'd, demanding an indemnity of 500,000 Egyptian pounds, a public apology, and the withdrawal of all Egyptian troops from the Sudan, as well as the prosecution of the assassins. What most galled the Egyptians, though, was Allenby's statement that the murder, which Sa'd could not have countenanced, was an act "which holds up Egypt as at present governed to the contempt of civilized peoples." The ultimatum also deprived Egypt of the Nile waters that the Sudan needed to irrigate its newly developed Gezira region, which planned to raise long-staple cotton in direct competition against the Egyptian product. The Foreign Office had not approved the text of this ultimatum, but the British government decided to stand behind Allenby. Sa'd, who could have rallied the Egyptian people by refusing some of its more extreme demands, chose instead to resign. His resignation enabled King Fu'ad to appoint a caretaker cabinet of his own men. On this sour note the first era of Wafdist rule ended.

The emerging pattern in Egypt's politics was that of a power triangle made up of the king, the Wafd party, and the British. King Fu'ad, the son of Isma'il, wanted to rule Egypt autocratically. He used his vast landholdings and his ability to make appointments to the army, the civil service, and al-Azhar University to expand his claque of loyal followers. The Wafd party enjoyed the support of the overwhelming majority of Egyptian voters; it could always win any unrigged election that it did not boycott. But note that even nominally democratic elections were marred by landlords who forced their peasants to vote en masse for themselves or their favorite parties or candidates. The British used the absence of a treaty with Egypt to preserve their influence, often invoking the 1922 declaration's "Four Reserved Points" to block any policy or appointment deemed likely to harm their interests.

There were also lesser Egyptian parties that could not compete with the Wafd for popularity but were able, in pursuit of power, to throw their weight to one or another of the legs of the triangle. The most extreme of these was the National party, which continued to uphold the principle of Mustafa Kamil and Muhammad Farid to oppose negotiations with the British until after they had withdrawn their troops from Egypt. The Nationalist stance had a theoretical rigor lacking in the more pragmatic parties, inasmuch as the British clearly used the presence of their troops in Egypt as a bargaining chip, but the other groups realized that negotiating would be the only practical way to get them out. The largest minority party, the Liberal Constitutionalists, consisted of the people who had supported Adli Yakan and Abd al-Khaliq Tharwat. Although they had all been members or backers of the Wafd in 1919, they had gradually left it because of their opposition to Sa'd's intransigence or what they saw as his demagogy. Its leaders were mainly landowners and intellectuals, strongly in favor of the 1923 constitution because of the powers it gave them. They would sometimes join with the Wafd to oppose King Fu'ad's usurpation of parliament's powers, but by the late 1920s they were cooperating with Palace politicians to form anti-Wafdist governments. King Fu'ad set up his own group, the Union party, in 1925. One of Egypt's cleverest politicians, Isma'il Sidqi, who headed a dictatorial and anti-Wafdist government in the early 1930s, set up one incongruously called the People's party. All of these parties entered into the triangular power struggle. Although several tried, none reached a treaty with the British that could have won popular acceptance. None tried to formulate policies to address any of Egypt's economic and social problems.

Egypt in the 1920s and 1930s was still an agricultural country heavily dependent on the export of long-staple cotton. Nile River irrigation was still increasing the amount of land under cultivation, but the population was growing faster. The distribution of landholdings was becoming increasingly lopsided, and the disparity was widening between a handful of rich landlords and the mounting number of desperately poor, landless peasants. Crop diversification and industrialization could alleviate these problems only if Egypt was able to find customers for products other than its long-staple cotton. This overdependence on cotton posed other problems as well: competition from rayon and other artificial fibers, infestation by the cotton maggot, and declining output per acre as a result of overwatering and salinization of the fields. In this state of ambiguous independence, the Egyptian government was free to spend more money on public education than it had done under the British protectorate, but the school system was starting to turn out more graduates than the government and private enterprise could absorb. The consequence was the unemployment or underemployment of many of Egypt's brightest and most westernized young people, which in turn created the potential for a revolution.

Egyptian politicians put off addressing such issues as these until later, but no one could ignore the need to reach a settlement with Great Britain. Allenby's successor as high commissioner, Lord [George] Lloyd, was an imperialist of the old school. He tried to maneuver Egyptian politicians in order to weaken the Wafd. He even asked for a British gunboat to be stationed outside Alexandria harbor to pressure Sa'd Zaghlul into refusing to serve as prime minister after his party had won the 1926 election by a resounding margin. As long as the Conservatives, who had appointed Lloyd, held power in London, the Egyptians did not try to negotiate with Britain. After Sa'd's death in 1927, Mustafa al-Nahhas became the Wafd party leader. When a British Labor government took power in 1929 and the Wafd won a free election in Egypt, Anglo-Egyptian negotiations briefly resumed, but the rivalry between the Palace and the Wafd led to Nahhas' downfall. King Fu'ad appointed as his new prime minister Isma'il Sidqi, who dismissed the Wafd-dominated parliament and replaced the 1923 constitution with a new one that concentrated power in his own hands. For five years Egypt was under a virtual Palace dictatorship, in which both the Wafdists and the Liberal Constitutionalists boycotted the elections. High Commissioner Lloyd's replacement, Sir Percy Loraine, kept a low profile, and there were no Anglo-Egyptian negotiations. But in 1934 a new high commissioner, Sir Miles Lampson, urged the Palace to bring back the 1923 constitution and to hold free elections, in order to form an Egyptian government with enough popular support to negotiate a treaty with the British. After a year of rising discontent and many student riots, King Fu'ad accepted Lampson's advice and reinstated the old constitution. A caretaker cabinet was formed, including ministers from most of Egypt's political parties, and Anglo-Egyptian negotiations resumed.

The Anglo-Egyptian Treaty

In 1936 both the British and the Egyptians were becoming eager to strengthen their ties, mainly because of the regional threat from Fascist Italy, which was occupying Ethiopia and already controlled Libya. Although King Fu'ad and his supporters had pro-Italian leanings, most Egyptians, including the Wafd, viewed the Fascists as a threat to their independence and democratic government. In addition, they feared that any war between the democracies and the dictators would probably become a replay of World War I, during which Egypt had, against its will, served as an Allied military base. An Anglo-Egyptian treaty might enable the Egyptians, in case of a war, to limit more effectively British interference in their government. The British, deeply concerned about their deteriorating position in Europe and the Middle East, needed a stronger basis for their military presence in Egypt and were eager to deal with Nahhas, the leader of the Wafd, which alone could influence Egyptian popular opinion. In the 1936 parliamentary elections, the Wafd won by a huge majority. Soon afterward, Fu'ad died and was succeeded by his 16-year-old son, Faruq, then a student in the British military school at Woolwich. The two sides started negotiating in earnest and, in August, reached a satisfactory agreement on the terms for a twenty-year treaty of alliance. The British recognized Egypt's independence, agreed to reduce their troops to 10,000 and to limit their bases to the Suez Canal zone, and promised to sponsor Egypt for membership in the League of Nations and to work for the abolition of the Capitulations. The Egyptians accepted a twenty-year British occupation of the Canal zone and allowed British troops to remain in Cairo until adequate barracks, roads, and bridges had been built at Egyptian government expense. Both sides put off any decision about the Sudan's future.

Conclusion

By the end of 1936, it looked as if Egypt would at last be ready to tackle some of its other pressing problems. Its relationship with Britain had been settled on a mutually satisfactory basis. A Wafdist government was firmly in power, backed by the Egyptian voters and the 1923 constitution. King Faruq, the first member of his family who could make a political speech in Arabic, was a handsome, pious, and well-behaved youth, genuinely loved by his subjects. Egypt could pursue its own foreign policy interests, now that there were no obvious crises in which Egypt had to become involved. But the country was on the verge of facing new challenges that would lead to the destruction of its monarchy, its parliamentary system, and even its traditional way of life. The greatest of these would result from its involvement with the political fate of its eastern neighbor, Palestine.

CHAPTER SEVEN

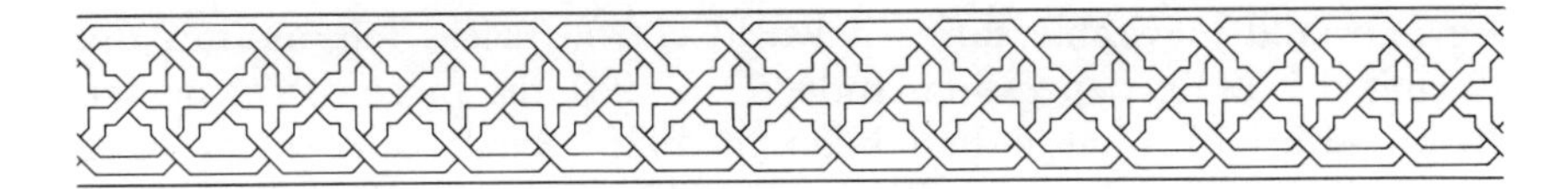

The Turning Point

The signing of the Anglo-Egyptian Treaty in August 1936 was then regarded by most Egyptians and foreigners as the final step toward Egypt's political independence. Representatives of all the Egyptian parties, except the Nationalists, signed the document. Although few Egyptians today look back at the treaty favorably, and the Nationalists were even then protesting that it legitimized Britain's military occupation of Egypt, the treaty was popular at the time. A portrait of Britain's foreign secretary, Sir Anthony Eden, appeared on a series of Egyptian postage stamps, in recognition of his role as a negotiator. More popular still was the 1937 Montreux Convention abolishing the Capitulations and phasing out the Mixed Courts over a thirteen-year period. After 1949 foreigners living in Egypt would no longer enjoy, before the law, privileges greater than those of the country's own citizens. Britain sponsored Egypt's application for membership in the League of Nations. The Egyptian government was now free to open embassies and consulates in other countries and to make its own domestic and foreign policies.

Socioeconomic Conditions

Since 1919, or perhaps even since the 1890s, most politically articulate Egyptians had focused their energies on ending the British military occupation of their country. But, they neglected many other problems as a result. In a country where possession of land was the primary source of power, most of the population either owned no land at all or owned too little to support themselves and their families. With the construction of the Nile irrigation works by the British, and as a result of improved rail and maritime transport, cash crops, especially long-staple cotton, had largely replaced subsistence agriculture. Hence, Egypt would inevitably suffer if world cotton prices fell, as they did during the 1930s depression. Indeed, in 1931 the price of cotton fell to one-third of what it had been in 1926. Small landowners were especially hard hit; between 1927 and 1937 more than 40,000 peasants, unable to pay their taxes, lost their lands. Land rents were so high that, even when the Nile flood was just right and cotton prices were high, it was hard for tenant farmers to raise enough to pay the landlord and still make an adequate living. An average daily wage for a cotton farmer fell from 8 piasters in 1920 to 2.5 (less than 13 cents) in 1933. Some peasants moved to Cairo, Alexandria, and the canal cities of Port Said, Ismailia, and Suez to seek employment, but there were more jobs in transport and services than in industry (where wages would have been higher).

Thanks to Bank Misr, founded by Tal'at Harb in 1920 and at the peak of its influence in 1939, Egyptians were beginning to invest in such industries as textiles, building materials, and food processing, but industrialization remained embryonic up to World War II, and most manufacturing firms were still owned by foreigners. To protect its infant industries, Egypt began to impose protective tariffs after 1930, but its membership in the sterling bloc still tied its economy to that of Britain. There was as yet no state planning, let alone any coordinated economic policy. Parliament, dominated by landowners and urban lawyers, did limit some land rents during the depression, but it never tried to redistribute landholdings. Land and buildings remained the most popular forms of investment.

Meanwhile, the income gap between rich and poor Egyptians grew wider. Along with poverty went ignorance and disease. Poor peasants could not afford tuition payments to send their sons and daughters to school; indeed, they could not do without even the meager income they received from their children's work in the fields. Mortality rates, especially for babies and small children in rural areas, were among the world's highest. Bilharzia (a disease carried by parasites of a snail that lives in stagnant irrigation ditches) and trachoma (an eye disease) were endemic. Few doctors or nurses would or could live in rural villages. There were still other causes of bad health conditions. Peasants could not afford piped water, let alone garbage and sewage disposal facilities that might have improved their hygienic conditions. Village ditches and ponds provided most of the water they used for drinking, cooking, washing clothes and cooking utensils, bathing themselves and their animals, and other purposes. Chickens and water buffaloes shared the mud-brick houses of the poor. The poorest did not even have houses; many vagabonds slept in doorways, under bridges, and on railroad rights-of-way. Most Egyptians endured hardship patiently, but these conditions could not be borne forever. Eventually, some would question the system by which the benefits and burdens of citizenship were parceled out. By 1936 Egyptian democracy was on trial.

King Faruq Versus the Wafd

The signing of the Anglo-Egyptian Treaty seems, in retrospect, to have been the high-water mark of liberal democracy in Egypt. The 1923 constitution had been restored after five years of government under Fu'ad's more autocratic version. Free elections had swept Egypt's most popular party, the Wafd, into power. Fu'ad, its royal arch-enemy, had died. His son and successor, Faruq, was young, handsome, and adored by the Egyptian press and people. Termed "the pious king," Faruq made frequent ceremonial visits to the Friday prayers, al-Azhar University, and the inauguration of new mosques. The Azharite leader, Shaykh Mustafa al-Maraghi, encouraged King Faruq's candidacy for the caliphate, the political headship of the world's Muslim community. There had been no caliph since 1924, when Kemal Ataturk had abolished the office, and it became increasingly unlikely that the world's Muslims would agree on any candidate, let alone one who was not (as the Shari'ah required) a descendant of the Prophet; but the idea appealed to Faruq's vanity. Britain's high commissioner (from 1936 its ambassador), Sir Miles Lampson, noted that Faruq was immature and insufficiently educated to rule Egypt, but most leading Egyptians wanted him to be only a figurehead king. The real power, they would argue, should belong to the cabinet, which was responsible to the people's representatives in parliament. The year 1936 was one of high hopes for Egyptian democracy.

But few of these hopes were realized. The Wafdist cabinet, led by Mustafa al-Nahhas, lasted for only eighteen months, before Faruq's advisers engineered its replacement by a coalition ministry made up of party leaders opposed to the Wafd. Ironically, the leaders of the Liberal Constitutionalist party, which had played the lead role in writing the 1923 constitution, defied that document by joining the anti-Wafd coalition. King Faruq turned out to be as dictatorial as his father had been, but because of his youth he reigned under the influence of his mother and his chief tutor (who may in fact have been her lover), Ahmad Hasanayn. They were helped by the Wafd's declining popularity. Two of its ablest politicians, Ahmad Mahir and Mahmud Fahmi al-Nuqrashi, bolted from the Wafd to establish the Sa'dist party, which joined the coalition cabinet.

Egypt and the Arab World

By the late 1930s, outside tensions were affecting Egypt internally. The rise of Nazi Germany was undermining the postwar peace settlement in Europe. Other countries could hardly ignore the changing balance of power and its effects on Britain and France, not only in Europe but also in their foreign colonies. Iraq, under a British mandate, had become independent in 1932. The countries mandated to France—Syria and Lebanon—seemed likely in 1936 to follow suit. Would these Arabic-speaking new states remain closely tied to Britain and France, or would they form a united Arab nation in opposition to their erstwhile rulers? The two Arab countries most apt to influence them were Egypt and Saudi Arabia, but the latter state was still extremely poor and owed what prestige it had to the dynamic rule of Abd al-Aziz, known in the West as Ibn Sa'ud. And there was one mandated country that was not advancing toward independence, at least not for most of its inhabitants. This was Palestine.

The Palestine question has received no attention thus far in this history, because it was not a major issue for Egypt until 1936. Let me try to sum it up. Palestine had belonged to the Ottoman Empire until it was taken by the British in 1917–1918. Shortly before this conquest, the British cabinet had issued a statement, called the Balfour Declaration, in which it had pledged to back the creation in Palestine of a national home for the Jewish people. Because the Jews were then a people scattered among many nations of the world, whereas over 90 percent of Palestine's inhabitants were Muslims or Christians who spoke Arabic, the creation of a "national home" (or state) would take some time and could require the transfer of large populations. Jews would have to move to there from the countries where they were living in 1917. Palestine's Arab inhabitants would face an uncertain political status, although the Balfour Declaration did specify that nothing should be done to prejudice their civil and religious rights. Historians are still debating Britain's motives for issuing this policy statement. Probably it hoped to strengthen Jewish support for the Allied cause in Russia and the United States, to secure British control over the land east of the Suez Canal, and to restrict France's wartime gains to what are now Lebanon and Syria.

Understandably, Arab Palestinians resisted the Balfour Declaration and British efforts (amplified by a mandate over the country from the League of Nations) to implement it. They looked to neighboring Muslims and Arabs, including Egyptians, for support. As long as the number of Jews entering Palestine was small, the movement to create a Jewish state, called "political Zionism," posed no real threat to the Arabs. And while most Arabic-speaking countries were being ruled by Britain or France, their ability to help the Palestinian Arabs to combat Zionism was slight. By 1936, though, conditions were changing. With the rise of Nazi Germany and its fiercely anti-Jewish laws, mounting numbers of Central and Eastern European Jews were trying to flee. Palestine was one of the few countries to which they could go, although since 1922 the British authorities had limited Jewish immigration to the country's absorptive capacity. By the late 1930s the Jewish community made up about 30 percent of Palestine's population, up from some 7 percent in 1917. Palestinian Arabs feared they would soon turn into a minority in their own country. Divided hitherto by family and religious loyalties, they sank their differences in 1936 and began a nationwide revolt against the British and the Zionists. Newly independent Iraq and Egypt tried to help them, politically and economically more than militarily. Often individuals gave more help than their governments.

Egypt's rising involvement in the Palestine question, both popular and official, stirred up interest in Arab nationalism. The Egyptian people had not generally viewed themselves as Arabs. They still associated the Arab nationalist idea with the Syrians and the Hijazis who had rebelled during World War I against the Ottoman Empire. Egyptian nationalists had considered this Arab Revolt an act of treason, for they had wanted the Turks to liberate them from the British. They also regarded themselves as having progressed further toward civilization (which in the 1930s still meant European cultural standards) than any other Arabic-speaking country. Their strongest loyalty was to Egypt, or indeed the Nile Valley, for they saw the Sudan as Egypt's southward extension, severed by British imperialism, and thought that the Sudanese people wanted to unite with them. Both Muslims and Copts took pride in their descent from the ancient Egyptians and stressed the pharaonic character of their common culture. But political independence, together with the growing Palestine crisis, gradually reoriented the majority's loyalties from pharaonism toward Arab nationalism and Islam.

The Society of the Muslim Brothers

Egyptians were at the same time becoming disillusioned with European ideas and institutions, including parliamentary democracy, and felt drawn to Islamic beliefs and values. Arab nationalist parties and ideologies won few followers in Egypt before World War II, but

Egyptians of all classes and educational levels were joining a revolutionary movement, founded in Ismailia in 1928, that was called the Society of the Muslim Brothers. The Muslim Brothers rejected parties, parliaments, and constitutions. They called on Egypt's Muslims to restore the authentic institutions of Islam: the *ummah,* the Shari'ah, and the authority of the ulama. For Egyptian politicians, then, the country's pressing domestic problems could not be solved until after they had grappled with foreign policy and ideological issues: Egypt's stance between the democracies and the rising totalitarian states, the Palestine question, and the choice among "pharaonic" Egyptian nationalism, Arabism, and Islam.

Events in Europe almost forced the Egyptian government to adopt a policy on the first question. As Italy tightened its hold on Libya and Ethiopia, not to mention its eastern Mediterranean islands, it cast covetous eyes on the Nile Valley. Its powerful radio transmitters in Bari beamed Fascist propaganda into Egypt, where some 60,000 Italian residents also helped spread the influence of Mussolini (locally, "Musa Nili"). Nazi Germany, meanwhile, was remilitarizing the Rhineland, occupying Austria, persuading Britain and France to concede the Czech-ruled Sudetenland, and threatening to march into Poland to reassert German control over Danzig. Although Britain and France did their utmost to appease Hitler while rearming themselves, a new European war seemed inevitable. Naturally, the British wanted to be assured of military bases and support in the now-independent Arab countries, even if these needs were already being met by the treaties they had signed with Egypt and Iraq. To lessen the danger of popular opposition in those countries, the British government took a pro-Arab stand on the Palestine question by issuing a new White Paper in May 1939, placing severe limits on Jewish immigration and land purchases and promising independence to a predominantly Arab Palestine in ten years. Although the Egyptians did not resent the British government's actions in Palestine as much as they did Britain's policy of separating the Sudan from Egypt, the White Paper may have helped draw them nearer to Britain's side when World War II broke out in September 1939.

World War II

Several points must be made at the outset about Egypt's involvement in World War II. First of all, most Egyptians did not want to fight on either side; if their nationalism still alienated them from the British, their realism warned them that kicking their old masters out the front door could admit new ones in the back. Second, the new masters were most apt to be the Italians, who already held territory on three sides of Egypt. However, during the first year Nazi Germany fought without Italian help, so the Egyptians did not view the war at first as one likely to change their situation. Third, once the Germans overran Western Europe in 1940 and Italy did enter the war, the focus shifted to Eastern Europe and North Africa, regions closer to Egypt. During 1939 and 1940, the country, as in World War I, was turning into a major base for troops from all parts of the British Empire. Although the Anglo-Egyptian Treaty had limited the number of British troops and bases in Egypt during peacetime, it placed no restrictions in case of a general war (by 1945 their number would reach 200,000). It also did not require Egypt's government to declare war on Britain's enemies. But the presence of British troops did render Egypt—in Italian and German eyes—fair game for attack, invasion, or subversion. Egypt might resist pressure to enter World War II, but it could not, like Sweden or Switzerland, avoid it totally.

The attitudes of Egyptian politicians and people shifted as the war progressed. During the first year, they expected the British to defeat Hitler and cooperated with them, even though their prime minister, Ali Mahir, was a strong nationalist. The fall of France, the country most admired by the Egyptians, came as a dreadful shock to them. The British pressured Faruq to dismiss Mahir, and for the next two years the king and various ministries tried to minimize Egypt's role in the war. As German troops under General Erwin Rommel took control in Libya and swept across the border into Egypt, many Egyptians began demonstrating in his support. Wheat flour became scarce, as did many other basic necessities, owing to the demands of the foreign troops. Some Egyptian politicians (possibly Faruq) entered into secret talks with the Nazis, and some officers, led by the arch-nationalist general, Aziz Ali al-Misri, at a high level and by Colonel Anwar al-Sadat at a more humble one, plotted to cross the battle lines and link up with Rommel's forces. In Cairo the British burned embassy documents and planned to move into Palestine.

On 4 February 1942, one of Britain's darkest moments in the war, its ambassador took a drastic step to ensure Egyptian cooperation. Countering the king's attempt to replace his pro-British prime minister with Ali Mahir, Sir Miles Lampson ordered British tanks to surround Abdin Palace and handed Faruq an ultimatum, demanding that he appoint a cabinet that would uphold the 1936 Anglo-Egyptian Treaty. This, in reality, meant an all-Wafdist ministry under Mustafa al-Nahhas. The king tried to avoid giving in to Lampson, but his only alternative was to sign a letter of abdication. He finally submitted. Britain's action, understandable given that German forces were only 50 miles west of Alexandria, had a traumatic effect upon the main actors on Egypt's political stage. King Faruq, shorn of his power, went into a moral decline that led to his fall from power in 1952. The Wafd party ceased to be the vanguard of the nationalist resistance and came, in the eyes of the Egyptian people, to stand for collaboration with the British. In his memoirs, General Muhammad Nagib, leader of the 1952 Revolution against the monarchy, recalls that he asked Faruq for permission to resign from the army out of shame for Egypt. Other Egyptian officers, including Nasser and Sadat, grieved over this latest humiliation that their country was suffering at Britain's hands.

But during the war, most Egyptians acquiesced in their situation. They did not like being a giant army camp for British, Canadian, Indian, Australian, New Zealander, South African, and even U.S. troops. They resented the rising prices of food, clothing, and housing, but martial law and press censorship muffled their protests. Some hoped for a Nazi triumph to free them from British imperialism and the possible threat of Zionism, but most thought that German or Italian rule would be equally bad. Once the Allies had stemmed the German tide in November 1942 at El Alamain (located on Egyptian soil), there was little to gain from supporting Britain's enemies.

Many Egyptians benefited from wartime prosperity. The British government borrowed heavily from Egypt, running up a 400 million sterling pound debt by 1945. The presence of Allied troops and support personnel created additional demand for Egyptian-made goods and services. More than 200,000 Egyptians found jobs with the Allied forces. Although cotton acreage had to be cut back, food prices skyrocketed, thereby enriching landowners whose peasants grew wheat, corn, and rice (but also setting off food riots in the large cities). The war ended imports of Western-manufactured goods, sparking the growth of local industries. By 1944 Egypt was self-sufficient in sugar, alcohol, and cigarettes, and nearly so in cotton thread, soap, shoes, glass, cement, and furniture. It had also become the hub of a new British-formed organization called the Middle East Supply Center, which tied Egypt's economy to those of other Arab states and opened more markets for its nascent manufacturing industries.

Egypt and the Arab League

During the war, some British officials urged the Arabs to build political unity on this economic integration. A union of the Fertile Crescent states—Iraq, Transjordan, Palestine, Syria, and Lebanon—was proposed by Nuri al-Sa'id, Iraq's prime minister, in 1943. Fearing that such a union would diminish Egypt's own influence over the Arab world, Premier Nahhas successfully proposed a different form of unity, a league of independent Arab states. This looser association, commonly called the Arab League, was organized at a conference in Alexandria in 1944. Its formal existence began in March 1945, under the direction of a dynamic Egyptian secretary general, Abd al-Rahman Azzam. Saudi Arabia and Yemen joined Egypt, Transjordan, Iraq, Syria, and Lebanon in the organization, which vowed to oppose efforts to set up a Jewish state in predominantly Arab Palestine. Most observers saw British encouragement behind the formation of the Arab League, although the initiative came from the Wafd. Britain's policy was to focus Egypt's concern on regional economic affairs, in order to weaken agitation against its efforts to promote Sudanese independence from Egypt.

Disillusionment with Democracy

If Egypt prospered because of wartime conditions, it should not be assumed that the Egyptians were happy. If King Faruq remained the symbol of the nation, his increasingly blatant carousing and sexual infidelity embarrassed the people. If Mustafa al-Nahhas and the Wafd still claimed to bear the standard of the struggle against British imperialism, they could never evade accusations of having taken power behind British tanks. They were embarrassed when their secretary general, Makram Ubayd, the brightest and most respected of the Wafdist leaders, quit the party and published a burning exposé of their corruption. Egypt may have had the trappings of independence, but it remained a British dependency in reality. Embittered young Egyptians were losing faith in parliamentary democracy and the prewar political parties and were turning to militant, antidemocratic movements. Even before World War II, many had flocked to an ultranationalist group called Young Egypt, whose members wore green shirts, took paramilitary training, and adopted a Fascist salute. After the Axis defeat, Young Egypt recast itself as the "Islamic Socialist party." Hitherto obscure, Egypt's Communist party scored propaganda gains while the USSR was allied with the British. It gained influence after the war among the growing number of urban industrial workers, especially in the unions, which were legalized for the first time during the war.

But the most popular antidemocratic movement was the Society of the Muslim Brothers. It is hard to know how much power to ascribe to this organization, which was banned by Gamal Abd al-Nasir in 1954 and later allowed by Anwar al-Sadat to reappear as a counterweight to the Marxists. Recent history is often colored by the concerns of the present. It did not enter the kaleidoscope of cabinets in the last years of the Egyptian monarchy, but its members and sympathizers became notorious for their well-organized demonstrations, terrorist actions, and political assassinations. They set up schools and welfare institutions in rural villages and urban slums, winning the support of thousands, perhaps millions, of Egypt's poor people. They organized huge protest rallies against Britain's presence in Egypt and the Sudan. When the British announced in 1947 that they were turning their Palestine mandate over to the United Nations, whose General Assembly voted (against the wishes of Palestine's Arab majority) to partition it into Jewish and Arab states, the Muslim Brothers were the first to volunteer to fight on the Arab side.

The Postwar Independence Struggle

The Egyptian government, during the early postwar years, tried to persuade the British to revise the 1936 Treaty, which governed relations between the two countries. Owing in part to the Atlantic Charter and to the subsequent creation of the United Nations, the peoples of Asia and Africa were demanding the same freedoms, democracy, and national independence for which the Allies had fought in World War II. In 1945–1946 Egypt may not have experienced a popular revolution like that of 1919, but unrest was rife. On 9 February 1946 a student demonstration got out of hand when Egyptian police opened a drawbridge on which the students were marching. Many demonstrators fell into the Nile, and some sources claim that as many as 20 were killed. Riots and protest marches now became a daily occurrence, as the students for the first time made common cause with the organized workers. On 21 February they stormed the British army barracks in Ismailia (now Liberation) Square, and the soldiers opened machine-gun fire, killing 23 and injuring about 120. Anglo-Egyptian relations hit a new low.

Egypt resented being treated like an independent country in name but like a British colony in practice. Britain's new Labor government understood Egypt's concerns and withdrew its troops from Cairo and Alexandria, concentrating them in the Suez Canal zone. It is an irony of history that the canal, which de Lesseps had hoped to keep open to all nations and free of any fortifications, would become the largest military base in the non-Communist world between 1945 and 1952. The British, especially those with wartime experience in Egypt, saw

Suez as their imperial lifeline, even after they had granted independence to India and Pakistan in 1947. The canal remained important, they argued, for Gulf oil shipments and for defense against Communism. Others felt that basing soldiers in a country where they were unwanted would be too costly, politically and economically—hardly an idle consideration given that the British government owed large sums to other countries, including Egypt.

Successive Egyptian governments tried to minimize Britain's presence in Suez and to gain control over the Anglo-Egyptian Sudan. Since the withdrawal of Egyptian troops from the Sudan after the assassination of Sir Lee Stack, joint rule there had been a fiction, although the 1936 Treaty did allow Egyptian troops to return to the Sudan. Britain was in fact governing the "condominium" as a private colony. The British claimed that, just as the Egyptians wanted to be independent of Britain, the Sudanese did not want to be a colony of Egypt. Egypt argued that it had been paying for the conquest and administration of the Sudan, and that the two countries had to unite because of their common dependence on the Nile. Late in 1946 Foreign Minister Ernest Bevin and Prime Minister Isma'il Sidqi drafted a treaty that would have provided for the complete withdrawal of British forces from their Suez Canal base by 1949 and acknowledged "the framework of unity between the Sudan and Egypt under the common crown of Egypt," but it also called for preparing the Sudanese for self-government. This compromise was vehemently opposed by the Wafd, by the Sudanese Ummah party, which wanted independence from Egypt, and by British Conservatives appalled at Bevin's concessions to Egyptian nationalism. After Bevin denied, in the House of Commons, that he had handed the Sudan to Egypt, Sidqi resigned and the treaty was never ratified. His successor, Mahmud Fahmi al-Nuqrashi, carried the Sudan issue to the UN Security Council in the summer of 1947. Unable to justify freeing the Sudanese people from Britain, only to subject them to Egypt, the member-states called on the two countries, now almost at loggerheads, to resume negotiations. Although Nuqrashi tried to disguise it, the UN decision was a defeat for Nile Valley unity and for Egypt.

It was also in 1947 that Egypt took a fateful step that would eventually destroy both the monarchy and the 1923 constitution. King Faruq met with the representatives of the other Arab governments at Inshas Palace and agreed to commit Egypt's forces to war against any plan to partition Palestine and to create a Jewish state there. The Arabs expected to win easily. They were wrong, and many of their regimes did not survive their shameful defeat in 1948–1949. Egypt's regime would ultimately share their fate.

CHAPTER EIGHT

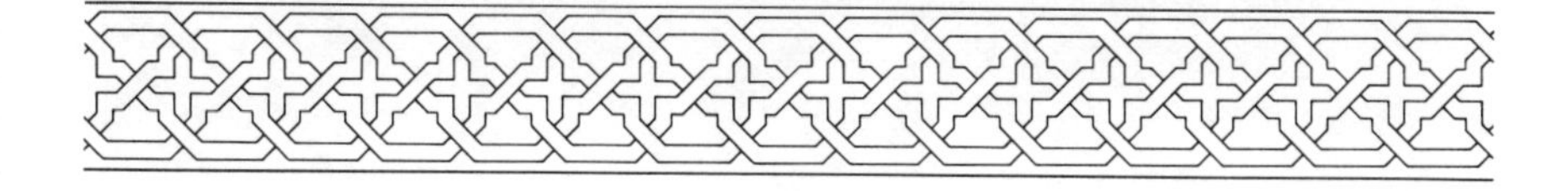

The 1952 Revolution

Some Arab countries seem to have revolutions annually, but the Egyptian people are proverbially easy to govern. The fact that 99 percent of Egypt's population live in the valley or the delta of the Nile puts them within easy reach of their rulers. Their culture places a premium on obedience to persons in authority and to governments. But now and then the incompetence of a ruling elite exhausts the patience even of the Egyptians and, once conditions permit, revolution erupts. As King Faruq grew ever more inept, the Wafd and its rival parties more corrupt, and parliamentary democracy more decrepit, a rebellion was inevitable. But which rebels could speak for the Egyptian people? Many looked to the Muslim Brothers, some to Young Egypt, and a few to the Communists. Few expected the army to act. But its 1948 defeat in Palestine by a seemingly smaller, less well-equipped Israeli force shamed the officers, the soldiers, and the Egyptian people. As revolutions broke out in Yemen in 1948 and in Syria in 1949, and after Jordan's King Abdallah was killed in 1951, a forceful change of Egypt's government seemed imminent.

More than one generation of Egyptians has come to maturity since the 1952 Revolution. A well-established interpretation has grown up around those now historic events, their antecedents, and their consequences. The personalities and institutions of prerevolutionary Egypt have been painted in the darkest hues, while the purest motives have been ascribed to the men who carried out the revolution or at least to those who did not lose power afterward. Although I do not mean to detract from the accomplishments of the colonels who overthrew the monarchy in July 1952 and set up a more efficient government, this book will try to present a balanced picture of their revolution.

MAP 2. The Egyptian Delta

Trouble at the Top

Egypt was a troubled country between 1945 and 1952. King Faruq embarrassed the Egyptians by his womanizing, gambling, and gluttony. The Wafd party lost credibility as the standard-bearer of Egyptian nationalism when it formed a British-imposed government in 1942, and Makram Ubayd's *Black Book,* published the following year, discredited Mustafa al-Nahhas as its leader. The Egyptian people—or, rather, the 90 percent whom history ignored—were hobbled by poverty, illiteracy, and disease. Revolution takes place when the ruling group is losing its ability to govern and other leaders are trying to take over its power. Although bad economic and social conditions may anger the mob and light the revolutionary fires, the root cause is either the disillusionment of the old regime or the ideas of the new leaders who are striving to take its place. It may be both.

King Faruq was a tragic figure. His father died before the young prince had finished his schooling. He lacked both the emotional maturity and the political judgment to rule Egypt. There were many courtiers and politicians who exploited his inexperience to weaken their rivals or to enrich themselves. He was further weakened by his hostile relationship with Britain's ambassador, Lord Killearn (Sir Miles Lampson), who tried more than once to depose him during World War II. Although Faruq rejoiced when the British Labor government replaced Killearn in February 1946, in that same month his wisest counselor, Ahmad Hasanayn, was killed in a car crash. Faruq's own accident in 1943 had left him with a glandular disturbance, which some Egyptians thought had been deliberately maltreated in a British military hospital. After that, he became more and more obese. His reputation as a ladies' man and as a pornography collector hardly disguised his sexual impotence. He suffered the failure of his marriage to Farida, beloved by the Egyptians, and began spending his nights in cabarets or in the boudoirs of various other women (often already married to officials or officers) whom he desired. He often stole property as well.

Faruq's political activities were usually directed against the Wafd, especially Nahhas. Most of the cabinets formed during his reign were led by rivals who lacked any popular constituency and had to govern by force. Unrigged parliamentary elections still produced large Wafdist majorities, and Nahhas remained Egypt's most popular politician, but even the Wafd resorted to corrupt methods to assure itself both public employment and peasant support. The king and his advisers sought ways to maneuver the Wafd out of power and to appoint politicians whom they could control.

One possible strategy would have been to implement a program of economic and social reforms that would address Egypt's real ills: poverty, illiteracy, and disease. Americans (of whom Faruq seems to have been genuinely fond) often urged the king to start an Egyptian New Deal from Abdin Palace. Aside from Faruq's lack of political acumen and stamina, another reason this policy was never adopted is that the royal family owned about a tenth of Egypt's arable land. Even if Faruq had agreed to give up his land and real estate holdings, he could not have persuaded the other heirs of Mehmet Ali and Isma'il to follow his example. Egypt had growing numbers of doctors, lawyers, economists, teachers, and other educated people. Nearly all agreed that the gap between the richest and the poorest Egyptians would have to be narrowed, but the landowning politicians in government posts, in the judiciary, among the ulama, and in the clergy—and of course those in parliament—all stood to suffer from any redistribution of Egypt's lands. Faruq felt, correctly, that he was powerless to act. He quipped to a deposed Balkan monarch: "Soon the world will have only five kings: spades, hearts, diamonds, clubs, and England."

The Palestine War, 1948–1949

If the people's material needs could not be met, the smartest strategy was to distract them with foreign adventures. The fateful decision to commit the Egyptian army to fight in the 1948 Palestine War was made not by the Sa'dist cabinet of the time but by Faruq himself, who had been manipulated by a wily Lebanese journalist, Karim Thabit. The prime minister, his cabinet, and indeed the Egyptian general staff believed that the army was not ready to fight. But many politically articulate Egyptians favored intervention. The UN decision of November 1947 to partition Palestine (thereby legitimizing the creation of the Jewish State of Israel) offended Muslim and Arab opinion everywhere. The Muslim Brothers started recruiting volunteers even before Britain's withdrawal from Palestine and Israel's declaration of independence precipitated the war in May 1948. The Arab League, led by Egypt's Abd al-Rahman Azzam, had resolved to go to war against Israel. But Faruq's main motive for sending Egypt to war was to prevent his arch-rival, Amir Abdallah of Transjordan, from taking control of Palestine if the Arabs won.

The Egyptian army's performance in the Palestine War was humiliating. So ill-prepared was Egypt's general staff that it needed to borrow road maps of Palestine from Cairo's Buick dealer. Nagib remembered hiring twenty-one trucks from Palestinians to move his troops from the Sinai to Gaza. Faruq insisted on making decisions on strategy, pointedly ignoring the repeated warnings that his current mistress, Lilianne Cohen (the young film star "Camelia"), was passing his orders along to Israeli spies. Only two brigades of Egyptians and Sudanese infantry, fewer than 3,000 men, made up the first force sent into Palestine. Although they advanced on Tel Aviv in the early days of the war, they did not score the victories that Karim Thabit boasted about in his press releases and that were broadcast over Egyptian state radio. In the war memoirs that he published after taking power, Nasir alleged that the Egyptian general staff had made no plans for feeding the troops, caring for the wounded, reconnoitering enemy positions before battle, drawing up a strategy for advance, or preparing fallback positions in case of a retreat. It was, for them, a political war.

During the first cease-fire, ordered by the United Nations, both sides combed Europe's used-weapons markets, but Israel replenished its arms more effectively with the timely aid of Czechoslovakia. Once the fighting resumed, the Israelis pushed back its enemies on all fronts. The various Arab armies, far from coordinating their plans, often fired on one another. The largest and best equipped were the armies of Transjordan and Iraq; these countries were ruled by Hashimite kings, whom Faruq regarded as his hereditary enemies. Transjordan's Arab Legion was especially well trained. Its commander, an Englishman named Sir John Bagot Glubb, was truly devoted to the Arabs and wrote in his memoirs that the Egyptians often undercut the Legion. By contrast, the Israelis did surprisingly well, taking and holding lands in Palestine not allotted to them by the UN partition plan.

One fateful consequence of the Arab armies' failure was the exodus of most Palestinian Arabs from their homes. Some Zionists claim that they fled of their own accord, or because Arab leaders had ordered them to leave; but during the second stage of the fighting, the Arabs in such strategically located towns as Jaffa, Lydda, and Ramleh were actually expelled by Israel's army. Some fled to lands within Palestine remaining in Arab hands, the areas now known as the West Bank and Gaza. Others went to neighboring Arab countries other than Egypt, which had no room for them. As the Egyptian army fell back on Gaza, it took a heroic stand near the village of Faluja. After withstanding a four-month siege, the troops, led by General Nagib, were allowed under the armistice to leave as heroes. They were welcomed back with a "victory parade" in February 1949.

There was little else for the Egyptian people to cheer about. Their vaunted army (vaunted, that is, by Faruq, Azzam, and Karim Thabit) had proved to be a hollow shell. The Israelis would have invaded the Sinai Peninsula but for Britain's threat to invoke the 1936 Anglo-Egyptian Treaty (the very pact the Egyptians hated) by way of defending the canal. On the island of Rhodes, an Egyptian delegation negotiated an armistice agreement with Israel, using UN Representative Ralph Bunche as a mediator. The other Arab states (except Iraq) gradually followed Egypt's lead but attacked its leaders for letting them down. Egypt administered (but did not annex) the lands around Gaza, which were crowded with angry Palestinian refugees. Thousands of Egyptian soldiers had been killed or wounded; many were missing. Their officers, especially those who had spent time in the field, were embittered against the king, his court, parliament, and the old regime in general. Whom should they blame for Egypt's unexpected defeat? Many leading politicians, some of them close to the king, were accused of selling defective weapons to the army. The arms scandal was one more nail in the coffin of Egypt's parliamentary democracy.

Political Parties and Movements

Egypt had a bewildering array of parliamentary parties. Most cabinets were coalitions made up of politicians from several parties and factions. The only popular party was the Wafd. Indeed, its members regarded the Wafd not as a party but, rather, as the embodiment of the Egyptian nation, comparable to the Indian National Congress. It had become notorious, however, for corruption and administrative incompetence. In 1919 nearly every politician belonged to the Wafd; in the following years, most leading figures in Egypt's political life either resigned from the party or were forced to leave it. The first breakaway party was that of the Liberal Constitutionalists, led originally by Adli Yakan and Abd al-Khaliq Tharwat and later by Muhammad Mahmud and Muhammad Husayn Haykal. All were men of learning and integrity, but their outlook was that of the landowning nobility and they increasingly backed the palace against the Wafd. The Sa'dist party split off from the Wafd soon after the 1936 Treaty, claiming (as its name implies) that it was more faithful to the principles of Sa'd Zaghlul than was Wafd party leader Nahhas. The Sa'dist party founders, Ahmad Mahir and Mahmud Fahmi al-Nuqrashi, both died at the hands of assassins. Makram Ubayd's splinter group, which broke away when he published his *Black Book* in 1942, was called the Wafdist bloc. Isma'il Sidqi, Egypt's ablest (but least liked) politician, headed the so-called People's party. All these groups wanted independence from Britain, union with the Sudan, and parliamentary government. The Nationalist party was the most intransigent, as it called for Britain's unconditional withdrawal. It had split when its leader, Hafiz Ramadan, twice joined anti-Wafdist cabinets, but it was no longer a strong contender for power. Some politicians, such as Ali Mahir, managed to be independent; but most were caught in the maelstrom of partisan rivalries, which left them little time or energy to devote to their country's real needs.

The Society of Muslim Brothers stayed aloof from parties, but it was politically active in its call for a return to Qur'anic values and traditional Muslim institutions and in its assassination of politicians, judges, and police officers who stood in its way. Young Egypt still espoused extreme nationalism; though weakened by the Fascists' defeat in World War II, it influenced many young army officers. Renamed the Islamic Socialist party, it was effective mainly in league with other groups, such as the National Committee of Workers and Students formed during the 1946 student demonstrations. The Communist party appealed mostly to the educated members of ethnic and religious minorities: Jews, Greeks, Armenians, and Copts. The early support given Israel by the USSR and its satellites weakened Communism's appeal to rank-and-file Egyptians. Even though Faruq, his entourage, and some Westerners feared the spread of Communism, the Muslim majority despised its atheistic doctrines and did not care to take up common cause with the minorities. In contrast, approximately half a million Muslims joined the Society of the Muslim Brothers.

This organization reached its apogee during the Palestine War, in which the Brothers distinguished themselves as volunteer soldiers and auxiliaries. By 1948 they had 2,000 branches in Egypt, most of which ran schools, clinics, and various welfare institutions. They had a women's auxiliary section, appropriately named the Muslim Sisters, and a youth movement, 40,000 strong, called the Rovers. Their supreme guide, Shaykh Hasan al-Banna, was respected for his religious principles, even as he was feared for his followers' frequent resort to violence. Some Egyptians hoped for a coalition between the Muslim Brothers and other power centers, such as the Wafd or the Palace; many foreigners believed the Society to be in the pay of Germany (during World War II) or Britain (after the war). The group was starting to falter, however. During the Palestine War, while Egypt was under martial law, Prime Minister Nuqrashi outlawed it for its revolutionary activities. Hasan al-Banna countered by having Nuqrashi assassinated. In this stressful time, Faruq set up a tough government, under Ibrahim Abd al-Hadi, which began arresting the Brothers and seizing the Society's assets. Hasan al-Banna was not imprisoned, but in February 1949 he was murdered, probably by the government agents. By July, when Faruq dismissed Abd al-Hadi, 4,000 Brothers were in prison. A series of trials ensued. The most notorious was the "Jeep Case," named for a government-captured vehicle filled with documents that incriminated the Brothers for attacking Jewish property in Cairo, allegedly to foment a Muslim revolution in Egypt. In spite of heavy state pressure to execute the indicted Brothers, the judges acquitted some of them and gave others light jail sentences, owing to insufficient evidence. The council of state allowed the Society to appeal its dissolution in 1951 and, after hearing its case, ordered the government to restore its funds and property. But Abd al-Hadi's repressive measures in 1949 had weakened the Society. Even the election of a new supreme guide, Hasan al-Hudaybi, a judge with strong Palace connections, did not restore its strength.

The Revival of the Wafd

During the dark days following the Palestine defeat, one ray of hope for Egypt was the government's decision to hold parliamentary elections in January 1950. The Wafd took part in the elections and again won most of the seats, but with only 40 percent of the vote. For the next two years, Egypt was governed by Mustafa al-Nahhas at the head of the Wafd party, which implemented a number of major reforms intended to better the welfare of Egypt's workers and peasants. The education minister, Taha Husayn (the famous writer), abolished fees for the state secondary and technical schools, while Ahmad Husayn (no relative) set up health centers in many of the villages. For the first time, the government established a social insurance program for widows, orphans, and disabled and aged persons. The Wafd even proposed to distribute a million feddans (one feddan equals 1.039 acres) of state land to poor peasants. At last the government seemed to address Egypt's real problems.

Predictably, though, the Wafd resumed its campaign to oust the British from Egypt and the Sudan. Negotiations were difficult. The civil war in Greece (1946–1950), the loss of Palestine, and the outbreak of the Korean War (June 1950) all increased Britain's determination to keep its Suez Canal base, manned by 80,000 troops and holding equipment and supplies worth more than a billion dollars, lest a war should break out between the Soviets and the West. For the Egyptians, however, the main enemy was not the USSR but Israel. If they were to be drawn into an anti-Communist war, they wanted better terms than they were apt to get from an unpopular alliance treaty that allowed British troops to remain on their soil and could still permit London to interfere in their politics.

Britain also seemed more responsive to the demands of the Sudan's Ummah party for self-rule than to the Egyptian desire for Nile Valley unity, based on Egypt's total dependence on that river's waters. In 1947 British administrators in Khartum had prepared a draft constitution for the Anglo-Egyptian Sudan, setting up a popularly elected legislature. The Egyptian government, fearing that the British presence would bias the elections toward the Ummah and against the pro-Egyptian Ashiqqa party, opposed the new constitution and ignored the subsequent elections. The Sudan's separation from Egypt now seemed inevitable.

Direct negotiations and UN debates had not helped Egypt's cause. In October 1951 Nahhas (imitating Musaddiq, who had just nationalized the Anglo-Iranian Oil Company) unilaterally renounced the 1936 Anglo-Egyptian Treaty and declared Faruq king of Egypt and the Sudan. The radical nationalists could now claim that the British troops' presence in the Suez Canal was illegal and could be opposed by force. Egyptian workers at the British camps went out on strike, customs officials held up the clearance of goods destined for the base, longshoremen balked at unloading British supplies, and tradesmen refused to sell their merchandise or their services. British troops retaliated by occupying the roads and bridges in the canal area, as well as the Suez customs house. The Egyptian government summarily dismissed its British employees (mainly teachers) without severance pay and openly encouraged the students, workers, and auxiliary police (plus, significantly, the Muslim Brothers newly freed from prison) to form groups of *fida'iyin* (Muslims who sacrifice themselves for a cause) to harass the British troops on the canal.

On 25 January 1952 the British besieged and sacked the police headquarters in Ismailia, one of the main trouble spots. More than fifty Egyptians were killed. The next morning hundreds of auxiliary policemen, who were gathered at Cairo University, met students affiliated with the Muslim Brothers, the Wafd, and Young Egypt, and marched into downtown Cairo. An argument broke out at Badia's cabaret in Opera Square between some of the demonstrators and an off-duty policeman, who was sitting with a woman and drinking whiskey. Enraged, the demonstrators set the casino on fire. Soon mobs materialized throughout the westernized downtown, carrying cans of kerosene and igniting such landmarks as Shepheard's hotel, Groppi's restaurant, Cicurel's department store, St. James's bar, the Cinema Metro, Barclay's bank, the Ford motor company's showroom, the TWA office, and the Turf Club. If any wind had been blowing that day, most of Cairo would have burned to the ground. More than 30 people perished, many hundreds were injured, and 400 buildings were destroyed. Estimates of the property damage ran to $500 million. After several hours' delay (during which the mobs looted the burnt-out shops), the army stepped in to restore order, martial law was declared, and the fires were put out. Soon afterward, King Faruq, who had done nothing to stop the rioters, dismissed the Wafdist cabinet.

No one has ever proved who started "Black Saturday." It was probably not the Society of the Muslim Brothers, which was still trying to recover from its earlier repression and to expunge its reputation for fanaticism. Some suspected that Young Egypt had started the burning of Cairo but that other groups, street gangs, and individuals had quickly joined in. Faruq may have sent in some of his agents, to prove the Wafd's incapacity to govern. Some Egyptians accused the British of using the fire to discredit all of Egypt's nationalist movements and to oblige the Egyptian government to invite Britain's troops back in to restore order. The consensus is that no one group was solely to blame. Black Saturday was the collective expression of many Egyptians' hostility to Western wealth, power, and cultural influence. It also exposed the bankruptcy of the old regime.

Exactly six months remained for Faruq to reign. Some observers think that he could still have saved his throne through resolute action. During this time, he appointed four different cabinets, some of which were headed by honest and energetic men. Cairo was under a dusk-to-dawn curfew for several months. Some of the looters were arrested and tried, and the public prosecutor's office tried to find out who had started the fire. In a final attempt to win popular support, King Faruq had one of the ulama proclaim him a descendant of the Prophet Muhammad. He also tried to strengthen his hold over the officers of the armed forces by concentrating his loyalists against the dissidents. But by 1952 there was little he could have done to save Egypt's monarchy.

The Free Officers

Egypt contained many secret societies plotting to overthrow Faruq. The one that succeeded was called the "Free Officers," a cabal of some 300 commissioned Egyptian officers, most of them in their thirties. One of the results of the 1936 Anglo-Egyptian Treaty, little noted at the time, was the opening of the Egyptian Military Academy (hitherto a school for pashas' sons who excelled in sports but had no aptitude for higher education) to secondary-school graduates who passed a competitive examination. This change caused a significant rise in the quantity and quality of the entering cadets. These young men, ambitious for themselves and their nation, came from lower- and middle-class backgrounds. Many were supporting Hasan al-Banna, General Aziz Ali al-Misri, or Ali Mahir's nationalistic war minister, Salih Harb, in the late 1930s, when, according to Anwar al-Sadat, some of them secretly pledged to drive the British from Egypt. The decisive event was Lampson's ultimatum to Faruq in February 1942. After that, the young officers felt that Egypt's welfare depended on destroying all points of the power triangle: the Wafd, the king, and the British.

Several inside accounts purport to tell the true story of when—and by whom—the Free Officers' society was formed. The personal association of Gamal Abd al-Nasir, Anwar al-Sadat, and such other young officers as Zakariya Muhyi al-Din and Abd al-Hakim Amir began before World War II, but they organized their society later, possibly in 1942, more probably after the Palestine War. Sadat wrote that it was organized into cells of five members (each of whom was expected to form another cell) containing either officers or civilians. A minimum of twenty cells constituted one section. He went on to say (other accounts differ) that each section had a specific function: fund-raising, recruitment, security, terrorism, and propaganda. Overall direction was supplied by a twelve-man revolutionary committee headed by Gamal Abd al-Nasir, whose appointment as an instructor at the Military Academy enabled him to spot likely recruits. As individuals, the Free Officers had contacts with various parties or revolutionary societies, especially the Muslim Brothers. Young Egypt and the Communists also had ties with the Free Officers. As a group, though, they chose to operate independent of all other organizations.

The Free Officers lacked a clear ideology. The following six points, put forth by the secret society in 1951, would remain their guiding principles long after they had taken power: (1) destroying the British occupation and its Egyptian supporters, (2) eliminating feudalism, (3) ending capitalism's domination of political power, (4) establishing social equality, (5) forming a strong popular army, and (6) establishing a healthy democratic life. These points were open to a variety of interpretations: liberal, nationalist, and Marxist. They were not a detailed blueprint for governing the country.

At first, the Free Officers were planning to take over Egypt's government in 1954, but they advanced their timetable after "Black Saturday" revealed the incompetence of the old order. Realizing that their relative youth would probably weaken their authority, they sought a senior officer to serve as their figurehead leader, finally choosing General Muhammad Nagib (after pondering such alternatives as Aziz Ali al-Misri). Because of the officers' ties with the Muslim Brothers, Ibrahim Abd al-Hadi had interrogated Gamal Abd al-Nasir in 1949, but the government underestimated their strength. It was first tested when they put up Nagib for the presidency of the Officers' Club in December 1951. Faruq delayed the election and then tried, unsuccessfully, to get one of his favorites chosen instead. One of the king's last premiers was dismissed when he dared to propose Nagib as his war minister.

More influenced by what was happening in the army than by events in the rest of Egypt, the Free Officers decided to move their revolution up to early August 1952; they then advanced their plans to the night of 22–23 July when they found out that the king was convening his generals to move against them. The actual power seizure, carefully planned by Nasir, proved easy. But there were a few hitches: Anwar al-Sadat had taken his family to a movie, and a policeman stopped Nasir's car because of a burnt-out taillight. By 3 A.M., though, the revolutionaries had taken all the key military posts in Cairo, with only two casualties. Most Palace and high government officials had gone to Alexandria for the summer, but that city, too, soon fell. In fact, there was almost no resistance at all. King Faruq asked the U.S. and British embassies to help stop the coup, but both refused. After debating whether to kill Faruq, try him, exile him, or retain him as a constitutional monarch, the Free Officers agreed to let him abdicate in favor of his 6-month-old son and to leave Egypt. Although a three-man regency council was set up, all real power was held by the Free Officers.

Several writers aver that Nasir and the Free Officers were put in power by the U.S. Central Intelligence Agency. Their rationale is that the Americans, fearing a Communist takeover, wanted to turn power over to army officers who, having been British trained and traditionally apolitical, were presumably pro-Western. The most reliable accounts available maintain that the coup's timing surprised the CIA, like nearly everyone else. However, the Agency quickly made contact with the new regime and later helped it to fend off power bids by the Muslim Brothers, the Communists, and the old political parties.

The Revolutionary Regime

But what would these young officers do with the power they had won so easily? In *The Philosophy of the Revolution,* Nasir (or, to be more accurate, his ghostwriter, Muhammad Hasanayn Haykal) wrote:

> Before July 23rd, I had imagined that the whole nation was ready and prepared, waiting for nothing but a vanguard to lead the charge against the battlements, whereupon it would fall behind in serried ranks, ready for the sacred advance toward the great objective. I had imagined that our role was to be this commando vanguard.

The Free Officers soon realized that they could not carry out their revolution so easily. Divided, the masses were filled with egotism and proposals for vengeance, not visions of national reconstruction:

> We needed order, but we found nothing behind us but chaos. We needed unity, but we found nothing behind us but dissension. We needed work, but we found behind us only indolence and sloth. . . . We were not ready. So we set about seeking the views of leaders of opinion. . . . Every man we questioned had nothing to recommend except to kill someone else. . . . If anyone had asked me in those days what I wanted most, I would have answered promptly: To hear an Egyptian speak fairly about another Egyptian. To sense that an Egyptian has opened his heart to pardon, forgiveness, and love for his Egyptian brethren. To find an Egyptian who does not devote his time to tearing down the views of another Egyptian.

Once Faruq had sailed into exile, the Free Officers handed Egypt's government over to an old-regime politician, Ali Mahir, whom they admired for his patriotism, and planned to go back to their barracks. Meanwhile, Nahhas returned from a European vacation to say that the Wafd wanted new elections under the 1923 constitution to confirm its hold over parliament and public opinion. The Free Officers responded by ordering all political parties to cleanse themselves of corrupt politicians, including Nahhas. The Muslim Brothers insisted that the Qur'an was Egypt's constitution and demanded veto power over any laws passed by the new government. In early August the textile workers at Kafr al-Dawar (near Alexandria) rioted in the name of "the peoples' revolution," seized the factory buildings, set fire to several, and damaged the machinery. The new government repressed them violently, killing eight, trying the ringleaders, and putting two of them to death. This glaring contrast with the bloodless coup against the king disillusioned the Egyptian Left. So did the new government's formation of a state security department to combat Communism and Zionism. The Free Officers dropped Ali Mahir and set up a watchdog committee to oversee the government, which was called the Revolutionary Command Council (RCC). A few competent old-regime politicians, such as Sayyid Mar'i, found their way into the new order, but most withheld support until they could see how the wind was blowing. The Free Officers appointed a capable finance minister, who adopted stringent measures to balance the government budget. Foreign investors were reassured by a relaxation of the laws, passed earlier by royalist cabinets, specifying that a majority of shares in local companies had to be owned by Egyptians and that a certain percentage of their payrolls had to go to Egyptians. The abolition of such Turkish titles as "pasha" and "bey" was accepted stoically. Male officials no longer had to wear fezzes.

Of the many accomplishments of the Free Officers, the first and most revolutionary was the September 1952 land-reform decree. It limited to 200 feddans (about 208 acres) the amount of agricultural land that any individual was allowed to own. This was not a new idea. Even more radical legislation had been proposed in parliament before the 1952 Revolution. But this time it was enforced. The lands belonging to ex-King Faruq and his numerous relatives were confiscated and, eventually, redistributed to landless peasants. Other land-tenure abuses were also reformed. Especially important was the abolition of family *waqf*s, Muslim endowments that had been used not for pious purposes but to keep estates within one branch of a family from being fragmented under the Qur'anic inheritance laws. The reforms weakened the large landowners, although the government was committed to reimburse them for their confiscated property. Some of Egypt's destitute peasants became small landowners for the first time, but they were expected to pay for the lands they received. The real purpose was political: to weaken the power base of the Wafd and other old-regime parties. The land reform may have been a revolutionary step, but its ends were conservative, not radical.

Hoary political issues, especially Egypt's relationship with Britain, still exercised the Egyptians. In 1952 British troops were still guarding the Suez Canal, a link in the West's chain of defenses against the USSR. Nearly all Egyptians wanted them to get out. Negotiations with Britain, stalled since Nahhas' unilateral abrogation of the Anglo-Egyptian Treaty in 1951, resumed one month after the military coup. The Sudan, nominally an Anglo-Egyptian condominium, remained in fact a British colony. Before the revolution, all Egyptian politicians had called for Nile Valley unity. General Nagib, who was born in Khartum and had a good rapport with the people of the Sudan, accepted their right to decide whether they wanted complete independence or unification with Egypt. In January 1953 Egypt agreed to a national plebiscite by the Sudanese people, thus removing an important cause of Anglo-Egyptian antagonism. Backed by the United States, Egypt expected that it would eventually persuade the British to give up their Suez Canal base. Nagib and Nasir even hinted that Egypt might make peace with Israel. In international relations, too, the new regime seemed patriotic, but hardly xenophobic.

Conclusion

To sum up, the change of government that occurred in July 1952 was more than a military coup; it ushered in significant tranformations in Egyptian society. The old regime had clearly shown itself to be incompetent. Some historians believe that the fate of Egypt's royal family was sealed in 1882, when the British occupied the country and restored Khedive Tawfiq to his throne. After that, the monarchy was never able to combine the protection of the British with the support of the nationalist leaders. By 1952 the landowning elite had become a useless burden to the peasants, and the foreign businesspeople and technocrats constituted a barrier to the advancement of educated young Egyptians. The level of frustration had become intolerable. The revolution was, if anything, overdue.

But, at first, the new regime did not know how revolutionary it was, what its goals were, or, indeed, how much it wanted to rule. It was anxious to maintain order, concerned about national unity, and cautious about radical policies. Speaking to Egyptian and foreign journalists, Nagib stressed his commitment to civil liberties, free elections, and the 1923 constitution. He and his young officers were technically educated and middle class. Only after they had consolidated their power and realized the extent of Egypt's problems could the Free Officers truly turn into revolutionaries.

CHAPTER NINE

The Revolution Matures

A common challenge faces all revolutionaries once they come to power: how to make the transition from resisting others' authority to imposing their own. Until 23 July 1952 the Free Officers had been a conspiratorial cabal within the Egyptian army, presumed loyal to the king, the symbol of the nation. After King Faruq had been deposed and exiled, the Egyptian people looked to the Free Officers for leadership and order, for new beliefs, symbols, and national myths. What sort of government might they expect from these young colonels, whose spokesman was a homely, pipe-smoking general named Muhammad Nagib?

Democracy Versus Dictatorship

The real leader was Gamal Abd al-Nasir. His eventual successor, Anwar al-Sadat, wrote in his book, *In Search of Identity,* that on 27 July the Revolutionary Command Council debated whether the new Egypt would become a military dictatorship or remain a democracy. By a seven to one vote, the RCC leaders chose dictatorship. Incensed by the vote, Nasir left the room in a huff and went home. The other officers were so afraid of ruling without him that one of them pursued him and persuaded him to return, with promises that Egypt would be ruled democratically. It is a strange story, for Nasir, once he took over full executive power two years later, would rule for the next sixteen with little regard for parliamentary democracy. But it does show the dilemma facing the Free Officers. The Egyptian nation (or at least its politically articulate minority) wanted a democratic government. Except for the extremists, it viewed the 1923 constitution, whatever its faults, as the guarantor of civil liberties and of the people's right to participate in their own rule. Government under the 1923 constitution meant that sovereignty would reside in the monarch (now, symbolically, the regency council) and that free elections, with universal male suffrage, would be held for a new parliament. The winner would probably be the Wafd party, however tainted by corruption and collaboration with British imperialism, because of its appeal to most of the rural landowners, who could force their tenant farmers and hired laborers to vote for Wafdist candidates. Such a regime would not end corruption or restore order. Egypt needed strong and decisive leadership to solve its problems. But repudiating democracy would anger Egypt's educated elite, the press, the students, the labor unions, and the foreigners whose support the revolutionaries still needed. Indeed, no one could have predicted with confidence whether the Free Officers would be able to govern the country.

Their answer was to give lip service to democracy and to govern by decree. For a time, Egypt would have cabinets made up of civilian politicians. Behind them, though, sat "secretaries general" from the Revolutionary Command Council who observed the ministers as the "advisers" had done during the early days of the British occupation. Nagib ordered the political parties to get rid of their corrupt elements. Only the Wafd resisted purging itself, but it was the sole party with a real constituency. The others vanished once parliament was dissolved in December 1952. Most of the members of Young Egypt (whom no one remembered to call the Islamic Socialists) embraced the new regime, whose pronouncements reflected its founders' views. The Muslim Brothers assumed that their officer contacts, one of whom was Anwar al-Sadat, would guarantee their influence over the new regime. The Society did indeed win privileges denied to the parliamentary parties. When the officers shelved the constitution and put off the elections, they banned all parties and confiscated their assets. The Muslim Brothers, however, remained free to agitate for their program. This license did not mean that the new regime espoused their religious fanaticism, for Nagib and his colonels publicly visited churches and synagogues and sent appropriate holiday greetings to the leaders of Egypt's minorities. Most old-regime politicians were barred from public office, tried by a revolutionary court using exceptional judicial procedures, and sentenced to prison terms of various lengths. Only Ibrahim Abd al-Hadi, who had severely repressed the Muslim Brothers in 1949, received a death sentence (this was later commuted to life imprisonment). People's rights to free speech and assembly were restricted by military censorship, but they were not totally denied.

The Internal Power Struggle

During the first year of the new regime, Egyptian and foreign observers admired the Free Officers' energy and efficiency, although some noted their inexperience in running a complicated government. All agreed that reforms were vital, that corruption must be rooted out and punished, and that Egypt should negotiate with the British for a peaceful evacuation of their Suez Canal base. But people began asking whether the Revolutionary Command Council would be willing to give up its power to a civilian government. In June 1953 the RCC formally ended the monarchy. Fu'ad II, a one-year-old child living with his parents in exile, ceased to be Egypt's nominal king. Nagib became its first president, as well as its prime minister and RCC chairman. He had become popular in his own right, but this was a development not desired by most of the younger Free Officers lurking behind the limelight and making the critical decisions. As the date for a new constitution kept receding, Nagib seemed to be Egypt's man on horseback. A power struggle was brewing.

The 1952 Revolution had been a classic army coup, not a popular uprising. If the Free Officers wanted to gain and hold the people's support, they needed to appeal to other groups and individuals whose interests and attitudes often clashed with their own. Some officers had family or friendly ties with the royal family, the big landowners, old-regime politicians, Young Egypt, the Muslim Brothers, the trade unions, or various foreign embassies. As long as these ties strengthened the RCC's power over the government and the people, Gamal Abd al-Nasir tolerated and even exploited them. But once the RCC was clearly in control, it could no longer share its power with rival movements.

Nagib came to symbolize a pluralistic polity, one in which the RCC would compete with the Wafd, the Muslim Brothers, and the Communists for the minds and hearts of the Egyptian people. Nasir did not want this. If the Egyptians wanted their country to have strength and dignity, all power would have to be concentrated in the RCC. Even if some of its members had loose ties with competing power centers (as long as their help was needed), the RCC was strong because it did not belong to any of them. Now that the monarchy and the old parties had been abolished and the landowning classes had been weakened by the 1952 land reforms, the RCC could do without the rival movements. Moreover, Nasir was determined to build a new popular consensus behind the officers. This was hard to do, given that the army had never enjoyed much prestige and had been further discredited by its loss in Palestine, but the RCC set up a mass movement called the Liberation Rally (the term *Front* was tried but dropped after someone explained what the word meant in Western countries). The organizers of the Liberation Rally made concerted efforts to attract workers and students, but, ironically, its most zealous backers were often Muslim Brothers. Within the government, RCC members took over from civilians the lion's share of the ministries. Nasir became deputy premier and interior minister. He soon gave up the latter position, but he made sure that his RCC allies dominated the cabinet and that his best friend, Abd al-Hakim Amir, became the commander of the armed forces. Another backer, Shams Badran, purged the officer corps of Nasir's opponents.

These events alarmed the Muslim Brothers, who got up mass demonstrations in January 1954 in commemoration of the Egyptian guerrillas killed by the British in the Suez Canal zone two years earlier. They were challenged by the Liberation Rally on the Cairo University campus, leading to a brawl that resulted in many injuries and arrests. The RCC promptly banned the Society, but divisions among the officers encouraged RCC foes to believe that the Muslim Brothers would make a comeback. Nagib became the standard-bearer for their hopes.

Nagib objected to Badran's reorganization of the officer corps and opposed Nasir's measures against the ex-party leaders, including Nahhas' house arrest. He thought that the other RCC members were flouting his leadership and that Nasir was turning the press against him. On 23 February 1954 he resigned as RCC chairman and president. Several of his backers followed suit. At first, Nasir responded by putting Nagib under house arrest, but mass demonstrations forced him to rescind the measure. Realizing that Nagib commanded widespread backing and that many Egyptians were clamoring for a return to constitutional government, Nasir made a tactical retreat. After three days, he asked Nagib to resume his posts. He then promised to dissolve the RCC by July and to hold free elections for an assembly that would write a new constitution. Nagib's restoration was celebrated in Abdin Square by a mass rally, during which he invited one of the leading Muslim Brothers to join him at the podium. He may have meant to co-opt the society, but to Nasir this act betrayed Nagib's true loyalties. Having proved he had the support of Egypt's students, workers, and other articulate groups, Nagib flew to the Sudan to help open its new legislative assembly.

It looked as if Nagib had won, but he underestimated Nasir's ability to mobilize the support of the Free Officers, the forces of state security, and his few allies in the trade unions. A chess player in his spare time, Nasir was a master tactician, willing to withdraw at first in order to advance later. While Nagib was in the Sudan, Nasir cultivated ties with the union leaders and convinced them that Nagib's opposition to the RCC threatened the revolution. By the end of March he had mobilized his backers within the Liberation Rally for anti-Nagib demonstrations. In April Nasir took over the premiership and purged Nagib's backers from the cabinet. He reneged on his promises to abolish the RCC and to allow elections for a constituent assembly by July. Nagib's leading backers were jailed or exiled, and Nasir emerged as Egypt's new dictator. Nagib retained the presidency, but this was merely a figurehead position.

Nasir in Power

Even though books written during the 1950s do not mention Nasir's foreign backers, later works reveal that the CIA (especially Kermit Roosevelt, who had helped to overthrow Musaddiq in Iran) facilitated Nasir's takeover. One concrete form of U.S. aid was a suitcase containing $3 million that Roosevelt had ordered to be delivered to one of Nasir's aides. Although he was sensitive to any imputation of taking bribes, Nasir decided to keep the money but not to reward those who had demonstrated in his support. Instead, he built a decorative tower, topped by a revolving restaurant and a blinking antenna, officially named the Cairo Tower but (at first) sardonically called *al-waqif Rusfel* ("Roosevelt's erection") by the Egyptians. Ironically, Nasir used to avoid the tower, fearing that the CIA was using it to spy on him. In 1954, though, Nasir did work with the Americans, who preferred the dour colonel over the smiling General Nagib (with his Communist backers).

Unlike Nagib, who was born in Khartum of a Sudanese mother, Nasir was a pure Egyptian. His father was a postmaster in Alexandria, where Gamal had been born in 1918, but the family had come from the Upper Egyptian village of Beni Murr and Gamal spent his summers there. He identified closely with Upper Egypt, in a reaction against the stereotyped image of Upper Egyptians (among their city cousins) as strong but stupid hicks. Nasir did most of his schooling in Cairo, often living with an uncle. His mother's early death, news of which was long hidden from him, wounded him deeply. Resenting his father's quick remarriage, he became moody and introspective, but he excelled in his studies. A fervent nationalist, he took part in many schoolboy demonstrations, sustaining a bullet wound when he was seventeen.

Upon graduating in 1936 from one of Cairo's best secondary schools, he tried to enter the Military Academy but was rejected. He entered law school instead, but reapplied for officer training after the Wafd opened the Military Academy to secondary-school graduates who had passed a competitive examination. He completed the program in eighteen months and, after being commissioned in 1938, served in Upper Egypt, the Sudan, and El Alamein before becoming an instructor at the Military Academy. He was rare among Egyptians for his serious disposition and purposeful behavior. His methodical organization of the Free Officers movement, the 1952 Revolution, and Nagib's fall from power demonstrated Nasir's talents as an organizer and tactician. But he lacked Nagib's popular appeal.

The Egyptian people cared most about their relationship with the British. Almost all wanted the British to leave their Suez Canal base, but the two sides held lengthy negotiations over the terms of the evacuation. Even after Britain had conceded that the West's defense needs could not be met by occupying lands belonging to a hostile people, it still wanted to retain technicians at the base—civilians if military ones were unacceptable—in case a general war broke out with the Communist countries. Both Britain and the United States pressed Egypt to join an anti-Communist military alliance, including Turkey and Pakistan, similar to NATO. Nasir rejected both the stated conditions. He argued, with good reason, that his domestic opponents would attack him for making any agreement prolonging the British presence in Egypt. If Egypt needed defense, it was against Israel. Even if Communism threatened Egypt as much as Zionism did, which Nasir doubted, the menace would be more apt to take the form of an internal revolution than an invasion from the USSR, more than a thousand miles from Egypt's shores. From Britain's side, evacuating the Suez Canal meant abandoning its largest and best-equipped military base and admitting that the end of the British Empire was near. Even the independence of India and Pakistan in 1947 was a less bitter pill for diehard imperialists to swallow than the 1954 agreement to leave Suez.

At last, British and Egyptian negotiators hammered out an agreement. Initialed in July and ratified in October 1954, it provided for the evacuation of all British troops from the Suez Canal within a twenty-month period. For the next seven years, Egypt would permit announced flights by Royal Air Force planes to land in Suez Canal zone airbases. Britain would have the right to reoccupy the canal in the event of an armed attack by an outside power against any Arab League member or Turkey. The inclusion of Turkey, which was being more directly menaced by the USSR than was Egypt or any other

Arab state, seemed to tie Egypt into the West's defense system. Naturally, both the Egyptian Communists and the Muslim Brothers assailed the treaty, as did many less ideological nationalists who rallied behind the tattered standard of President Nagib, now powerless against the RCC. For them, the pact pushed the British out the front door but let them back in through the rear; it seemed to be a revised version of the abandoned 1936 Anglo-Egyptian Treaty. To this historian, the agreement resembles one nearly reached in 1887 between Britain and the Ottoman Empire (blocked at the time by France and Russia) that would have ended the British occupation of Egypt, but with a three-year right of reentry.

Nasir nearly paid for the 1954 Treaty with his life. A week later, while he was making a speech in Alexandria, nine shots rang out, but they hit nothing but a lightbulb above his head, and he managed to go on. The police quickly caught the assailant and several of his accomplices, and they proved to be Muslim Brothers. The revolutionary court was promptly reactivated and the conspirators were tried and executed, as were several of their leaders. Then the Egyptian government launched a campaign, lasting for several years, to wipe out the Society of the Muslim Brothers, including all its branches, schools, and welfare institutions. The Society had put down deep roots in Egypt and several other Arab countries, and Nasir's vendetta against it ranks among his least popular policies. Nagib was put under house arrest. The presidency of the republic (offered to the venerable intellectual, Ahmad Lutfi al-Sayyid, who declined because of his age) was declared vacant. Egypt's prisons were now crammed with old-regime politicians, Communists, Muslim Brothers, and other dissidents. After 1954 there was no legal opposition to Nasir's policies.

Rising Egyptian-Israeli Tensions

The military junta, like any government, needed legitimacy. As political scientist Michael Hudson has noted, gaining legitimacy has been the major problem for most Arab governments since their independence. Legitimacy is the ability of a leader to command the voluntary obedience of his subjects. Nasir might have argued that his regime should be obeyed because it was trying to build Egypt's economy, but economic development may have seemed too slow for a revolutionary. The country's fiscal policies from 1952 to 1955 were conservative. Technical assistance, coming from the United States, Britain, and the United Nations, was modest.

The stronger case for obeying a military junta should be its ability to defend the country. Defense might have seemed an easy task, if British troops were poised to occupy the Suez Canal in case an Arab country were attacked, but few Egyptians expected Britain to defend them for their own sake. The most obvious menace to Egypt was Israel. Even though Egypt had a larger land area, more soldiers, and a population ten times greater than that of Israel, it was poorly equipped to withstand an Israeli attack. It needed all kinds of arms, but the United States, France, and Britain had reached an agreement in 1950 not to arm either the Arab states or Israel. Several U.S. aid missions had visited Cairo, but up to the 1954 Treaty, British opposition deterred the Americans from selling any sort of weapons to Egypt. Even after the treaty was signed, Israel's vociferous supporters in Congress argued against arms sales to any enemy state. It is interesting that the Egyptian government did explore various ways to make peace with the Jewish state, using mainly U.S. intermediaries. Egypt's terms would have included the repatriation of some of the Palestinian Arab refugees, mainly those in Gaza who were chafing under Egyptian military administration, and territorial concessions to create a land bridge across the Negev Desert to Jordan (access to Saudi oil was a later desideratum).

The cause of peace between Israel and Egypt was not helped by the abortive attempt of several Israeli agents to attack U.S. cultural institutions in Cairo and Alexandria in 1954. The attempt led immediately to David Ben Gurion's return from retirement to the defense ministry and later to the notorious Lavon Affair, a cause célèbre in Israeli politics. Ben Gurion advocated a strong defense posture against military actions (or threats) from Israel's Arab neighbors. On 28 February 1955 Israel's army raided Gaza, in retaliation against armed attacks by Egyptian-trained Palestinian *fida'iyin.* This raid exposed the glaring weakness of Egypt's army. Four days earlier, Iraq and Turkey had signed an alliance treaty—joined shortly by Britain, Pakistan, and Iran—that came to be called the Baghdad Pact. Leading Americans (especially John Foster Dulles) had worked for such an anti-Communist alliance for years, but the U.S. government did not join it in 1955.

The Gaza raid and the Baghdad Pact presented a double challenge to Nasir. He now intensified his quest for arms, still looking first to Britain and the United States; but neither government was willing, without conditions, to sell him the quantity of arms he needed. His reprisals against Israel, therefore, took the form of intensified raids by the Palestinian *fida'iyin.* As the tension grew, he also intensified economic measures against Israel, confiscating Israel-bound cargoes on ships transiting the Suez Canal. As for the Baghdad Pact, Nasir argued that it served the interests, not of the Arab countries, but of Western imperialism in the Arab world. The inclusion of Iraq, next to Egypt the most powerful and influential Arab state, meant that the Hashimites in Baghdad and Amman were challenging Cairo's preeminence and undermining Arab solidarity. Egypt pointed out that the Arab countries had already signed a collective security pact under the auspices of the Arab League. Nasir could not countenance the defection of one state, especially Egypt's historic rival for Arab leadership.

Nasir's prestige received a big boost when he attended the first meeting of "nonaligned" Afro-Asian leaders, held in Bandung, Indonesia, in April 1955. There he was received as a hero (for having persuaded the British to withdraw their troops from Suez) by such leaders as Sukarno, Nehru, and Chou En-lai, whom he was meeting for the first time. They also encouraged him to buy arms from the Communist countries, if Britain and the United States refused to sell sufficient quantities to meet Egypt's needs. Nasir began to view himself and Egypt as star actors on the international stage. Radio Cairo started beaming propaganda into other Arab countries discrediting their leaders, if they were already independent, or inciting them to overthrow their colonial masters.

Hitherto, despite Egypt's role in forming the Arab League, Egyptians had rarely identified themselves as Arabs. Indeed, Nasir had never seen another Arab country, except the Sudan, and knew few Syrians, Iraqis, or other Arabs personally. But this new combination of Arab nationalism and anti-imperialism raised Egypt's dignity and self-esteem (or, to its detractors, its nuisance value). Nasir became a hero, especially in the eyes of frustrated youths in other Arab countries. As his troops trained *fida'iyin* for raids into Israel, and as his "Voice of the Arabs" transmitters (a gift, ironically, from the U.S. government) broadcast anti-Zionist propaganda, Nasir became a special hero to the Palestinians.

It is hardly surprising, then, that Nasir found it easier to make large arms deals with Communist countries than to buy smaller quantities from Britain or the United States. In September 1955 he announced that he had agreed to buy up to $200 million worth of weapons from Czechoslovakia, to be paid for through exports of Egyptian cotton. Only later did it become known that the real seller was the USSR, which had hesitated to reveal its role just after its leaders had met with President Eisenhower in the first postwar summit at Geneva. The arms sales were on a scale larger than any made before in the Middle East. They effectively nullified the 1950 agreement to limit such sales; now an Arab-Israeli arms race began in earnest. France hastened to sell more weapons to Israel and assailed Nasir for stirring up anti-French feeling in Tunisia, Morocco, and especially Algeria, where 1 million European colonists faced a bloody rebellion by 10 million native Muslims. This upward spiral in instruments of death has been going on ever since. It also signaled a much more visible Soviet role in Middle Eastern politics. Nasir turned a deaf ear to Americans who pleaded with him to cancel the arms deal. He was determined, after the Gaza raid, not to be humiliated by Israel again.

The Western countries were hampered in their ability to deal with Egypt by their support for Israel, but they were better able than the Communist states to provide economic aid. Aside from strengthening his armed forces, Nasir's surest path to legitimacy was his implementation of projects that showed his government's determination to develop national pride. One such showcase project was the Nile Corniche, or shore drive. Cairenes had long been cut off from portions of the river by princely palaces, the British Embassy in Garden City, and the British army barracks, whose lands extended to the water's edge. The completion of the Corniche and the replacement of the barracks (between the Qasr al-Nil Bridge and the Egyptian Museum) by the Arab League Headquarters and the Nile Hilton Hotel inspired civic pride and gave ordinary Egyptians a long river promenade (poorly maintained and choked by construction and car traffic since Nasir's death) and a big public square in which to mingle on hot summer nights. In addition, a huge statue of Ramses II was erected in front of Cairo's main railroad station, with an immense fountain cooling the public square (also defunct in recent years). It replaced another statue, "Egypt's Reawakening," the best-known work of sculptor Mahmud Mukhtar, which was moved from the station to grace the head of an avenue of trees leading to Cairo University. Other statues were put up in Cairo and Alexandria to honor Egypt's nationalist heroes.

The Aswan High Dam

But the project that most notably came to symbolize Egypt's reawakening was the High Dam at Aswan. One of Britain's greatest achievements in Egypt had been the extension of large-scale, year-round irrigation, up and down the Nile Valley. Since the reign of Mehmet Ali, barrages, canals, and water-raising devices had increased the lands of Egypt that, thanks to perennial irrigation, could grow two or three crops in one year. The British had built a large dam at Aswan, completed in 1902 and later raised twice, that had made perennial irrigation possible in much of Upper Egypt. The country had also benefited from various river projects in the Sudan.

By the 1950s, though, most engineers recommended building still more dams to store and regulate the Nile water, if the Nile Valley's agricultural output was to keep up with its rapid population growth. The plan preferred by most experts before the 1952 Revolution was called the "Century Storage Scheme." It proposed the creation of additional reservoirs, mostly on the White Nile and its sources, to hold enough water to ensure supplies to Egyptian and Sudanese farmers throughout the year—regardless of the height of the flood, which depended on how much water flowed down the Blue Nile. The plan would have made Egypt heavily dependent on public works projects located in the Sudan. Once it became clear that the two countries would probably never unite, the Century Storage Scheme (even if it could have been implemented) would have subjected Egypt to the ongoing good will of the Sudan.

The alternative plan was to build a much larger Aswan dam, wholly within Egypt, creating a reservoir large enough to hold a year's flood waters. No longer would Egypt's farmers worry about the Nile flood being too high or too low to sow and harvest their crops. Such a dam would also enable the Nile to irrigate 1–3 million more feddans of farmland and to generate sufficient hydroelectric power to meet all of Egypt's electricity needs. The "High Dam" project had been advocated by some engineers before the 1952 Revolution, but the Free Officers soon seized on the idea and made it the centerpiece of their program. It would be large and could be built in a decade.

Although engineers foresaw some technical problems in the High Dam project, the most obvious obstacle was financial in nature. Egypt was too poor to pay the billion dollars that most experts expected the dam to cost. If the High Dam was to be built, large foreign loans would be absolutely necessary. The risks were far too great for private investors or even for a single government to undertake. Therefore, Egypt turned to the International Bank for Reconstruction and Development (the World Bank) for financial assistance. Its director, Eugene Black, was cautiously in favor of the project, sending out World Bank engineers and economists to make a new feasibility study.

In December 1955 he made a package offer, consisting of a $200 million loan for the first phase of construction, combined with $56 million in grants from the United States and $14 million from Britain. The two countries were also expected to lend larger amounts to help finance the later phases of the project. The World Bank offer depended on Egypt's agreeing to the conditions placed on the U.S. and British grants. The suggested terms included close Western scrutiny and control of Egypt's economy, no new arms purchases, open bidding for contracts (but excluding any Communist countries), and prior agreement with the Sudan over allocation of the Nile waters. Nasir's government did not want to accept a package deal that reminded the Egyptians of the Dual Financial Control; he hinted that Egypt would seek offers from other countries, hoping that the Soviets might rise to the bait. This was the era in which Egypt was trying to get the superpowers to outbid each other for its support.

It was clear to the Egyptians (and everyone else) that the West was making a political offer, mainly to counter the rising Communist influence on Egypt and other Arab countries after the announcement of the Czech arms deal. In fact, both Syria and Yemen followed Egypt's example by buying Communist arms, ending what had been a Western monopoly. Rioting mobs (inspired by Radio Cairo) greeted Britain's representative when he visited Amman late in 1955 to sign up Jordan for the Baghdad Pact. So fierce was the nationalist opposition in that country that King Husayn's government decided not to join Iraq in the anti-Communist treaty. A few months later, while Britain's foreign secretary was visiting Nasir, King Husayn publicly dismissed Sir John Bagot Glubb, the British commander of Jordan's Arab Legion. A pro-Nasir (but constitutionally chosen) government was ruling in Amman. The French were fighting a bitter war in Algeria against Muslim rebels, who were being backed morally (and maybe materially) by Cairo. With Tunisia, Morocco, and the Sudan all gaining formal independence in early 1956, the tide of Western imperialism was clearly receding in the Arab World. To the West, it looked as if Nasir and the Communists were filling the void it had left behind.

The U.S. secretary of state, John Foster Dulles, was a strong-minded, inflexible Calvinist who tended to regard the world as divided between the democratic nations and the Communists, with no true neutrals in between. He viewed with alarm the leftward drift of the Nasirite Arabs, especially when Nasir (perhaps in an effort to secure more arms) recognized the Communist government in China. Meanwhile, Congress, whose approval would have been needed for the U.S. government's part in the Aswan High Dam deal, began raising objections about the danger to the southern states that Egypt would increase its cotton exports (here Congress erred, for one purpose of the High Dam was to diversify export crops), the long-term costs of the project, and the rising hostility between Egypt and Israel. The final outcome was that, when Dr. Ahmad Husayn, Egypt's ambassador in Washington, finally came in on 18 July 1956 with Nasir's consent to the U.S. offer, in spite of its objectionable conditions, Dulles replied that the deal was off.

The Suez Crisis

Withdrawing the High Dam offer was the worst diplomatic blunder Dulles ever committed. Nasir, who was visiting Yugoslavia at the time, was furious over what he and his followers regarded as a calculated (though not unexpected) insult. His riposte came eight days later. In a speech marking the fourth anniversary of Faruq's abdication, as Nasir repeated the code name, "Lesseps," Egyptian military and naval units occupied the offices, wharves, encampments, and other facilities of the Suez Canal Company. He then announced its nationalization, saying that the canal tolls would pay for the construction of the high dam. No previous Nasir speech had ever received so tumultuous a response, for the Suez Canal symbolized Egypt's exploitation by the West. Its governing board, still mainly French in 1956, virtually excluded Egyptians from its management. To the French, the canal was the main vestige of their role in Egypt's economy. To the British, it had been the lifeline of their empire during two world wars, and they had defended it as tenaciously as if it were their home territory (which, in one sense, it was, inasmuch as the British government owned 44 percent of the company's shares). To the Arabs (and other Third World states, such as India), Nasir became an instant hero for defying the imperialist West. The United States cared less about Suez, perhaps, but it did worry about navigation rights and the possible influence of Nasir's act on Panama.

How many knew that the Suez Canal was legally Egyptian, a fact recognized ever since it was built and confirmed most recently in the 1954 Anglo-Egyptian Treaty? The company had been chartered in Egypt, although its international headquarters was in Paris. The right of governments to nationalize companies within their borders, with appropriate compensation to their shareholders, is recognized under international law and was exercised by every country involved in the two world wars. Nasir's act was, nevertheless, loudly praised or stridently condemned because of its symbolic significance.

Britain and France reacted in several ways. The press and the public threatened to invade Egypt and to stop Nasir before he seized control of the whole Arab world, notably the oil of Iraq, Kuwait, and Saudi Arabia. Zionists stressed Egypt's arms buildup, the crescendo of *fida'iyin* raids and of Radio Cairo propaganda against Israel, and the probable use of the canal to blackmail the West. Westerners doubted that the Egyptians had the technical expertise or discipline to manage the Suez Canal. Neither Britain nor France was capable of invading Egypt immediately to seize the canal, and President Eisenhower, campaigning for reelection, insisted that the United States would not join in or support military action without congressional approval. He and Dulles called for a diplomatic response. Western Europeans, who imported most of their oil on ships transiting the canal, wanted it placed under international administration. A conference was held in London, but Egypt refused to send representatives, and India and the USSR (among others) blocked unanimity on a resolution calling for international control of the canal. The eighteen nations that did support that plan sent a delegation to Cairo, headed by Australia's prime minister, but Nasir firmly rejected internationalization. Dulles, while reiterating U.S. opposition to any use of force against Egypt, proposed to set up a Suez Canal Users Association (SCUA) to collect the tolls. Nasir rejected that idea, too, and no one knew if Dulles would order U.S. shippers to pay tolls to SCUA (nicknamed "screwya" by the Americans, "skewer" by the Egyptians). Another London conference proved inconclusive, but Egypt was surprisingly conciliatory at the next UN Security Council meeting. French, British, U.S., and Egyptian diplomats agreed to meet in Geneva in late October to devise a compromise, but the first two governments persisted in their threats to use force to regain the canal.

The Egyptians did not flinch. They set up a Suez Canal Authority, headed by Colonel Mahmud Yunis, to replace the old Canal Company administration. When most of the European pilots, who had guided convoys of ships transiting the canal, walked off their jobs in an effort to paralyze its operation, Yunis managed to import replacements from Communist and neutral countries and to train enough Egyptian pilots (in a crash program) to keep it running. Tolls did not become extortionate; Egypt allowed users to pay them to the Suez Canal Company's European offices. Egypt also offered to pay stockholders for the value of their shares, as determined by their selling price on the stock exchange just before nationalization was announced. In short, the country tried to show that it could manage the canal as well as the company had done, such that there was no need for international control.

Britain and France reacted by preparing for war. Concerned about Nasir's influence over their people, some pro-Western Arab leaders would have supported the European powers but for their ill-concealed collaboration with Israel. France, angry at Nasir for aiding the Algerian Revolution, was arming Israel heavily. Ben Gurion wanted to attack Egypt to stop the *fida'iyin* raids and to wipe out its military potential before it could absorb the new Communist guns, tanks, and planes into its operations. He also hoped to break Egypt's Tiran Straits blockade, which had barred Israeli ships from using the Gulf of Aqaba.

On Ben Gurion's initiative, Moshe Dayan traveled secretly to meet with British and French leaders to coordinate an attack on Egypt.

On the very day when British, French, U.S., and Egyptian diplomats were to have met in Geneva to devise a compromise deal over Suez, Israeli paratroopers landed at the strategic Mitla Pass, deep in the Sinai, and Israeli ground forces began spilling across the border. Although the Egyptians had known about Israel's mobilization, they had expected its attack to be directed against Jordan, and thus they fell back in shock. On the following day an ultimatum came from London, calling on Egypt to withdraw its forces to 10 miles (16 kilometers) west of the canal (as if that were the border with Israel), so that the British could secure the canal region, as provided for in the 1954 Anglo-Egyptian Treaty. Predictably, Egypt refused. British planes started bombing targets in Cairo, Alexandria, the canal zone, and the coastal region, while an immense Anglo-French armada steamed slowly into positions in the eastern Mediterranean. Nasir vowed that Egypt would never surrender, but he ordered the army to pull back from the Sinai to prepare for the European invasion.

Britain and France seriously misjudged their ability to rally support against Nasir. Even though the Americans were near the end of an election campaign, Eisenhower risked losing the votes of Israel's backers by demanding an Israeli withdrawal and condemning the British attacks. Even while the Soviet army was crushing a revolt in Hungary, Premier Nicolai Bulganin threatened to bomb London, Paris, and Tel Aviv if the "Tripartite Aggression" against Egypt did not stop. Many of the British Commonwealth members (including Canada) opposed the attack; India and Pakistan assailed it in the strongest possible terms, as did London's Arab allies, Iraq and Jordan. The British prime minister, Sir Anthony Eden, who was broken in health and spirit, decided to abort the attack just as British and French ground troops were going ashore at Port Said to capture the canal. Nasir would later exalt the heroic resistance of Port Said's citizens to the invaders, but their heroism was due in part to his army's hasty abandonment of the city, in part to Eden's failure of nerve, and mostly to the superpowers' joint condemnation of the Tripartite Aggression. British and French troops lingered in Port Said for seven weeks. The Israelis stayed in Sinai a little longer. Canada's foreign minister proposed the stationing of a UN Emergency Force in Gaza and in strategic areas of the Sinai, such as Sharm al-Shaykh, letting Israeli ships use the Gulf of Aqaba. Under heavy U.S. pressure, the Israelis pulled out.

The Suez War was a military defeat but a political triumph for Nasir. He lost most of his new airplanes, Egypt's postrevolutionary army lost some credibility, and Israel's military reputation was enhanced. But it also showed the Egyptian people that Nasir, unlike Urabi seventy-five years earlier, could withstand British pressure. Even if no diplomat said so publicly, it was clear that Britain had hoped to overthrow Nasir's regime, but without knowing who would replace him. In the eyes of most other Arabs (if not those of their leaders), Nasir was now the foremost foe of both imperialism and Zionism. The Suez War weakened British and French influence throughout the Middle East, raised U.S. prestige slightly, and improved the USSR's reputation greatly. Indeed, many British and French subjects who had spent their entire lives in Egypt were expelled without their property. So, too, were most Jews, even if they were anti-Zionist Egyptian citizens. The nationalization of British and French companies in Egypt after the Suez War set a precedent for many later seizures and sequestrations of private property. Egypt boycotted British and French products. It broke diplomatic relations with the two countries and influenced other Arab states to do so. It renounced the 1954 Anglo-Egyptian Treaty. As for the canal itself, Egypt had sunk enough ships to make it impassible; it then refused to allow the canal's clearance (by the United Nations) until the British, French, and Israeli invaders had all withdrawn.

Egypt and the Arab World

Amid all the clangor and strife over Aswan and Suez, one could hardly have expected any domestic progress in Egypt during 1956. But in June of that year the people finally got to vote on the new constitution that had been promised since the revolution. The constitution set up a government with a strong presidency, thereby centralizing power in the hands of Gamal Abd al-Nasir (who received 99.9 percent of the popular vote, there being no opponent) but creating a new consultative assembly in the place of the abolished parliament. For the first time, Egyptian women were allowed to vote and hold public office. Political parties were banned. Having served in March 1954 to legitimize Nasir against his foes, the Liberation Rally had subsequently faded away. Nasir now called for a new mobilizing organization, the National Union, which was to serve Egypt rather as the Communist party does the USSR—namely, as a means of gathering ideas, discovering political talent, and sending government directives down to villages and neighborhoods. The 1956 constitution was also the first to state specifically that Egypt was an Arab country and a part of the Arab nation.

This commitment opened opportunities to spread Cairo's influence from the Atlantic Ocean to the Gulf, but it was also the cause of new troubles for Egypt. Once Nasir had weathered the Suez Crisis, the country might have fared better if he had tried to solve some of its domestic problems. Nasir's dedication to Arab nationalism, widely denounced in the West as a ploy to grab the oil fields of Arabia, was certainly sincere. His pursuit of Arab unity, however, was in reaction to expectations placed upon him by Arabs in other countries. If Nasir could stand up to Israel and the two main imperialist powers the Arab world had known, in defense of Egypt's dignity and the Suez Canal, then Palestinians expected him to dictate policy to King Husayn, Syrians belonging to Arab nationalist parties wanted him to rescue them from both CIA and Communist plots, and the Muslim Lebanese hoped he would free their country from Maronite Christian (and Western) domination. Nasir often claimed that he did not act—that he only reacted to the moves of others. This is a strategy for the weak; it is not a policy.

The United States, too, learned by trial and error how to formulate its Middle East policy. Its so-called Eisenhower Doctrine, passed by Congress in January 1957, promised economic and military aid to any Middle Eastern country facing aggression from a state controlled by "international Communism." Some governments accepted the U.S. offer, but they agreed to fight Nasirism, not Communism. During 1957 King Husayn faced down a group of rebellious army officers, ousted his Arab nationalist cabinet, and established a royal dictatorship, thereby angering his mainly pro-Nasir Palestinian subjects.

Later in that year, Syria asked for Soviet help against threats (which were allegedly CIA-inspired) by Turkey. Then the Syrian government, led by the Arab socialist Ba'th party, asked to unite with Egypt before its few but highly disciplined Communists could take control. Nasir insisted on an organic unification of Egypt and Syria. The result was the United Arab Republic (UAR), a union of two noncontiguous countries, with Israel and Lebanon between them. The UAR's creation aroused the Arabs in neighboring countries, especially Palestinians and young people, to their governments' discomfiture. Civil war broke out in Lebanon, and the pro-Western side promptly accused Nasir of sending agents, arms, and propaganda to the rebels. Then a revolution toppled the monarchy in Iraq and set up a military regime that professed Nasirite aims. The Iraqi Revolution led to the landing of U.S. Marines in Lebanon (an action that invoked the Eisenhower Doctrine) and to the entry of British paratroopers into Jordan. Britain, France, and the United States pursued their national interests while claiming to fight Communism, but their real target was Gamal Abd al-Nasir. They failed. By late 1958, he seemed to be dominating the Arab world. After King Sa'ud's foolish attempt to bribe a Syrian Nasirite to assassinate Nasir, Saudi Arabia turned his powers over to Faysal, who was presumed to be an Arab nationalist. The U.S. occupation enabled Lebanon to end its civil war by electing a new president acceptable to the UAR. The Sudan, too, had a military coup, but the resulting regime proved not to be Nasirite. Iraq's new rulers decided that Arab nationalism did not require them to join the UAR and hence to turn over their oil revenues to Cairo. This discovery caused some Syrians to regret having joined Egypt, for Iraq was nearer to them.

In the course of pursuing Arab hegemony, Egypt neglected its real problems of overpopulation, undercapitalized agriculture and industry, and inadequate technicians, in favor of showcase projects like the Hilwan steel mill, the Ramses auto assembly plant, and "Liberation Province" (a large-scale project for desert reclamation). Countless arguments arose among Egyptians as to whether they really were Arabs; the United Arab Republic had at first stirred up more fervor in Damascus than in Cairo. The Syrians viewed themselves as more clever than the Egyptians, and their politically articulate leaders, especially the Ba'th party, assumed that they would wield influence over the less ideologically sophisticated Egyptian colonels. Nasir, for his part, was astonished when he saw how strong were Syria's capitalists and how simple was their government. Compared with Egypt's heavy-handed bureaucracy, the Syrian administration seemed minuscule; its annual budget, Nasir said, would hardly suffice for an Egyptian grocery store. Before long, Egyptian officers, administrators, accountants, and technocrats were pouring into Syria to reorganize what was now the UAR's "Northern Province," as if it were their latest colony—hardly what Syrians had been asking for.

Arab Nationalism and Communism

At the end of 1958, liberal democracy was but a vague memory in Egypt and the rest of the Arab world. Parliamentary government had been discredited as a playpen for palace hangers-on, rich landowners, capitalist merchants, and shrewd lawyers. Egyptian nationalism seemed old-fashioned; now the competing ideologies, Arab nationalism and Communism, were both supranational. The idea of uniting all the Arab countries appealed to many citizens, partly because it sounded like a respectably modern version of the older idea of pan-Islam. Pan-

Arabism seemed even better: It did not exclude Arabic-speaking Christians, and it would combine oil-rich countries having few people, such as Saudi Arabia, with populous ones poor in petroleum, such as Egypt. The Arabs had served, for the past millennium, as a doormat for foreign invaders and colonists: Turks, Crusaders, Mongols, French, and British. Having now become independent, except for Algeria, Palestine, and a few fringes of Arabia, the Arab peoples had to join together to become rich, strong, and respected. Nasir would lead them.

The Communists accused the Arab nationalists of clinging to a romanticized version of their past and of lacking a plan by which to shape their future. Only through class struggle could societies progress from slavery to feudalism to capitalism to socialism. Arabism might unlock the shackles of Western imperialism and to destroy its lackeys in some countries, but it was not a program to develop free peoples. Because Nasir had banned all parties but the National Union and had jailed Egypt's Communists (Syria's Communist leaders fled as soon as the UAR was formed), Arab nationalism dominated in Cairo. In Iraq, however, the revolutionary regime, after denouncing the Baghdad Pact, steered a cautious course between Arabism and Communism, turning Nasir against both Iraq and the USSR. Some Americans began to hope that Egypt might even become reconciled with the West.

In October 1958 the USSR announced that it would provide the aid needed to build the first phase of the Aswan High Dam. The Communist states in many ways strengthened their ties with the UAR. Yet, within a few months, Nasir was exchanging insults and criticisms with the Soviet leaders—ostensibly over ideology, but really over who had the most influence in Iraq. Egypt resumed diplomatic relations with Britain, and ties with the United States warmed up slightly. As long as the UAR depended on the Communists for its weapons and replacement parts, though, the West's ability to influence Cairo remained limited. The UAR still refused to let ships carrying Israel-bound goods through the Suez Canal. Consequently, New York longshoremen refused in April 1960 to unload an Egyptian freight vessel, thus chilling U.S.-Arab ties. Influenced in part by the Syrian Ba'thists, the UAR government began strengthening its commitment to socialism, nationalizing more foreign-held property (e.g., Belgian companies in Egypt, following the outbreak of disorders in the newly independent Congo), and placing public utilities, banks, and newspapers under state control. Another harbinger of change was the publication of Egypt's first five-year economic plan in 1959.

Conclusion

Under Nasir, Egypt had at last become an independent country, free of British troops and indirect control. The processes of nation building were now under the command of a native Egyptian—indeed, an Upper Egyptian—and were being harnessed in the name of the Egyptian people. If free press and assembly had disappeared, if the students' excess energies were being diverted from politics into soccer and other sports, if censors were looking at incoming books, magazines, and letters—well, most workers were making more money, people were getting better housing, and more children were going to school and receiving medical care. More than half a million feddans of farmland had been redistributed to needy peasants. The Aswan High Dam, on which Soviet and Egyptian engineers began work in 1959, promised even higher living standards in the future.

Equally if not more important was the new respect that Egypt now received from other countries. Formerly, foreign residents or visitors had seen the natives as wogs, gyppos, dirty beggars, and sellers of filthy pictures. These terms and images were now fading away. Beggars, touts, and prostitutes were being chased away from tourists by the police. Drug smugglers were vigorously prosecuted. Belly-dancers had to cover their torsoes with body stockings. The police even tried to quell reckless driving in Cairo and Alexandria. Nasir's incorruptibility impressed Egyptians and foreigners alike. His devotion to Arab unity won him widespread support from Arabs everywhere and, in particular, from Palestinians. In the late 1950s, most Arabic-speaking peoples believed that the union of Egypt and Syria would be the first step toward a wider federation of all Arab states; Yemen (still a monarchy) did federate with the UAR. Nasir's ability to play off the two superpowers, which he called "Positive Neutrality" (critics called it "working both sides of the street"), won aid for Egypt from the United States and the USSR—and respect from the other new nations of Asia and Africa. Students from many of these countries flocked to its universities, perhaps gaining lasting impressions of Egypt as a country worthy of emulation. Nasir's quest for national dignity and strength seemed to have succeeded. It was time to seek social justice and equality.

CHAPTER TEN

The Socialist Phase

The regime of the Egyptian officers began as a nationalist revolution with no general ideology. Nasir was essentially pragmatic; he deliberately shaped his program around the needs of the moment. It gradually became clear, though, that the revolutionary regime did need guiding principles if it was to cure the various ills of Egypt's society. In an influential article first published in the *Atlantic Monthly*, Sir Hamilton Gibb, a well-known scholar of Islam, pointed out the "Factor X" that he discerned as missing in the reform programs of the Middle East's westernizing reformers: "No stable state can arise or endure without a basic social philosophy, accepted by the mass of its citizens, more or less consciously pursued in public life and private associations, and guaranteed by its laws, whether it be the *Respublica Christiana*, or the ideology of the Islamic Community, or *Liberté, Egalité, Fraternité*, or 'Life, Liberty, and the Pursuit of Happiness.' Nationalism by itself is not such a philosophy."

What Gibb thought Egypt lacked in the 1950s was a feeling of Islamic solidarity, buttressed by the once-powerful religious brotherhoods that had been weakened by two centuries of state-imposed westernization. Modern Egyptians had earlier expressed their need for this type of organization by joining and supporting the Society of the Muslim Brothers, but this group had been ruthlessly extirpated by Nasir's government—ostensibly for having tried to assassinate him, but actually for challenging the primacy of the state. Nasir looked in a different direction in the late 1950s and came up with what soon would be called "Arab socialism."

Socialism in Egypt

The ideological development, not only of Egypt but of most Asian and African countries, has been shaped by the power, the wealth, the social institutions, and the ideas of Western Europe and North America. If the peoples of Asia and Africa have at various times viewed Britain and France, or Germany and Italy, or the United States and the Soviet Union, as militarily strong, economically prosperous, and socially cohesive, they have also chosen to adopt the organizing ideas, as well as the material goods and other attributes, that have made them so. The presence of European merchants in Egypt helped to promote a capitalist form of economic organization, together with the ideas of individual freedom and parliamentary democracy associated with liberal capitalism. The power of the British occupation to manipulate the Egyptian government enhanced the growth of nationalist feelings. The challenge of the USSR and other Communist states to the West's hegemony in the Middle East up to 1955–1956 lent an attractive luster to the ideas of socialism.

"Socialism" has many meanings. It can mean state ownership of factories and other means of production, workers' participation in the management of industries, national policies aimed at equalizing personal incomes, state economic planning, or charitable actions by individuals to share their material goods. In predominantly Muslim states, such as Egypt, it is rarely used in the purely Marxian sense, for Muslims can never deny the primacy of the one God above mundane material interests, nor can they accept a historical dynamic based on a struggle between classes. In Egypt, the term *socialism* has commonly been applied to state ownership and management of the means of production. In that sense, it is hardly novel, for the factories of Mehmet Ali and Isma'il (not to mention their irrigation works, which were so extended by the British) were state enterprises. Even such nascent capitalist enterprises as Bank Misr had sought and received government subsidies and tariff protection. The Free Officers, with a few exceptions, were not socialists; the RCC's first economic policies initially favored foreign investors and domestic capitalists. The 1955 Bandung Conference first brought Nasir into contact with Asian socialist leaders. The 1956 constitution pledged the government to strive for social justice by raising living standards, providing old-age benefits, public health, and social insurance, but free enterprise and private property were also respected. In 1957 several state planning agencies were established, notably the Economic Development Organization, with authorization to set up new companies and to dispense state funds to existing firms. Land reform continued, with additional distribution of *waqf* lands to needy peasants, followed by reductions of peasant payments and landlord compensation for the lands that had been redistributed earlier.

The formation of the United Arab Republic in 1958 brought Nasir and his fellow officers into contact with a more articulated socialism than any they had ever known before. Syria's Ba'th party was the first Arab movement to attempt a synthesis of nationalism and socialism. Its leaders were at first among the staunchest advocates of union with Egypt, although they became disenchanted when Nasir abolished their party along with all the others. However, it left major traces, including the slogan "Freedom, Socialism, Unity," which the United Arab Republic adopted for itself.

During its three years of existence, the UAR applied itself to developing a distinctively Arab interpretation of socialism. Traditional Arabism had stressed the pre-Islamic virtues of generosity to the poor, hospitality to visitors, and subordination of each person's interests to those of his or her tribe. Islam itself could be seen as socialist, or at any rate egalitarian, in its injunctions to be charitable toward the orphaned and the needy and in its institution of *zakat,* roughly corresponding to a tithe. The early nationalists had assailed the foreign ownership of utilities and factories, a situation corrected by the nationalization decrees that proliferated after the Suez War. Now the country saw a widening economic gap between such oil-rich countries as Saudi Arabia and those poor in petroleum and natural gas like the UAR. If the Arabs could combine their military and political power, they would have to share their economic resources to create a strong and respected state that could guarantee a decent minimum living standard to everyone.

As a practical step, the government required new industrial firms to be licensed, barred any person from being a director of more than one corporation, placed thirteen public utility companies under the state audit department, nationalized the large banks, subjected most newspapers and publishing houses to the National Union, and drew up its first five-year plan, which expressly aimed at doubling the national income in ten years. These small steps toward socialism led to the great leap known as the July Laws of 1961. Featured among those laws were (1) the regulation of most industries; (2) the nationalization of such businesses as textiles, tobacco, pharmaceuticals, shipping, and all banks and insurance firms not already under state ownership; (3) income redistribution, whereby no Egyptian could receive an annual salary above LE 5000 (then worth $11,500) and incomes above LE 10,000 were to be taxed at 90 percent; and (4) land reform, under which the maximum individual landholding was reduced from 200 to 100 feddans, with the excess to be distributed among the landless peasants, and all future peasant loans would be free of interest. The real July Revolution took place in 1961—not in 1952, as Egyptians claim.

The effect of these laws, and of those that would follow for the rest of Nasir's presidency, was the weakening of the Egyptian bourgeoisie and the destruction of what had been the overwhelming power of the large landowners. They could no longer effectively oppose Nasir and his policies. The industrial workers were now somewhat better off than ever before. They were guaranteed a minimum wage (although it remained abysmally low) and various fringe benefits, such as health care and disability benefits. A few became leaders in the state-controlled labor unions, or even members of the boards of directors in the companies for which they worked. Some peasants benefited from the land reforms, although they were hard-pressed to meet even minimal payments for the lands they had acquired. Rural cooperatives for the sharing of supplies and equipment helped, even though they were tied to the government bureaucracy. There were still many landless peasants, however, working for daily wages on lands owned by others.

Public education at all levels expanded rapidly, but school buildings and teaching staffs could not keep up with the burgeoning numbers of pupils, and so educational standards fell below their prerevolutionary levels. But improved school discipline reduced the number of days lost to political demonstrations. Egypt's private schools, once the training ground for the elite, were greatly reduced in number and increasingly subjected to state regulation. Government employees rose drastically in number, especially after so many manufacturing, financial, and commercial firms were nationalized. Nasir's 1962 guarantee of a government job for every university graduate also swelled the bureaucratic ranks. Salaries were low, as was productivity. Subsidized housing, health care, and old-age and disability pensions were offered as fringe benefits.

Unity of Goals, not Unity of Ranks

One unforeseen result of the new Arab socialist laws was Syria's secession from the United Arab Republic in late September 1961. Many explanations have been given for this breakaway: intrigues by other Arab regimes (especially Jordan) or by foreign powers, the low salaries paid UAR government officials and military officers relative to what Syrians had been accustomed to getting, Syrian resentment over the imperial attitudes of many Egyptians working in Syria (especially their chief, Abd al-Hakim Amir, who was Nasir's right-hand man), several years of poor harvests (hence higher food prices), and disillusionment with Arab nationalism once it became clear that Iraq and other oil-rich countries would not join the United Arab Republic. Paradoxically, Syria had not only more doctrinaire socialists than Egypt but also more recalcitrant capitalists, who were alienated by the July Laws. Although Nasir was chagrined by Syria's defection, he did not use force to regain control of the country, nor did he oppose its readmission to the Arab League. Egypt went on calling itself the United Arab Republic, hoping that other countries would join it some day.

Nasir did conclude, though, that the National Union had failed to mobilize UAR citizens behind his regime; on the contrary, he viewed it as having been infiltrated and corrupted by reactionary elements. In October 1961 he proposed a nationwide conference, the National Congress of Popular Forces, to form a revolutionary organization, not a party, that would be the "highest political authority" in the country: the Arab Socialist Union (ASU). The Congress would be open to workers, peasants, intellectuals, professionals, military men, and owners whose property was not based on exploitation. Students and women were also to be represented. To the Congress, which met in May 1962, Nasir presented a new national charter. It summarized the modern history of Egypt, explained why Arab socialism had become the country's guiding ideology, stated the ASU's aims and organizational framework, and reiterated the basic domestic and foreign policies of the UAR government. It included a declaration that "Woman must be regarded as equal to man. She must shed the remaining shackles that impede her from taking a constructive and vital part in shaping Egyptian society." For the first time, Nasir accepted family planning as a necessary means of combatting Egypt's overpopulation. For six weeks the Congress debated the charter and even openly criticized some of Nasir's policies—but without any practical results. The charter was passed unanimously.

On all domestic fronts—political, economic, intellectual, and social—Egypt was now committed to an ambitious modernization program, one that could hardly be achieved unless the country remained at peace with its neighbors and managed to obtain large grants of aid from foreign countries. Fortunately, with the USSR building the High Dam, the United States selling wheat for Egyptian pounds (thus saving Egypt's hard currency for other purchases abroad), and other countries (notably West Germany) giving aid independently, it seemed likely that the latter condition would be met. Despite their political differences, Nasir exchanged cordial letters with President Kennedy, whose ambassador, John Badeau, knew Egypt intimately and was a good friend of Nasir.

Egypt's relationship with other Arab countries, not to mention Israel, was the greater problem. In the wake of Syria's secession from the UAR, Nasir felt isolated within the Arab world. Iraq under its revolutionary leader, Abd al-Karim Qasim, was as fierce a rival as it had been under the Hashimite kings and Nuri al-Sa'id. Jordan and Saudi Arabia, as monarchies, opposed republican socialism. Lebanon had recovered from its 1958 civil war and was dedicated to the pursuit of freewheeling Arab capitalism. Syria was attacking Egypt in the Arab League. Tunisia and Libya had long opposed Nasir, and Morocco under King Hasan II (who had succeeded to his father's throne in 1961) was aligning itself with them. Algeria's independence in June 1962, after a bitter eight-year war (aided by Egypt) against French rule, was the sole bright star in the Arab firmament, for President Ahmad Ben Bella was closely allied with Nasir. Then came the death, in September 1962, of Yemen's aging Imam, who had repented of his federation with the UAR after Syria's secession. A week later, an army rebellion in San'a overthrew his son, or so most people thought. Egypt promptly recognized Yemen's military regime, headed by General Abdallah al-Sallal. When it became evident that the imam had escaped to the hills and was stirring up a counterrevolution among loyal Yemeni tribesmen, Egypt began sending advisers, arms, and troops to help Sallal's republicans. Saudi Arabia's regent, Faysal, viewed Nasir's aid as an attempt to extend his influence into the Arabian Peninsula (a perception shared by the British, who still ruled Southern Arabia). Before long, Saudi Arabia and Britain were aiding the Yemeni "royalists," and Egypt was ensnared in a five-year civil war often termed "Nasir's Vietnam."

If republican Yemen was a weak breach in the wall of isolation, Nasir's allies increased when, early in 1963, successive military coups brought Ba'th party sympathizers to power in Iraq and Syria. The new governments petitioned Nasir to start talks to create a new United Arab Republic, the formation of which was (a bit prematurely) announced in Cairo on 17 April. The three countries, despite their leaders' common belief in Arab unity and socialism, differed on the terms of their union. Nasir contended that Egypt, with its larger population and longer adherence to Arab socialism, deserved more of the power. He distrusted the Syrian Ba'thists, accusing them of having sabotaged the earlier United Arab Republic. He liked Iraq's new leader, Abd al-Salam Arif, who had aided Qasim in his 1958 Revolution and had then broken with him over Arab unity, suffered exile and imprisonment, and now emerged as a Nasirite. But even the Iraqi Ba'thists rejected Nasir's no-party dictatorship, and so Egypt put off the new federation indefinitely. By the year's end Egypt, Syria, and Iraq were back to their usual state of mutual estrangement. As an Arab proverb says: "I can protect myself from my enemy, but let God defend me against my friends."

The cause of Arab unity was better served by the actions of its enemy than by those of its friends. Israel, faced with recurrent water shortages, had begun its National Water Carrier Project, tapping Lake Tiberias to irrigate new lands and bring water to its cities, development towns, and other settlements. In 1954 Eisenhower had sent a special envoy, Eric Johnston, to the Middle East to promote a plan for developing the Jordan River valley and sharing its waters among Israel, Jordan, and Syria. The Arab states, although they approved its technical aspects, had rejected the Johnston plan for the political reason that it would mean recognition of Israel. In 1963 Israel began diverting what would have been its share of Jordan River waters under the plan, much to the alarm of its Arab neighbors. Nasir proceeded to call a summit meeting of all Arab kings and heads of state, held at the Arab League headquarters (and the adjacent Nile Hilton) in January 1964. He managed to convince the other Arab leaders that no one was ready for war against Israel. They agreed to study ways to divert the Jordan River's sources, mostly in Syria and Lebanon, so that Israel could not take the Arabs' water, but nothing concrete was accomplished. They also proposed to form the Palestine Liberation Organization (PLO), as a means of concentrating the political clout of the Palestinian Arabs and deflecting their pressures from their own governments. In May 1964 Palestinian delegates met in East Jerusalem (then ruled by Jordan) and founded the PLO under the presidency of Ahmad Shuqayri, a Nasirite Arab nationalist. The summit decisions enhanced Nasir's stature as an Arab leader, but they achieved little for Arab unification or the liberation of Palestine.

Early in 1964 the UAR got its new constitution, and elections were held for the local, provincial, and national councils of the Arab Socialist Union, as well as for the reorganized National Assembly. All Assembly delegates had to be over 30 years old and able to read and write. At least half had to be either workers or peasants, a stiff requirement in a country where most of the adult population was illiterate. If Nasir seemed to grant these representative bodies supreme authority over the government, in practice the ASU served to mobilize the people and recruit local leaders, and the National Assembly's powers were purely consultative. The country's laws still took the form of "Republican Decrees." Many of the Free Officers were now leaving the UAR cabinet, mainly due to their opposition to Nasir's

Arab socialism. The new ministers were mostly civilian technocrats, who lacked an independent power base. The executive branch, too, had become a rubber stamp for Nasir's unbridled will. Several separate secret police forces "protected" the UAR against foreign and domestic spies—or dissidents.

Problems in Egypt's Foreign Relations

After having declined many invitations to visit Egypt, Soviet leader Nikita Khrushchev finally came in May 1964 to celebrate the completion of the first stage of the High Dam. During his visit, he got into many arguments with Nasir and other Arab heads of state over their emphasis on Muslim values and Arab nationalism at the expense of Marxian scientific socialism. But Soviet aid, whether economic or military, kept coming, whereas U.S. wheat sales became ever more tied to politics, especially once Lyndon Johnson (who was distrusted by the Arabs) had succeeded the revered John Kennedy as president of the United States. U.S. differences with Egypt over the internal power struggle in the Congo (now Zaire) led to a protest demonstration by Africans studying in Cairo that caused the total destruction of the American library there. A few days later, Egyptian jets shot down a U.S. civilian plane that had strayed into the country's airspace without authorization, angering Johnson because the plane happened to belong to a personal friend, a Texas oil executive. Then Nasir, misunderstanding a talk between U.S. Ambassador Lucius Battle and Egypt's minister of supply over the terms for renewing the wheat sales agreement, said in a public speech that if the Americans objected to his policies, they could "drink from the sea" (the Egyptian Arabic equivalent of "go jump in the lake"). Such incidents as these delighted Egypt's Communists (out of prison since Khrushchev's visit), American Zionists, and anyone else opposed to friendly U.S.-Egyptian relations. After 1964 U.S. grain sales became sporadic and limited; as the USSR tried to take up the slack, Egypt edged toward the Communist camp. West German arms sales to Israel, followed by diplomatic recognition, caused the radical Arab states to strengthen their ties with East Germany, and the Middle East became more polarized than it had ever been before.

One of the interesting misconceptions the United States had about Nasir's government was that it was split between a doctrinaire pro-Communist wing led by Ali Sabri and a pragmatic pro-Western one personified by Zakariya Muhyi al-Din. The truth is that both men espoused various cold war positions during the many years they served under Nasir. By 1964 even his fellow Free Officers while in Nasir's presence were cautiously saying what they thought he wanted to hear. Ali Sabri, as prime minister from 1962 to 1965, was trying to carry out Nasir's program of modernization via Arab socialism. When Zakariya replaced him, Ali Sabri took over the senior vice-presidency and a leadership post in the Arab Socialist Union. Prime Minister Zakariya was less interested in Egypt's cold war stance than in its budget and balance of payments, both of which had run deficits for years. Without either an austerity program or a greater infusion of aid than the Soviets could afford, Egypt's economy was in danger of a total collapse. Zakariya did take one fateful step when he let Egyptians emigrate freely to other countries. In every year since 1965 up to half a million Egyptians have gone out to other Arab countries or to the rest of the world, sometimes to seek greater freedom but usually to make more money. By the 1980s their remittances were providing Egypt $2 billion in foreign exchange annually, a valued contribution to its balance of payments. Some people believe that these emigres may also have helped to reduce Egypt's overpopulation problem, but in fact the rate of population growth has not diminished.

Zakariya's government did not appreciably relax Egypt's police-state atmosphere. The Muslim Brothers, after a decade of severe repression, had been released from prison in 1964 and allowed to resume their propaganda. Their undiminished ability to attract support in Egypt and the other Arab countries alarmed Nasir, who would brook no dissent from his Arab socialist program. By the end of 1965 their leaders (especially their most respected writer, Sayyid Qutb) were back in jail. In a show trial, he and several other Brothers were convicted of plotting against the Nasir regime, condemned to death, and hanged in August 1966, horrifying many Muslims outside Egypt. As for the Communists, both the pro-Soviet and Maoist parties agreed in 1965 to dissolve themselves and join the ASU, where they played an increasingly powerful role in shaping public opinion, especially those who found jobs as journalists and professors. Pro-Western Egyptians, if they had not left the country, kept a low profile; many had been accused of antirevolutionary sympathies and had lost their property or their positions in earlier purges. Nasir's government even turned against Mustafa Amin, the influential editor of *al-Akhbar,* accused him of being a CIA agent, and put him behind bars.

Nasir's relations with the Saudis, even after Faysal officially succeeded King Sa'ud in 1964, remained strained—partly due to their differing views on Communism, but mainly because of the Yemen civil war, which was still tying up 70,000 Egyptian troops (and costing both Egypt and Saudi Arabia much money). More than once, Faysal and Nasir reached an agreement to end their involvement and settle the war, only to have it dissolve amid mutual recriminations. Late in 1965 King Faysal visited the shah of Iran, and the two rulers issued a joint statement calling for an Islamic pact to combat elements and ideas alien to Islam, thereby alienating Nasir further.

Foreign politics continued to fascinate—and also distress—Nasir. Many of his neutralist allies were disappearing: Nehru by death in 1964, Ben Bella by an internal coup in 1965, Sukarno by a bloody civil war in Indonesia soon after that, Kwame Nkrumah of Ghana by a military coup in 1966, and Abd al-Salam Arif of Iraq in a plane crash later the same year. Nasir was haunted by the rumors he had heard about the CIA's role in ousting Musaddiq from power in Iran and in toppling the Communist government of Guatemala. U.S. agents, he believed, had gotten rid of South Vietnam's Ngo Dinh Diem in 1963 and had often tried to assassinate Castro. As many of his political allies fell from power, Nasir wondered when his turn would come. He suspected the worst when the United States and Britain agreed to sell the Saudis arms worth $350 million, after which the International Monetary Fund denied Egypt a $70 million loan and Washington put off negotiating with his government on further grain sales.

Background to the June 1967 War

Of all the troubled countries of the Middle East, the one viewed as the least stable was Syria. Damascus was a capital in search of a larger country; in 1918–1920 it had housed the provisional Arab government of the Hashimite dynasty, claiming to rule all the Fertile Crescent and the western half of the Arabian Peninsula. The Hashimites' subsequent displacement by the French, the creation of separate mandates in Syria, Iraq, and Palestine, the truncation of Syria to form the Republic of Lebanon and later to deliver Alexandretta to Turkey, and finally the formation of Israel combined to infuriate the Syrians. They viewed these events as imperialist machinations at the expense of the Arab nation and vowed some day to regain their stolen lands, reunite the Arabs, and redeem their dignity. In the meantime, Syria was also a bone of contention for the other redeemers of Arab dignity. These included the rival regimes in Egypt and Iraq, whose rivalries had taken the form of Faruq versus the Hashimites in the 1940s and Nasir against Qasim in 1958–1963. Each would try to install its favorite Syrian colonel in power or to win Syria to its side.

The Syrians who had taken power in March 1963 were a coalition of Nasirite and Ba'th party pan-Arabists; by the end of that year the Ba'th alone held power and vowed never to sacrifice its existence or its principles to join a Nasir-dominated union. In February 1966 a cabal of officers belonging to a new Ba'thist faction seized power in Syria. Most of these men belonged also to a religious minority called the Alawites, but they felt obliged to prove their loyalty to pan-Arabism by strongly opposing Israel. The number of border incidents increased, for the Syrians were arming, training, and organizing a new Palestinian guerrilla group called al-Fatah to attack Israel from Jordan. Israel retaliated with a massive raid on the Jordanian village of al-Samu' in November 1966, but many Israelis felt that they should have gone after Syria as the instigator of the attacks. Days earlier, hoping to curb the neo-Ba'thists' zeal, Nasir had made a well-publicized defense pact with Syria.

The new alliance did not calm the Syrians; in April 1967 border tensions with Israel increased. An aerial dogfight between Israeli warplanes and Syrian MiGs, fought within view of Damascus, resulted in the downing of six MiGs as all Israeli fighters returned to their bases. Relying on its Egyptian pact, Syria started calling for war with Israel. Economically, neither Egypt nor Israel could afford a war. Egypt had exhausted its hard-currency reserves and could no longer buy spare parts to run some of its factories or to fly its United Arab Airlines passenger jets. Israel was in a recession, and more Jews were leaving than entering the state for the first time since the 1920s. But at a time when Jordan and Saudi Arabia were taunting Nasir for hiding behind the skirts of the United Nations Emergency Force (UNEF) in the Sinai, Israel's army was raiding al-Samu', and its fighters were downing Syrian MiGs, his pride would not let him keep quiet. Accepting Soviet reports (which could easily have been refuted) about an Israeli buildup at the Syrian border, Nasir decided to send his soldiers—except for the best ones, who were still fighting in Yemen—into the Sinai. Once Egypt's radio stations began competing with those of the other Arab countries to see who could make the most violent threats against the Jewish state, Israel started calling up its reserves and getting ready for what it believed would be its war for survival.

At this point, Nasir and his Soviet advisers should have spent more time on strategy and less on tactics. The best outcome for Egypt would have been to make itself look stronger than Israel without ever firing a shot, assuming that its main object was to impress the other Arabs and not to wipe out the Jewish state. Instead, Nasir asked the UNEF to pull back from its strategic posts in Gaza and the Sinai. Rather than haggle with Egypt, UN Secretary General U Thant quickly withdrew the UNEF, because Yugoslavia and India were already pulling out their contingents. Once Egypt's army was facing the Israelis without a buffer, something had to happen. Egypt announced that it

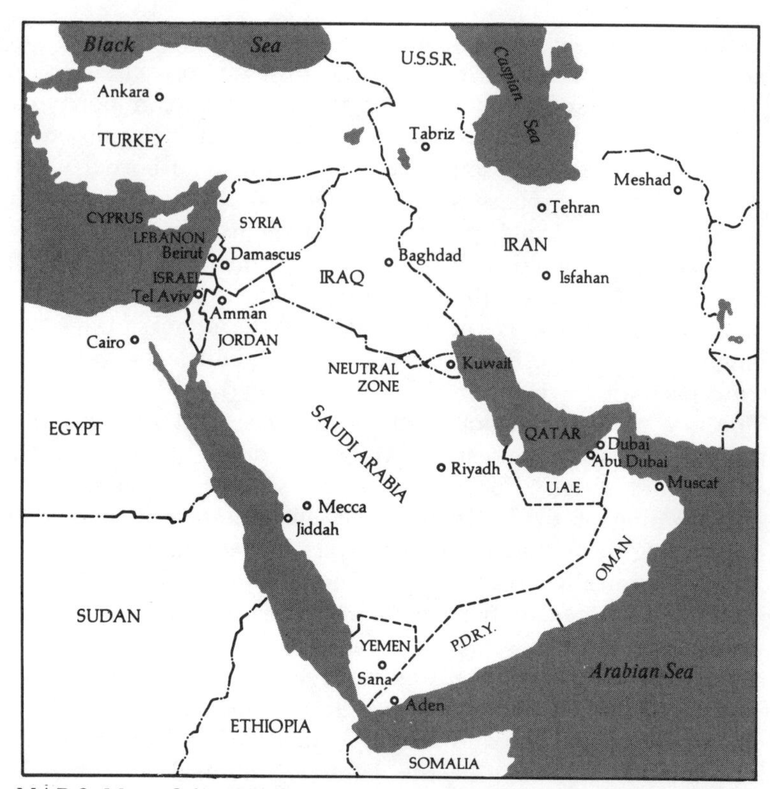

MAP 3. Map of the Middle East, Showing Internationally Recognized Borders. Reprinted by permission from Arthur Goldschmidt, Jr., *A Concise History of the Middle East,* 3d ed. (Boulder, Colo.: Westview, 1987).

was restoring the naval blockade across the Tiran Straits against Israeli ships and cargos, a reversion to the status quo before 1956. Even though the number of Israeli naval or merchant vessels using the Gulf of Aqaba was small, the blockade could stop Israel's oil imports from Iran and was objectionable in principle to both Israel and the United States. Having half a million troops in Vietnam left Johnson little room for maneuver, so the Americans hoped either to defuse the issue diplomatically or to test the blockade by sending a multinational flotilla through Tiran to Israel's port of Eilat.

This was not a war that anyone wanted. Both Egypt and Israel promised the outside powers not to fire the first shot, the UN Security Council met in almost continuous session, and various secret efforts were made to avert an armed conflict. Johnson proposed to send Vice-President Humphrey to Cairo while Nasir was to dispatch his deputy, Zakariya Muhyi al-Din, to Washington, where he was to make the magnanimous gesture of "lifting" the Aqaba blockade (purely a paper one) in return for unnamed Israeli or U.S. concessions that would redeem Egypt's reputation in Arab eyes.

Nasir's biggest error was that, by playing to the passions of an Arab audience in his speeches and interviews, he aroused the deepest fear of the Israeli Jews—the fear that he was preparing to wipe them out. No one heeded Nasir's insistence that Egypt would not start the war. While Egypt's forces remained curiously lackadaisical and its planes were lining up on their airfields, Israel's general staff drew up a sophisticated scheme to defeat all its Arab enemies. Prime Minister Levi Eshkol reluctantly made Moshe Dayan his defense minister by forming a coalition cabinet of all the Israeli political parties except the Communists. Early on 5 June Israeli fighter planes, flying below the Arab radar, swooped down on its enemies' airbases and wiped out 80 percent of the military aircraft of Egypt, Syria, and Iraq. As Radio Cairo broadcast reports of Arab victories more fantastic than those claimed by Faruq and Karim Thabit in 1948, Jordan plunged into the war on Egypt's side; but Egyptian and Jordanian ground forces, only recently placed under unified command following a dramatic reconciliation between Nasir and Husayn, fell back before the Israel Defense Force. Syria did nothing until after Jordan had lost Jerusalem and the rest of the West Bank. The reason for Syria's passivity was that the two countries had been quarreling on the eve of the war, but this lack of cooperation left Syria to face the Israelis alone and caused it to lose the Golan Heights. Without air cover Egypt's forces could not stop the Israelis, who in three days captured the Gaza Strip, all of Sinai, and at least 5,000 Egyptian prisoners. Some officers deserted their troops. About 20,000 soldiers died, often from thirst and exposure rather than from battle wounds. On 8 June Egypt accepted the Security Council's call for a cease-fire in place, as Israel's troops encamped on the east bank of the canal. Alleging that U.S. planes were flying air cover for Israel, Nasir broke diplomatic relations with Washington. At the same time, the USSR broke with Israel.

If Nasir had faced acute economic problems before the June 1967 War, he was now confronted by a worse political crisis. He had gambled on challenging Israel, expecting the Americans to restrain the Jewish state and the USSR to back him. He had misled his people and all the other Arabs to expect that Egypt, despite Israel's preemptive strike, would win the war. His vaunted arsenal of medium and light bombers, MiG-21 fighters, SAM-2 missiles, tanks, artillery, and rifles, for which Egypt had promised to pay billions of dollars in commodities or hard currency, had turned to smoking ruins. His army was battered, tattered, and scattered. He could make neither war nor peace. His wisest course was to resign.

The way in which Nasir did so demonstrated his masterful talent for turning defeat into victory. In a televised speech he admitted losing the war, assumed total responsibility for defeat (all the while carefully deflecting criticism for the specific mistakes of his regime), and announced that he would give up all his posts. The new leader would be Zakariya Muhyi al-Din. The speech sparked mass demonstrations, most of which were spontaneous, as men and women filled the streets, begged Nasir not to quit, and even serenaded the darkened U.S. and British embassies on Zahra' Street: *La Zakariya, la isti'mar, la stirlini, wa la dular* ("No to Zakariya, imperialism, the sterling, and the dollar," meaning British or U.S. rule). Zakariya, although he had privately advised against confronting Washington, had remained publicly loyal and was mortified by Nasir's announcement. Powerless to refuse the nomination, he now became the whipping boy for everyone who still favored Nasir's confrontationist policy against Israel and the United States. Although he would stay in the cabinet for a few months, he never forgave Nasir for ruining his career. At first Nasir resisted the people's entreaties, but he finally withdrew his resignation after the National Assembly unanimously asked him to stay. He used this mandate to oust his best friend, Abd al-Hakim Amir, from his post as commander-in-chief of the armed forces (Amir later took his own life) and to jail other officers, such as Defense Minister Shams Badran, for mismanaging the war.

For Nasir the war was a defeat that he would never live down. Egypt's armed forces had been destroyed, its enemy had captured the Sinai with its oil wells and strategic control over the Suez Canal (which, as in 1956, Egypt had closed), and its economy was in a shambles. The people forgave Nasir because he symbolized their national dignity, but grumblings against his regime increased once the people realized how many of their boys had fallen in the war and how shamefully some of their officers had fled. The Egyptians started criticizing the Russians and urging the Palestinians to regain their own land. But the war was no unalloyed victory for Israel. True, Arab radio threats to destroy the state had been lifted (or at least postponed), and the lands under Israel's control had tripled in size. But the Arabs had made those threats not so that they would be carried out but to impress one another. Israel denied that it had made war to expand its territory; it called for peace negotiations and recognition. But perhaps it also wanted new leaders in Cairo, Amman, and Damascus. Above all, it wanted security. It got none.

No War and No Peace

As the UN Security Council reached an impasse and the General Assembly held a highly touted but inconclusive session, Moscow resumed its schizophrenic policy of arming the Arab states while calling for a peaceful resolution to the conflict. But the U.S. government no longer cared enough about Egypt to repeat its 1956–1957 demand for an unconditional Israeli withdrawal from the Sinai. In fact, Nasir's relations with the United States hit an all-time low, for he had accused its forces of collusion in Israel's attack against Egypt. Although an American book, Stephen Green's *Taking Sides,* has recently alleged that the United States secretly carried out aerial photography for Israel during the war, no one admitted it at the time. Most Americans, therefore, overlooked Israel's unprovoked attack during the war on the *Liberty,* an intelligence ship in the eastern Mediterranean, in which seventy U.S. servicemen were killed. Washington was preoccupied with the Vietnam War, and it wanted the Arab states to make peace with Israel. Some of the defeated Arabs, possibly including King Husayn, put out tentative peace feelers; but most chose to dig in their heels, buy more Russian arms, and renew the struggle. Meeting at Khartum in late August, the Arab leaders adopted a negative policy: no negotiations, no recognition, and no peace with Israel. Egyptians and Israelis were already firing across the Suez Canal, which had been closed since the outbreak of the war. Egypt sank the Israeli destroyer *Eilat,* and Israel retaliated by blowing up the Suez oil refinery. Egypt had to evacuate 700,000 civilians from Port Said, Ismailia, and Suez.

These incidents made the search for peace more urgent than ever. In November, after conferring privately with Israel and the Arabs, Britain's UN ambassador, Lord Caradon, drafted Security Council Resolution 242 and secured its unanimous acceptance. In essence, it advised Israel to make peace with the Arabs by returning lands it had taken, but its wording had to be ambiguous to get the assent of both sides. Israel was to withdraw its forces from "territories occupied in the recent conflict," but not (in the English version) *all* the territories. The resolution stressed "the inadmissibility of the acquisition of territory by war," implying that all of the captured lands had to be returned. It called for recognition of the right of "every state in the area," implicitly including Israel, to "live in peace within secure and recognized boundaries." It guaranteed freedom of navigation through international waterways (e.g., the Gulf of Aqaba and the Suez Canal). It demanded a "just solution of the refugee problem," thereby fueling Israeli arguments that Jews fleeing from Arab countries were just as entitled to fair treatment as the Palestinian refugees. That clause angered the Palestinians, who no longer cared to be viewed as mere refugees but wanted their own nation-state in Israel's place. Jordan, Egypt, and Israel each accepted Resolution 242 on its own terms. Then U Thant named Gunnar Jarring as his personal emissary to talk with them about its implementation.

Jarring's mission proved fruitless. Both sides got new arms and resumed sporadic fighting. The most arresting development during 1968 was the emergence of the Palestinian *fida'iyin,* notably Fatah, a guerrilla group led by Yasir Arafat, which joined the Jordanian regulars in repulsing an Israeli raid east of the Jordan at a village called Karameh. Consequently, many Arabs began to expect the Palestinian people to take up their own liberation war, as the Algerians and the Vietnamese had done, and their guerrillas (called terrorists by the Israelis and freedom fighters by the Arabs) became heroes in an Arab world disillusioned with its regular armies after the 1967 "setback."

Internal Changes

The survival of the Nasir regime and its steadfastness in resisting Israel attest to the underlying strength of the Egyptian nation. The people were willing to endure austerity measures, a necessity under Egypt's near-bankrupt economy. Luckily, the 1967 cotton and rice harvests were abundant, and more oil was discovered in the Murjan fields just south of Suez. Saudi Arabia and Kuwait agreed to subsidize Egypt so that Nasir would not be tempted to make a separate peace with Israel. In return, he withdrew his troops from Yemen—another humiliation perhaps, but it stanched a drain on Egypt's resources. Outsiders scoffed, but another reassurance to the nation came in a miraculous apparition of the Virgin Mary, who is venerated by Muslims as well as by Coptic Christians. Thousands flocked to a small church in Matariyya, above which she seemed to hover as a light haze in this darkest hour for the Egyptian people. Interest in religion revived among both Muslims and Copts, to the chagrin of some Arab socialists.

For the first time since 1954, workers and students demonstrated in 1968, independent of the regime and its mobilizing organization. Nasir's police had clamped down on student political activity, outlawing unauthorized demonstrations, petitions, distribution of leaflets, and wall magazines. It had tried to co-opt student leaders into its Liberation

Rally, National Union, Socialist Youth Organization, and at last its underground Socialist Vanguard. Apart from these groups, all university students belonged to the Student Union, essentially a social and recreational group supervised closely by teachers holding administrative veto powers, under the so-called system of tutelage that students naturally resented. The June "setback" shook the students from their apathy, but the first impetus to action came from a demonstration by Hilwan workers against the lenient sentences passed by the military court on the air force leaders accused of negligence in the war. Due to an ASU mix-up, the police tried to stop an authorized demonstration by munitions workers on 21 February (observed in Egypt since 1946 as "Students' Day"), and scores were wounded in the ensuing clashes, in which some students took part. Thousands of Cairo and Alexandria University students demonstrated, causing numerous arrests and injuries. The student leaders even presented their demands to the National Assembly, occasioning lively debates about the lenient air force officers' sentences, the Hilwan workers' demonstration, and the repressive actions of the university security guards. The youths also called for an end to secret intelligence, abolition of the system of tutelage and of other repressive measures against students, and new laws guaranteeing political freedoms. After meeting for three hours with the student leaders, Nasir accepted some of their demands and promulgated what came to be called the 30 March Program, his first official promise to liberalize Egypt's political system.

Meanwhile, the Egyptian government's main preoccupation was with removing the Israelis from the east bank of the Suez Canal, whether by peaceful means or by force. Nasir faced a dilemma, regardless of the means he used. If Egypt fought the Israelis while the Soviets replenished the arsenal it had lost in the war, he could not get the offensive weapons needed to drive the Israelis back. Many suspected that the Kremlin was glad to keep the state of no-war-and-no-peace, as this condition would tighten its control over Egypt. If Egypt wanted the Israelis to hand back the Sinai, it would have had to enter direct talks, recognize Israel, and forgo its claim to lead the Arab countries. Nasir viewed this policy as a capitulation to the United States. Moreover, the Johnson administration, by not pressuring Israel to withdraw unconditionally (as Eisenhower had done in 1957) and by selling advanced weapons to Jerusalem, seemed to have abandoned the Arab world. The United Nations was snarled by the two sides' conflicting interpretations of its Resolution 242 and by the superpowers' rivalry. Nixon's electoral victory in November 1968, followed by William Scranton's fact-finding mission to the Middle East, which led to his call for a "more evenhanded" U.S. policy, raised Egypt's hopes for a change. However, Nixon, sensitive to pro-Israel feelings in Congress, soon adopted Johnson's policy of selling Phantom jet fighters to Israel. Talks among the foreign ministers of the United States, USSR, Britain, and France hinted at an "imposed solution" (presumably a pro-Arab one), but no agreement was reached.

The War of Attrition and the Rogers Peace Plan

Instead, Palestinian raids into Israel from neighboring Jordan and Lebanon intensified, as did Israeli reprisals. The shooting across the Suez Canal (which remained blocked) also became more frequent and severe. In March 1969 Nasir declared a "War of Attrition" against Israel. His strategy was to make the cost of the occupation to Israel in human lives (or manpower losses due to prolonged troop mobilization) unbearably high, or perhaps to convince the United States of the necessity (given its own interests in the Arab world) of forcing Israel to withdraw from the Sinai. This strategy proved costly for Egypt. Israel launched a "war of nerves" that included demonstrations of its ability to send tanks up and down the Suez Gulf coast, capture a new Soviet radar installation from a Red Sea island, buzz Cairo with jet planes at dawn, and bomb a military factory in Ma'adi and a school in the Delta. Nasir flew to Moscow and requested additional aid, including SAM-3 missiles and more military advisers. By late April 1970, aerial dogfights were taking place high above the Suez Canal, amid Israeli claims that Russian pilots were flying the Egyptian MiGs. Yet the War of Attrition was costly for Israel, too, and it ended with a peace initiative by U.S. Secretary of State William Rogers. The Rogers Peace Plan called for stopping the War of Attrition, reactivating the Jarring mission, and implementing Resolution 242. First Jordan, then Egypt (after Nasir obtained Soviet assent), and finally Israel accepted a ninety-day cease-fire, effective 8 August.

Although Nasir had an ineradicable reputation in the West for hostility to Israel, his acceptance of the Rogers Peace Plan was really his latest effort to put the Palestine problem into the deep-freeze. He realized that Egypt's ambitious policies in Yemen and Palestine had drained the nation's economy and placed him in a position of dependency on the contradictory poles of Communist Russia and royalist Saudi Arabia. Many writers believe that pride prevented him from negotiating directly with Israel, but Nasir also believed Israel to be the means by which successive U.S. administrations had tried to force a Pax Americana on the Middle East. But indirect negotiations, seemingly sponsored by the superpowers, were an acceptable step toward the peace Nasir needed. For months he had been advising Syria and other front-line Arab states that Egypt—and indeed the Arabs generally—were not ready to fight another full-scale war with Israel.

Most Palestinians remained unconvinced. On the contrary, they feared that Egypt was planning to make peace at their expense, just as it had done in the 1949 Rhodes armistice talks. Despite Nasir's friendly efforts to convince Yasir Arafat, the new leader of the Palestine Liberation Organization, that he could better resist Israeli rule in Ramallah or Jenin than in Amman (where he was fighting King Husayn's government), he opposed the Rogers Peace Plan. The *fida'iyin* stepped up their activities. On 6 September a splinter group called the Popular Front for the Liberation of Palestine hijacked four passenger jets and took three of them to an abandoned airstrip outside Amman, where they held 300 innocent passengers hostage, demanding the release of various Palestinians jailed in Europe. This action was taken as a direct challenge by King Husayn, whose troops responded by bombarding Palestinian refugee camps and neighborhoods in Amman. Meanwhile, Israel broke off talks with the Jarring mission because Nasir had installed newly acquired SAM-3 missiles close to the canal, an act Egypt justified by noting that the Israelis were digging in their forces on the east bank behind the "Bar-Lev Line." Peace talks, however indirect, between the Arabs and Israel had to await a peaceful settlement between Jordan and the Palestinians. To help the latter, Syria threatened to invade Jordan, an act likely to bring either the U.S. or Israel to Husayn's aid. Nasir convoked an Arab summit meeting in Cairo for 27–28 September and made an exhausting effort to reconcile King Husayn with Yasir Arafat. After accompanying the amir of Kuwait to see him off at Cairo International Airport, Nasir went home, lay down, and died.

The Contest for Nasir's Succession

Although Nasir had been diabetic for years and had suffered a heart attack in 1969, his death came as a shock to the Egyptian people. Millions turned out in the streets of Cairo, sobbing hysterically, shouting slogans attesting to his immortality in their hearts and minds, and following his flag-draped coffin to its final resting place in the Gamal Abd al-Nasir Mosque in Heliopolis. His last vice-president, Anwar al-Sadat, succeeded him provisionally, but no one knew how long he would hold power. He was regarded as Nasir's yes-man—as a political lightweight. Under the 1964 constitution his nomination required the approval of two-thirds of the National Assembly members, followed by a popular plebiscite.

Behind Sadat's back, several of Nasir's closest friends were contending for the succession. During Nasir's last year, when ill health had forced him to take prolonged vacations, several "power centers" had arisen to fill the vacuum. Men like Sami Sharaf (minister of state for presidential affairs), Sha'rawi Gum'ah (interior minister), and General Muhammad Fawzi (commander-in-chief of the armed forces), who had risen to power because of their direct ties to Nasir, seemed to be displacing the remaining Free Officers. Even Ali Sabri, who was often linked to these power centers and seen as pro-Communist, had been limited to working with the Arab Socialist Union. The Nasirites tended to be pro-Soviet, authoritarian in their governing style, and hostile to a settlement with Israel. They accepted Sadat's nomination by the National Assembly and approval by the ASU and the Egyptian people for the presidency, but they expected to rule Egypt from behind his back. Using their control of the secret police, the major ministries, and the information network (their "centers of power"), they hoped to ease him out and to continue the Nasirite program.

At first, they seemed to have guessed right. Sadat was nominated and elected by a relatively untampered vote of 90 percent of the Egyptian people. He agreed to continue Nasir's domestic and foreign policies. Although he extended the cease-fire several times, when Israel ignored his peace proposals (which included an offer to reopen the Suez Canal if the Israelis would pull their forces back a few miles), he warned that 1971 would be the conflict's "year of decision" and made highly publicized war preparations. He let the cease-fire run out, put his troops on full alert, ordered a partial blackout in Cairo, and asked for more Soviet arms to renew the war against Israel. He made a tentative agreement with Colonel Mu'ammar Qadhafi and Hafiz al-Asad (the new leader in Damascus) to form a federation of Libya, Syria, and Egypt. But in early May he suddenly dismissed Ali Sabri as his vice-president, just before Secretary of State Rogers came to Cairo on a trouble-shooting trip to revive the Jarring mission. A week later, apprised of a plot by the "centers of power" to seize control, he took charge of the army and dismissed General Fawzi, Sha'rawi Gum'ah, and Sami Sharaf from their positions.

This so-called Corrective Revolution of 15 May 1971 confirmed Sadat's hold on Egypt's presidency and marked the first step toward dismantling the Nasirite system of government. Sadat declared an end to the widespread use of wiretaps and tape recorders to spy on government officials—a popular move, as was the release of many dissidents who had been placed under house arrest in Nasir's time. New provisions for investment by private capitalists, both Egyptian and foreign, opened the way for needed infusions of capital from such oil-rich Arab countries as Libya and Saudi Arabia. The immediate cause of the Corrective Revolution was resistance by the centers of power to the proposed federation of Egypt, Syria, and Libya, but Sadat clearly wanted to set a new course. Even though he signed a friendship treaty with the USSR in late May 1971, Sadat tried to assume a more neutral stance between the superpowers. The oil-exporting Arab states promoted this change. The tide of Arab socialism was starting to ebb.

The End of Nasirism

Most people see Cairo's shift from Arab socialism to an Egypt-centered nationalism and capitalism as having started when Nasir died. This is only partly true. The Arabs' catastrophic defeat in June 1967 set events in motion. The changes started as soon as Nasir accepted annual Saudi and Kuwaiti subsidies during the 1967 Khartum summit, when his government agreed to abide by Security Council Resolution 242, and then took part in indirect negotiations under the Rogers Peace Plan in 1970. The transition would not be complete until after Sadat had indeed found the decisive moment in Egypt's struggle against Israel to redeem its honor in battle. That moment, though promised in 1971, did not come until October 1973.

CHAPTER ELEVEN

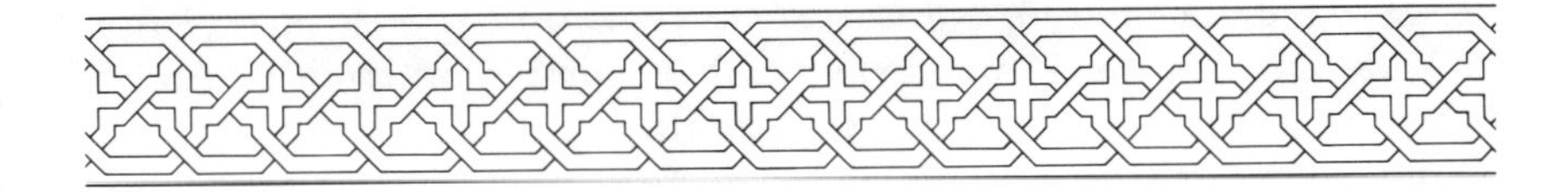

The Opening and the Crossing

Anwar al-Sadat ruled, practically unopposed, from May 1971 until October 1981. Although he turned out to be as dictatorial as Nasir had been, the less obtrusive character of his government made Sadat's regime seem more democratic. Outsiders assumed, therefore, that the lives of the Egyptian people must have become less tense and driven than they had been under his predecessor. Because Sadat dramatically reversed Nasir's policies toward the superpowers, socialism, and the conflict with Israel, he was highly lauded in the West. But his place in the hearts and minds of his own countrymen has not been so secure.

Sadat Before His Presidency

Originally from the Delta village of Mit Abu al-Kum, Sadat had actually spent most of his youth in Cairo in the humbling position of second son of his father's second wife (of four). Like Nasir, he climbed the social ladder by becoming an army officer. The two became friends in 1938 when they were both stationed in Manqabad, where Sadat claims that he started the secret society that Nasir came to lead. Always among the most zealous of the Free Officers, Sadat served time in jail and was even discharged from the officer corps for his revolutionary activities. He was implicated in the 1941 attempt to smuggle Egypt's popular nationalist general, Aziz Ali al-Misri, through the British lines to Rommel. In 1942 he aided Nazi agents who had infiltrated Cairo to make contact with Muslim Brothers and extreme nationalists. Accused of conspiring to murder Amin Uthman in 1946, he was finally acquitted. He wanted to blow up the British Embassy in 1948 and to hang King Faruq and his courtiers in front of Abdin Palace in 1952, but Nasir restrained him.

During Nasir's presidency, Sadat became one of his most visible henchmen. His account of the 1952 Revolution, written in French and English as well as in Arabic, was among the first to see print. He also wrote a laudatory Egyptian children's book, *This Is Your Uncle Gamal.* He broadcast the revolutionary manifesto over Radio Cairo on 23 July 1952, just as he would also announce Nasir's death on 28 September 1970. It was Sadat who called on Ali Mahir to become the civilian prime minister for the Revolutionary Command Council. He edited the government daily *al-Gumhuriyya* ("The Republic"), served as secretary general for the Islamic Congress, presided over meetings of the National Assembly, and performed other odd jobs for Nasir; but he rarely held any power. Other RCC members gradually drifted away; Sadat stood by him until the end. For his fidelity, he earned the sardonic nickname *Bikbashi Sah-sah* ("Colonel Yes-Yes") from his colleagues, for he dissimulated any differences he might have had with Nasir. Nasir rewarded him with the post of vice-president in 1969 but probably did not want him as his successor. He was disturbed when Sadat used his position to take over a villa (overlooking the Nile) that belonged to a retired general, but he was too busy during his last months to think of replacing him.

Sadat's Corrective Revolution

After eight months of collective leadership, during which most experts predicted that Nasir's closest supporters would ease Sadat out of office, he staged his Corrective Revolution in May 1971, taking uncontested control of Egypt. The general reaction to Sadat's purge of Nasir's "centers of power" was probably one of relief. The new president had outgrown his conspiratorial and revolutionary youth and hence—unlike Nasir—no longer cared about spying on dissidents and taping their telephone conversations. Huge bonfires of secret police tapes illumined Sadat's pledge to respect civil liberties. Meanwhile, Sadat kept on hailing the USSR's contributions to Egypt's development. He invited the Soviet president to attend the inaugural festivities for the Aswan High Dam and signed the Soviet-Egyptian Treaty of Friendship and Cooperation, but he harped constantly on Egypt's need for more arms and extended Nasir's tentative contacts with the West. This policy shift resulted in part from the United States' role in seeking a comprehensive Arab-Israeli settlement under the Rogers Peace Plan, and in part from the anti-Communist stance of Saudi Arabia's King Faysal. Egypt's anti-Soviet lurch also stemmed from the real fear engendered by the Communists' near takeover in the Sudan in July 1971. Sudanese President Ja'far al-Numayri would have been overthrown but for the timely intervention of Libya's nationalist but anti-Communist Colonel Qadhafi, and Sadat was almost as vulnerable as his upstream neighbor. Some Egyptians feel that Anwar and his highly visible wife, Jihan, wanted to imitate the American way of life as it was depicted by the films they had imported from the United States. By 1971, too, Egypt's armed forces were becoming more professional and less eager to be a vanguard of socialism.

Egyptians tell how Sadat, upon attaining power, got into the presidential limousine and, when asked by the chauffeur where he wanted to go, replied: "Take me the way Gamal used to go." Shortly afterward, the driver reached a fork in the road and stopped for further directions. "Would Gamal have gone left or right here?" Sadat asked. "Left, sir." "Very well," said the new leader, "Signal left but turn right." The joke expresses the common idea that Sadat used to give lip service to Nasirism while edging away from Nasir's policies. He went to Moscow in October 1971, seeking more arms to renew the war with Israel. He signaled to Washington that 1971 would be the "year of decision," a year in which either the Arabs and Israel would make peace on the terms outlined in UN Resolution 242 (following the application of appropriate U.S. pressure on Israel) or the War of Attrition would resume. He was disappointed when Israel and the United States ignored his offer to reopen the Suez Canal in return for a partial Israeli pullback in the Sinai. But 1971 ended with no progress toward either peace or renewed war with Israel, thus causing a spate of Egyptian jokes about Sadat's year of decision. It was said, for example, that he had decreed the addition of six months to the calendar, that he had made up a separate excuse for not fighting Israel to fit each day of the week, and that the locally manufactured "Nasr" bus, when it broke down, was renamed a "Sadat." The Indo-Pakistani War, fought in December 1971 over the Bangladesh secession, provided a pretext to delay fighting Israel; it also angered Sadat that India was receiving new Soviet weapons that Egypt could not buy. He felt that the Soviets were using arms sales to manipulate Egypt, just as Nasir had accused the West of attaching strings to its 1955 aid offers.

The chasm between Sadat and the Kremlin widened. The USSR wanted to slow down the arms race by reaching a détente with the U.S. government. It viewed the fall of Ali Sabri and the "centers of power" as a sign that Egypt would soon abandon the kind of Arab socialism that could have turned into Communism. The proposed "Federation of Arab Republics," involving Syria, Libya, and Egypt, alarmed the Soviets, especially if it seemed likely, as Qadhafi hoped, to lead to an organic union between Egypt and Libya. So enamored was the new Libyan leader of Nasir's role as leader of the Arab Revolution that he offered to put his country and its burgeoning oil wealth under the control of Nasir's chosen successor. Cynics predicted that Qadhafi would try to put himself in Sadat's place. At the time, the Kremlin considered the young Libyan leader a threat to its influence, even though he had already successfully removed British and U.S. bases from Libyan soil. The Soviets had hoped for Sadat's cooperation in the pro-Communist Sudanese coup of July 1971; they got the opposite. Egyptians resented the Russians' imperious demands for additional bases on Egyptian soil and their refusal to let high-ranking Egyptian officers into some of the ones they already had. Soviet-manned equipment in Egypt could be operated only on orders from Moscow. Soviet technicians, lacking any common language with the Egyptians they were training, often treated them with contempt. On a humbler level, Egyptian doormen, cab-drivers, and waiters complained that the Russians and their families were surly and tipped meanly. Their popularity had been great when Nasir had called them in after the 1967 war, but it had vanished five years later. As the British and the Americans had done before them, the Soviets underestimated Egyptian nationalism.

Sadat decided, therefore, to expel most Soviet technicians from Egypt, effective 17 July 1972. Those who stayed would work under Egyptian command. Although the Soviets kept their naval bases, the number of Soviet military personnel was reduced from 20,000 to fewer than 1,000. Most of the advanced weapons under their control were also withdrawn. The USSR government accepted all of these terms (many Russians were relieved to escape from a dangerous part of the world) but rejected Sadat's request for high-level talks. Both sides recalled their ambassadors, and Sadat began asking discreetly about buying new arms in Western Europe. When Palestinians killed eleven Israeli athletes at the Munich Olympics, however, anti-Arab sentiments increased in Europe and North America, thereby putting off Egypt's hopes of buying Western arms. Sadat renewed ties with the Soviets and extended their naval facilities, and the technicians started returning to Egypt; by April 1973 Sadat, in an interview with *Newsweek,* could claim that the Russians "are providing us now with everything that's possible for them to supply. And I am now quite satisfied." He also stated that Egypt was ready to end the current deadlock by resuming the war with Israel. He hinted to others that Egypt was planning a surprise raid on the occupied Sinai Peninsula. The Israelis called up some of their reserve troops, but no war ensued. Everyone else ignored him.

The October War

The sudden attack launched by Syria and Egypt on the Israel-occupied territories on 6 October 1973 was, as Sadat had meant it to be, a shock to the Americans. Intermittent war scares had broken out ever since the 1970 cease-fire, and Sadat had certainly given ample notice of his intentions, but most outside observers did not think that the Arabs were prepared for a war against Israel. All previous wars between Egypt and Israel had come after periods of mounting tension. The accepted wisdom was that, if Sadat were to start a war, Israel would quickly end it by totally defeating the Arab armies.

Sadat took the risks and made his preparations for four reasons. First, Egypt's economy could no longer endure the state of no-war-and-no-peace. The government had spent $8–9 billion since 1967 to rebuild and retrain its armed forces. (For the sake of comparison, Egypt's gross domestic product totaled about $5 billion in 1973.) Unable to buy U.S. grain with Egyptian pounds, it had to use its scarce hard currency to buy wheat and rice on the world market. Tourism income was negligible, and Suez Canal tolls had ceased in 1967. By 1973 Egypt's hard-currency supply was nearly exhausted.

Second, the country's morale was falling. Faced with long term military service upon graduating, the students in Cairo and other university towns had demonstrated against Sadat during 1972 and early 1973, even staging a sit-in at Liberation Square and speaking at the People's Assembly (Sadat's new name for the National Assembly). A group of older mothers held a mass protest in the Ezbekiyya Gardens. Fires of suspicious origin broke out. Two historic landmarks, the Opera House (one block from Cairo's main fire station) and Mehmet Ali's palace in the Cairo Citadel, burned down completely. A dishonest official was found to have torched twenty cheap trolley cars that he had bought abroad at what he had claimed to be a higher price, pocketing the difference. Government corruption was more widespread than it had ever been in Nasir's day, and some thought that it went straight to the top. The officers and soldiers on the front grew tired of being kept on constant alert. One captain led a convoy of three armored cars to the square beside the Mosque of al-Husayn and harangued the worshippers, saying that the army wanted to fight, not to eat sand. New laws tightened censorship on books and periodicals. Harsh sentences were imposed on rumor-mongers. Many writers were jailed on falsified charges. Sadat even tried (in vain) to stop Egyptians from telling political jokes.

Another reason for the war was that Sadat feared losing the material and moral support that Egypt had been getting from other Arabs, especially those in the oil-exporting countries. The Palestinian Arabs were increasingly restive. The *fida'iyin* committed many terrorist acts against Israelis at home and abroad, matched by equally fierce reprisals against Palestinians and their supporters. Israel's downing of a Libyan passenger jet over the occupied Sinai Peninsula, which resulted in more than a hundred deaths, angered Arabs everywhere and increased the pressure on Sadat to take revenge. Frustrated in his efforts to pin Sadat down to a date for their countries' unification, Qadhafi organized a well-publicized Libyan march on Egypt, demanding renewed war against Israel.

The fourth reason for starting the war was that Sadat needed the respect and cooperation of the superpowers. Although the USSR had resumed selling arms to Egypt, by 1973 it was seeking other Arabs as allies. The United States, although it had taken its troops out of Vietnam, was preoccupied with the growing Watergate scandal, which was sapping Nixon's energy and legitimacy. U.S. attempts to mediate between Israel and the Arabs had ground to a halt, whereas its arms sales to Israel increased, suggesting an increasing alignment of Israeli and U.S. policies. During the late summer of 1973, a hard-fought election campaign caused Israeli politicians to vie with one another in calling for the creation of new Jewish settlements in the occupied lands, including the Sinai. Referring to Israel's new port city near Rafah, Sadat said: "Every word spoken about Yamit is a knife pointing at me personally and at my self-respect."

Given these conditions, Sadat made a large arms deal with the USSR and proceeded to strengthen Egypt's ties with the nonaligned countries, the Organization of African Unity, and the leaders of the other Arab states. He paid special attention to Syria's new leader, Hafiz al-Asad, who, though no less militant than his precursors, had opened new links with the West. The two met several times to devise joint strategies for a war on Israel. They agreed to divulge their plans to Jordan's King Husayn, so that he could enter the war if he felt ready to fight, and to Saudi Arabia's King Faysal, because they needed his support. Owing to Qadhafi's erratic behavior, he was not informed, even though he had counted on an organic union between Egypt and Libya in September 1973 (it was postponed indefinitely). To throw off its enemy, Egypt twice held war maneuvers on so large a scale that Israel mobilized its armed forces at great expense. Sadat then lulled the Israelis by hinting publicly that he was planning to attend the UN General Assembly meeting in October.

Just before the October War, Israelis were worrying about the Palestinian capture of three Soviet Jewish emigrants on a train bound for Austria. To secure their release, Austrian Premier Bruno Kreisky had agreed to close Schönau Castle, which had become the main transit center used by the Jewish Agency for receiving the emigrants and persuading them to go to Israel. Golda Meir, Israel's prime minister, flew to Vienna and tried (in vain) to persuade Kreisky not to close Schönau. Meanwhile, Egypt and Syria agreed on a plan for a simultaneous attack on the Sinai and the Golan, to take place on 6 October, which happened to be the Jewish Day of Atonement and also the anniversary of Badr, Muhammad's first victory over the Meccan pagans. The Egyptians wanted to attack at dusk, so that the sun would be behind them and a nearly full moon would illumine their canal crossing, whereas the Syrians wanted to invade the Golan Heights early in the morning, when the sun would be in the Israelis' eyes. They settled on 2 P.M. The deception worked. Having grown accustomed to false alarms, Israeli intelligence did not pick up on the threats, maneuvers, or greater troop concentrations taking place at the front lines until the day before the attack. Most Egyptians and Syrians, too, were taken by surprise. If this period encompassed the High Holy Days for the Jews, it was also the month of Ramadan fasting for the Muslims.

The coordinated Arab attack worked as well as anyone could have hoped. On both fronts, the Israelis, outnumbered and outgunned, fell back in confusion. The Egyptian soldiers had rehearsed setting up pontoon bridges and transporting their equipment until they could cross the Suez Canal in their sleep. Armed with bazookas and fire hoses, backed by Soviet MiG fighters and their latest SAM-6 and SAM-7 missiles, five Egyptian divisions crossed the canal and broke through the Bar-Lev Line, which had been raised in places to a height of 38 feet (12 meters). Within 24 hours, they had penetrated 6 miles (10 kilometers) beyond that line. Could they have reached the strategic Gidi and Mitla passes? Given Israel's strategy of concentrating first on driving back the Syrians, the Egyptians should have found it easy to gain ground before Israel could bring its full might to bear against them. According to General Sa'd al-Din al-Shadhili, Egypt's five divisions needed time to consolidate their gains. By the time they got orders to advance to the passes, the central division was already vulnerable to an Israeli counterthrust. Muhammad Hasanayn Haykal, who served as Sadat's information minister and later became one of his severest critics, writes that Syria had counted on Egypt's ability to reach the passes (thus enabling its own army to finish taking the Golan Heights). But Sadat was only looking for a foothold in Sinai that would enable U.S. pressure to bring the Israelis back to the bargaining table. He was thinking of a quick victory to redeem Egypt's (and his own) dignity, not of a drawn-out war that could drag in the superpowers.

Once the Israelis had pushed the Syrians back off the Golan Heights, they managed to concentrate enough forces on their southern front to reverse the tide of battle. On the war's eleventh day, while Sadat and Golda Meir were giving well-publicized speeches to their respective parliaments, a battalion headed by General Ariel Sharon was leading the Israelis westward into Egypt's heartland. The Israel Defense Forces, aided by U.S. reconnaissance aircraft (according to General Shadhili), had found a weak spot between the Egyptian second and third armies, pierced through it, reached the canal, and crossed it just north of the Great Bitter Lake. Egypt's reserves had become dangerously thin west of the canal. While the superpowers hastened to rearm their Middle Eastern client states, the cutting edge of the fighting now moved into Egyptian and Syrian territory, with Cairo and Damascus both just an hour's drive away. The USSR now saw that it needed a cease-fire before Egypt and Syria lost the arms it was sending. Secretary of State Henry Kissinger flew to Moscow and, together with Foreign Minister Andrei Gromyko, drafted a cease-fire resolution that provided for negotiations among the belligerents "under appropriate auspices." Passed by the UN Security Council, it was to take effect on 22 October. It did not. As each side accused the other of violating the cease-fire, the Israelis tried to surround the city of Suez and isolate the Egyptian Third Army, while Egyptian units tried to fight their way out of encirclement. It took two more days and another Security Council resolution before the shooting stopped.

Although the crossing of the Suez Canal was hailed as a great victory for the Arabs and as the work of Sadat's strategic genius, others deserve more credit. The mastermind of the crossing was General Shadhili, who would be relieved of his military command soon after the war. The real Arab victory lay in the ability of the oil-exporting states, led by Saudi Arabia, to quadruple prices and reduce production, thus threatening Western Europe and Japan with severe oil shortages just at the outset of the winter heating season. Output was to be reduced by 5 percent each month until Israel withdrew from all the territories it had occupied in the 1967 and 1973 wars and recognized the Palestinians' right to self-determination. The Arab oil exporters, possibly in collusion with the big seven oil companies, proclaimed a total embargo against the United States for its massive arms airlift to Israel and against Holland for facilitating the shipment of weapons (or was it because of Rotterdam's role in setting the spot price of oil in Europe?). The psychological effect of such "oil diplomacy" was devastating, as the Common Market members hastened to befriend the Arabs, back their demands for Palestinian statehood, and distance themselves from Israel. This postwar trend explains why, when the Israelis had penetrated farther into Arab lands than ever before, they were grieving while the Arabs were rejoicing! Even so, the oil weapon would probably not have worked without the backing of Iran, which raised both its prices and its output to take advantage of the Arab oil embargo. Sadat's victory was real, all the same. Now he had reopened the issue of the Sinai and the other lands occupied by Israel. He had confounded his Arab detractors, who had previously denounced him as a hapless windbag. He would now set Egypt on its own national course.

Sadat After the Crossing

Sadat's triumph was played out concurrently on two planes—one worldwide, the other domestic. On the international level, he had restored the Arab-Israeli conflict to center stage; every country, large or small, near or far, had a stake in its outcome. One symbolic result of the October War was the decision by the black African countries to break diplomatic relations with Israel, even though most had hitherto shown little interest in the conflict and some had received technical assistance from Israel. Ever since the creation of the United Nations, Middle East issues have played a part in its deliberations out of all proportion to the number of countries and peoples directly involved. Both superpowers in October 1973 showed the depth of their involvement by the value of the arms they furnished to the combatants and by their efforts to manipulate events to further their own strategic positions. President Nixon put all U.S. forces on red alert just after the cease-fire in an effort to intimidate the USSR, which was reportedly shipping missiles with nuclear warheads through the Turkish straits. The more immediate cause was a Soviet proposal to set up a joint patrol with the United States to police the uneasy cease-fire between Egypt and Israel. Reportedly, Soviet troops had already entered Egypt for this purpose.

With Israeli troops west of the Suez Canal and Egyptians east of it, the danger of renewed fighting was extreme. Kissinger went out to the Middle East hoping to organize an international peace conference, to be chaired jointly by the two superpowers. His first meeting with Sadat proved to be far more cordial than anyone had expected, and the prospects for a peace settlement brightened. Sadat's immediate concern was to extricate his Third Army, which was completely cut off by Israeli troops, and Kissinger agreed to press Golda Meir's government to let Egypt truck in food and other nonmilitary supplies. Israel and Egypt were sufficiently eager to prevent new outbreaks of fighting on the front that they agreed to hold direct talks in a tent pitched at Kilometer 101 on the Suez-Cairo road. When the Americans and Russians issued a joint invitation to a peace conference in Geneva, to be convened in late December, both countries accepted. Syria refused, because the Palestine Liberation Organization had not been invited, but the Geneva Conference met anyway. After a day's speeches, however, the conferees agreed to an indefinite adjournment, during which time they hoped to facilitate technical negotiations to separate the belligerent forces.

As a facilitator, Kissinger mediated the indirect negotiations between Egypt and Israel, starting what came to be called "shuttle diplomacy" between Jerusalem and Cairo to hammer out a separation-of-forces agreement. By giving up his demand for an immediate Israeli pullback to the pre-1967 border, Sadat was able to secure Israel's withdrawal to a line about 10 kilometers (6 miles) east of the Suez Canal, corresponding to Egypt's farthest advance during the war. Later in 1974 Kissinger overcame the obstacles to a comparable agreement between Israel and Syria. This diplomatic feat paved the way for a visit to Egypt by Nixon, the first by a U.S. president since Franklin Roosevelt. U.S.-Egyptian relations improved dramatically, starting with the exchange of ambassadors and the resumption of U.S. aid, both of which had been suspended since June 1967.

The Revival of Egyptian Capitalism

The political honeymoon between Washington and Cairo coincided with Sadat's other major policy change, which he called *al-infitah* ("unfolding" or "opening"). During the heyday of Arab socialism under Nasir, major businesses owned by Egyptian citizens as well as by foreigners came under state ownership or sequestration. Although it is impossible to estimate the value of these assets, one economist has come up with the figure of 2 billion Egyptian pounds. This is not to say that Nasir's Egypt was a Marxist state, for most Muslim and Christian Egyptians rejected Communism, and Arab nationalism could not be reconciled with the class struggle. There were surviving pockets of private enterprise, including farming, retail sales, and even construction. Arab socialism no doubt weakened Egypt's capitalists, but many owned enough land and real estate to support themselves. Reducing the maximum individual landholding to 50 feddans in 1969 had hurt some people, but the income one could earn from this amount of land still sufficed for a comfortable living standard, especially if one grew specialty crops like fruit and vegetables, kept honeybees, or raised livestock. But Arab socialism had also created a new bourgeoisie, a class of managers that had arisen in the state-owned enterprises and (in a few cases) had discovered ways to milk the treasury for their own benefit. Both the old and the new bourgeoisie hoped to loosen the tight reins remaining as a legacy of Arab socialism. Moreover, Sadat saw the rising wealth of the oil-producing Arab states as a rich source of capital. He also hoped to lure back some of the Egyptian capital that (along with the capitalists) had fled abroad as a result of Nasir's Arab socialism, in addition to some of the money that other Egyptians had earned abroad in recent years.

The October War magnified the value of Arab oil and Egypt's attractiveness as a country in which to invest the proceeds. It also made Sadat popular in Egypt for the first time; Egyptians listened when he announced new initiatives, and civilian morale improved. Egypt could rebuild Port Said, Ismailia, Suez, and the other cities on the western side of the Suez Canal. Reconstruction was a bonanza for Egypt's contractors, greatest among whom was Sadat's friend, Uthman Ahmad Uthman, president of the Arab Contractors, Inc. This Egyptian company had worked on the High Dam and various construction projects in Arab oil-producing countries. People also compared the achievement of Nasir, whose policies had brought not only two defeats in 1956 and 1967 but also a standoff in 1970 that had made Egypt heavily dependent on the USSR, with that of Sadat, who took the credit for the crossing, the oil embargo, and Kissinger's ability to coax the Israelis to pull back. The natural result was an anti-Nasir reaction that enabled Egypt to renounce war as an instrument of policy against Israel, to rebuild ties with the United States, and to open the country to free enterprise and foreign investors.

The earliest expression of these changes appeared in the *October Paper,* which formally claimed loyalty to the principles of the Nasirite Revolution, including socialism and Arab nationalism, but argued that their mode of application must adapt to changing times. Nasirism's achievements would be preserved, but certain "deviations" of the late 1960s would be corrected by an "opening" to the new international economic environment. A few years later, Sadat would issue further pronouncements that effectively dismantled the Nasirite heritage; for now, he signaled left and turned right.

The positive case for *infitah* was Egypt's apparent economic revival. Its most visible aspect was an immense construction boom in the canal cities that enabled their residents to return after four to six disrupted years of exile. Cairo and Alexandria, too, were bursting out in new construction. As Egypt's population surpassed 40 million in 1977, plans were resurrected for building satellite towns in desert lands near Cairo or the Delta. Another sign of *infitah* was the return of foreign banks, including such U.S. firms as Chase-Manhattan and Bank of America, to do business in the new Egypt. Before *infitah,* the largest loan Egypt had ever received from the World Bank was for $60 million to widen the Suez Canal; in 1974–1975 it would get $227 million. Private foreign investment came mainly from the Arab states and Iran, which spent their new oil wealth more on real estate than on productive enterprises, but Sadat also coaxed large sums out of the kings of Saudi Arabia and Kuwait. In 1976, when the Egyptian government fell into arrears while trying to repay its short-term debts, the Arab states formed a consortium called the Gulf Organization for the Development of Egypt, which lent $1.475 billion on more favorable terms than the World Bank.

On the minus side, *infitah* failed to attract U.S., European, and Japanese investors in anywhere near the numbers that Sadat had hoped for. Its main beneficiaries were the Egyptian bourgeoisie, some of whom celebrated their return from the Nasirite wilderness by investing their money in urban land, new villas, apartments, and hotels, and less often in such productive enterprises as factories. Much money was spent on importing expensive cars, which further clogged the already infamous traffic of downtown Cairo and Alexandria. It was a sign of Sadat's sense of his main source of support that the Cairo Governorate invested heavily in new bridges and overpasses benefiting the minority of its population that could afford to own cars or ride taxis, while neglecting the need of the majority for improvements to the buses, trolleys, the "metro" line to Heliopolis, and the trains to Ma'adi and Hilwan. It speaks volumes that Egypt turned over to a German firm the operation of its luxury tourist trains connecting Cairo with Luxor and Aswan and licensed foreign companies to open such new hotels as the Meridien and the Ramses Hilton, while the state-managed Shepheard's Hotel (burnt in the January 1952 riots and then, under Nasir, rebuilt near the Nile Corniche) was allowed to deteriorate.

For the peasants, *infitah* meant an end to land reallocations from the large estates, deteriorating service from the rural cooperatives and health centers, and declining terms of payment for the food and fiber that they produced. If Egypt had been an exporter of cereal grains for almost its whole history, under Nasir and Sadat it became a net importer. Indeed, Sadat's new policy made Egypt a net exporter of its own people; peasants as well as engineers, doctors, teachers, plumbers, and electricians went off to wealthier Arab lands to earn higher wages. Given Egypt's annual population growth of 2.5 percent, emigration was a short-term benefit, but in the long run it separated families and created new income disparities and shortages of skilled workers and farmers. Workers in private firms gained more from *infitah* than those serving in public sector companies, which went into decline. With the bureaucracy swollen by the government's promise to employ every university graduate, price inflation outstripped salary raises for government clerks, teachers in schools and universities, doctors and nurses in public clinics and hospitals, and other state employees.

The Peace Initiative

But if Sadat could bring peace, the Egyptians still hoped for relief from the burdensome cost of the five wars they had fought (and the arms race they were still fighting) against Israel. Although Sadat still paid lip service to Arab nationalism, he moved toward an Egypt-first policy more consonant with his country's rapprochement with the industrialized West. The watershed came in September 1975, when Kissinger returned to perform his last feat of shuttle diplomacy—the second Sinai accord between Egypt and Israel. In return for a further Israeli troop withdrawal to the Gidi and Mitla passes, Sadat renounced war as a means to settle the Arab-Israeli conflict and agreed to limit Egypt's troops and tanks on the regained lands east of the canal and Gulf of Suez. Although Kissinger and Sadat argued that step-by-step diplomacy was gradually restoring to Egyptian control lands that it had lost in war, critics felt that Israel had driven a hard bargain and that the real price Egypt had to pay was its loss of leadership over the Arabs.

But that role, too, Sadat's supporters argued, had been devalued by the internecine quarrels of Arab rulers and factions. Their decision in 1974 to make Arafat's PLO the sole power entitled to negotiate for the Palestinians, at a time when that group was fomenting terrorist incidents against civilians in Israel, made it harder for Israel and the Arab states to settle the conflict. The assassination of Saudi Arabia's King Faysal and the outbreak of civil war in Lebanon added to the general picture of Arab political instability. Egypt should have learned from its five-year involvement in the Yemen civil war not to fish in troubled Arab waters, but, as Muhammad Hasanayn Haykal observed, Sadat committed Egyptian forces to fight in Oman against the rebels in Dhofar and to make raids into Libya to intimidate Qadhafi, after their proposed union had been abandoned.

The difference, of course, was that Nasir had fought in Yemen to help a republican military junta to replace a traditional monarchy, but Sadat had used Egypt's armed forces to aid the West and its backers. It was natural for the USSR to reduce and finally to cancel military aid, amid recriminations against Sadat for moving Egypt into the imperialist camp. Sadat's complaints were that the Soviets were withholding weapons and spare parts and refusing to let Egypt reschedule its debt repayments to the USSR. At the end of 1975, with Egypt's inflation rate exceeding 30 percent, foreign investment was lagging, the government was borrowing on the short term at rates up to 17 percent per annum, and the total amount owed to the USSR exceeded $7 billion. Moscow's refusal to reschedule the debt angered Sadat. In March 1976 he renounced the 1971 Treaty of Friendship and Cooperation, then canceled Russia's naval facilities in Egypt, and finally announced that he would cut off payments of $1.5 billion still owed to the USSR for past arms purchases. These acts were bound to antagonize the Soviet government and cause it to seek closer ties with other Arab regimes.

Worsening relations with the USSR did not guarantee better ones with the United States. Washington's strong commitment to Israel and its own apparent political instability during the Watergate scandal deterred Sadat from seeking closer U.S. ties. He did not welcome Jimmy Carter's election, both because of the traditional Democratic party bias toward Israel and because of Sadat's own attachment to Henry Kissinger. Sadat also disliked Carter's search for a comprehensive Arab-Israeli settlement involving the Palestinians and the USSR.

Early in 1977, though, Sadat had to retire from the glamorous world of diplomacy to counter a challenge to his power at home. Egypt's rising foreign debt led to burdensome repayments, which by this time amounted to more than half the value of Egypt's total annual exports of goods and services. Most of the Egyptian people had to pay for this somehow. The International Monetary Fund (IMF), trying to help Egypt strengthen its economy, suggested (among other measures) that government subsidies on certain consumer goods be reduced. The policy of subsidizing low prices for bread, rice, sugar, tea, cooking oil, bottled gas, kerosene, and a few other necessities had begun in World War II and was intended to ease the lives of the poor. But the policy had taken on a life of its own. As Egypt was importing (by 1976) more than half the wheat its citizens consumed, the government had to allot huge sums to pay for these imports while keeping bread and flour prices down to artificially low levels.

The IMF's advice alarmed most Egyptian ministers, but because of the rising foreign debt (as in 1881) Egypt was no longer the master of its economic destiny. What the government did was to end subsidies on goods that were not necessities for the poor, such as beer, refined flour, granulated sugar, French bread, and macaroni, and to reduce them on such foods as bread, cooking oil, broad beans, and lentils. The announcement of these measures sparked the fiercest rioting in Egypt since 1952. Mobs rampaged through downtown Alexandria and Cairo, pillaged boutiques of their expensive imported goods, set the Arab Socialist Union headquarters on fire, and tried to break into Abdin Palace, where Sadat had set up one of his offices. They shouted such slogans as *Sadat ala moda, wehna sab'a fi oda* ("Sadat dresses in style, while we live seven to a room") and *Gihan, Gihan, al-sha'b ga'an* ("Jihan [Sadat's wife, whose prominence in Egyptian public life was widely resented], the people are hungry"). The army was called in to quell the riots. In Cairo alone, 77 were killed, according to official figures; the total number of Egyptians killed in three days of rioting was more than 150. This protest against *infitah* was waged not because it was liberal but because it increased inequality. As *al-Ahram al-Iqtisadi* commented: "Sadly, the majority of the Egyptian people have come to feel that they are unwelcome in the new consumer society."

The immediate response from Sadat's government was to restore all the food subsidies and to allow them to increase, no matter what the cost to Egypt, as a way of fending off further disturbances. Indeed, this policy has been one of the real reasons behind the large sums in U.S. aid provided during the 1980s. A further response was a plebiscite, the questions of which were so worded as to give Sadat the appearance of unanimous support. But Sadat's main reaction was to plan his most spectacular act on the international stage—a journey to Jerusalem. No Arab leader had ever publicly talked to an Israeli leader, let alone traveled publicly to Israel, since the creation of the state in 1948, and Sadat had clearly told reporters that he was not about to recognize Israel or make peace without the concurrence of the other Arabs. Most experts assumed that the election campaign then taking place in Israel would retain the Labor Alignment in power. Sadat believed, therefore, that he would deal with Shimon Peres, who was seen as being liberal on Arab matters. Instead, the victor in Israel's election turned out to be Menachem Begin, the ultranationalist leader of the Likud coalition and erstwhile terrorist who had masterminded the 1948 Dayr Yasin massacre. Even so, Egypt's border war with Libya in July 1977, the rising tide of Muslim extremism that took the life of the *waqf*s minister, and the Carter administration's attempts (seen by Sadat as maladroit) to reconvene the Geneva Conference (a means of bringing the USSR and the Palestinians into the peace process) pushed him to this dramatic policy change.

In a speech given before the People's Assembly on 9 November 1977, Sadat announced that, in his search for peace with Israel, he was prepared to go to the ends of the earth, or even to the Knesset in Jerusalem. When asked later by U.S. reporters whether he had meant to be taken seriously, Sadat affirmed his willingness to negotiate directly with Begin's government. Indeed, when Begin was asked how he would respond to such an initiative, he replied that he would gladly invite Sadat to visit Israel and to make peace. Within two weeks, despite pleas by many Arab countries (and even by the head of Egypt's tolerated opposition party) that he not go, Sadat made the one-hour flight from Cairo to the David Ben Gurion Airport and was greeted by Israel's president, prime minister, and the entire cabinet. During his one-day visit, Sadat laid a wreath at the tomb of the unknown Israeli soldier, prayed at al-Aqsa Mosque, and gave an eloquent speech to the Knesset. Even though his peace terms were the same ones he had often stated before—withdrawal from all occupied lands and self-determination for the Palestinian people—the fact that Sadat had come to Israel and had recognized its existence (with Jerusalem as its capital) dramatized his desire for peace and put Begin into a position where most people expected him to make comparable concessions. He never did.

Many outside observers feared that Sadat would be assassinated during or after his trip to Jerusalem, as many Palestinians were extremely angry at him for going there. On his return to Cairo, however, he received a tumultuous welcome. It was quite clear that many Egyptians were eager to have peace with Israel, especially on the terms Sadat had stated in his speech. The Marxist Left and the fundamentalist Muslim Right did not share these sentiments. In addition, two foreign ministers resigned in rapid succession. The only Arab governments that openly approved were those of the Sudan (whose policies were closely aligned with Sadat's), Morocco (whose King Hasan had helped bring Sadat and the Israelis together), Oman, and Jordan (cautiously). Most Western governments and peoples hailed this new peace initiative. The Carter administration, though taken by surprise, quickly backed Sadat and scrapped its plans to reconvene the Geneva Conference (which would have involved the USSR) and to seek a comprehensive settlement including the Palestinians.

Sadat promptly convened an international peace conference at Mena House near the Pyramids. Only Israel and the United States came. Begin returned Sadat's visit on 25 December, but their talks did not help the peace process. During January 1978 the two sides set up military and political committees to work on the technicalities of a peace settlement. After an insensitive speech by Begin, Egypt broke off negotiations. The sticking point was the Sinai. Begin had offered, unequivocally, to hand back the peninsula; but the Israelis wanted the right to retain the existing Jewish settlements, such as Yamit, whereas Sadat wanted them evacuated and restored to Egyptian control. Issues involving the Palestinians under Israeli occupation were troublesome, but less so for Sadat than for other Arab leaders. Many Egyptians had come to feel that the Palestinians were ungrateful for the sacrifices they had made for them in five wars against Israel. Other Arab states, however, felt that Egypt likewise ignored the financial backing they had given since 1967. The militant ones set up the "Steadfastness and Rejection Front" in a summit meeting in Tripoli.

Domestic Political Changes

The Jerusalem initiative led to some domestic changes in Egypt. Sadat's government had been toying with a more pluralistic political system, first by creating three pulpits (Arabic: *manabir*) within the Arab Socialist Union; its center *minbar* was the Misr party, which served as his own faction. In February 1978 Fu'ad Sirag al-Din, an aging pre-1952 politician, revived the Wafd party, despite government obstructionism. The neo-Wafd proved surprisingly popular among educated upper- and middle-class Egyptians whose interests had been harmed by the 1952 Revolution. Even some leftist intellectuals who had backed the Wafd in the old days saw its revival as a means of resurrecting popular socialism. Most of its members, however, called for a total dismantling of state controls and a policy of liberal capitalism. Before long, Sadat concluded that the neo-Wafd posed too strong a challenge and shut it down. He also decided to replace the Arab Socialist Union with a "democratic socialist" party initially called the Arab Socialist party of Egypt and then renamed the National Democratic party (*al-Hizb al-Watani al-Dimuqrati*). Often reduced to *al-Hizb al-Watani* in the headlines, it recalls the heroic National party of Mustafa Kamil and Muhammad Farid—a choice of names that appealed to Egyptian patriotism. Adding the Socialist Labor party on the left and the Liberals on the right, Egypt had a full spectrum of political parties.

Egypt was not fully democratic, though, for peace with Israel, superpower relations, economic policies, and of course Sadat's person were all excluded from political debate.

The lingering authoritarianism became clear when Sadat held yet another plebiscite to gain popular approval for legislation to curb political dissent. Called "the Law of Shame," it prohibited advocating atheism or class war, setting a bad example to young people, publishing or broadcasting false news that could inflame public opinion, forming an illegal organization, or disparaging the government. Penalties could include deprivation of civil rights, withdrawal of passports, house arrest, or sequestration of property. Sadat put himself forward as the national equivalent of a village headman or the patriarch of an extended family. To oppose such a worthy man in public was disgraceful, according to village mores. Although many lawyers and civil libertarians objected to the Law of Shame, it handed Sadat a new muzzle for his political opponents.

The Egyptian-Israeli Peace Treaty

Sadat's peace initiative had raised people's hopes that the Arab-Israeli conflict would soon be resolved. Carter's administration was willing to resort to heroic measures to bring about peace in the Middle East. Sadat purported to seek a comprehensive settlement that included some provision for a Palestinian state, euphemistically called a "homeland." Israel and its supporters did not want to turn the occupied West Bank and Gaza Strip over to the Palestinians, lest these lands should come to be ruled by the PLO. If Carter, Sadat, and Begin all wanted peace, they would have to devise a mutually acceptable plan for the Palestinians. The parties tried visiting back and forth, a foreign ministers' conference at Leeds Castle (England), and finally an open-ended summit meeting at the presidential summer retreat in Camp David (Maryland), which went on for two weeks in September 1978. The end result was a draft treaty between Egypt and Israel that constituted, in all but name, a separate peace, and a vaguely worded "framework" providing "autonomy" for the inhabitants of the Gaza Strip and the West Bank, to be attained under the aegis of a transitional self-governing authority and over a five-year period. King Husayn was to be "invited" to enter the negotiations. He refused to join.

The appearance of fraternal feeling among the leaders was impressive but misleading. Begin's personality and persistence irritated Sadat—and indeed Carter—but he was looking after his own country's interests better than the others. The evacuation of the Sinai was to occur in very gradual stages, and Egypt would be required to establish full diplomatic relations with Israel, no matter how much they harmed its ties with other Arab states. The two sides would continue to negotiate to achieve "autonomy" for the Palestinians under Israeli administration. Cynics interpreted this to mean freedom to leave the occupied territories to enter other Arab countries. Begin's cabinet soon showed that these Palestinians would gain no effective control over their own lives; it said that Israel would continue to create new Jewish settlements on the West Bank and to "thicken" (i.e., enlarge) existing ones.

No one, therefore, should wonder why other Arab states condemned the Camp David accords. Jordan and Saudi Arabia joined the rejectionists, led by Iraq and Syria, even though Secretary of State Cyrus Vance visited Amman, Riyadh, and Damascus, seeking Arab support for the peace agreement. On the contrary, the other Arab states held a "Rejectionist Summit" in Baghdad to condemn Camp David and sent a delegation to Cairo with a $2 billion aid offer to dissuade Sadat from signing a peace treaty with Israel. Sadat refused to receive the delegates, and the Baghdad Conference voted to impose an economic and political boycott on Egypt if Sadat made peace.

Sadat's signature on a treaty with Israel was not yet assured, however, as he was demanding a detailed Israeli timetable for giving up control of the Gaza Strip and the West Bank. The best that Vance could get from Israel's cabinet was a vague commitment to negotiate. This was too little for Egypt, and a U.S. team of international lawyers and Middle East experts could not devise a formula that met the demands of Jerusalem and Cairo. Carter had to go in person to meet with the two governments before Israel's cabinet and Sadat agreed on a compromise wording. The treaty's price, for the U.S. taxpayer, included $3 billion to help Israel pay the cost of evacuating the Sinai and $2 billion in planes, tanks, and anti-aircraft weapons for Egypt. Both sides expected (and got) additional economic aid. An eleventh-hour visit by National Security Adviser Zbigniev Brzezinski failed to persuade Amman and Riyadh to support the treaty. The Israeli Knesset approved it after a bitter debate, and on 26 March 1979 Begin and Sadat signed the treaty on the White House lawn, formally ending the state of war between their countries.

The Egyptian-Israeli Peace Treaty was a significant step toward resolving the Arab-Israeli conflict. It helped Egypt to shed the burden of serving as a "blood bank" for Palestinians and other Arabs opposed to recognizing Israel; now it could devote more of its slender resources to internal economic development. But the treaty did not win autonomy for the inhabitants of the Gaza Strip and the West Bank, nor did any

Arab state hasten to follow Egypt's example, except (briefly and under U.S. pressure) Lebanon in 1983. Rather, the other Arab states, except for the Sudan and Oman, broke diplomatic ties with Sadat's government, ended all economic aid, ousted Egypt from the Arab League, and moved the League's headquarters out of Cairo. Sadat and the other Arab leaders exchanged angry recriminations, and some Arab investers took their money out of Egypt. But if the Arab governments had really wanted to ruin Sadat, they could have expelled all Egyptians working in their countries, thus costing Egypt $2–3 billion annually in emigrant remittances. In reality, the Arabs could not do without their skills and their relatively cheap labor.

Now that Egypt was at peace with Israel, the Egyptians hoped to reduce military expenditures, leaving more money for industrialization, education, social reforms, and general improvements in their standard of living. They also hoped that Menachem Begin's government would make a good-faith effort to negotiate toward Palestinian autonomy in the West Bank and Gaza. Backers of the peace process hoped that other Arab governments would see their error and line up behind Sadat. They expected improved ties with the United States to lead to increased investment and tourism from the Western world, to make up for the loss of income from the Communist countries and the recalcitrant Arabs.

Although Egypt was at peace from March 1979 and economic conditions did improve markedly, those hopes were realized only in part. Instead, Sadat's government started buying new and more expensive arms from the United States, presumably for defense against Libya, but really to ensure that the Egyptian military would go on backing Sadat's government and its policies. Israel's government, fearing that its turning over the administered territories to a self-governing entity might well lead to a terrorist regime that would endanger its own security, proceeded to block any progress toward Palestinian autonomy.

The other Arab governments, therefore, did not follow Sadat's example, even as their internal differences widened in the early 1980s. The revolution in Iran (although it was not an Arab country) stirred the hope of Muslims everywhere that they could affirm their own social and cultural values and free themselves from unwanted Western influences. Iraq's September 1980 invasion of Iran, however, split the Arabs. Most backed Iraq, materially as well as morally, but Syria and Libya broke ranks to back Iran. As Egypt also offered to support Iraq, the Ba'thist regime in Baghdad had to decide if it could accept aid from a government it was condemning for having made peace with Israel. It did. As a result, Egypt belatedly regained support from some Arab leaders, including King Husayn and even Yasir Arafat, without renouncing its peace with Israel. This support has led since 1981 to renewed investment in Egypt by Iraq, Jordan, and Saudi Arabia.

The number of tourists from Arab countries dropped briefly after the peace treaty but surpassed its previous level by 1980–1981, whereas the number of visitors from Western Europe and North America rose greatly in the last years of Sadat's presidency. The amount of money they spent was, however, almost the same in 1981 as in 1978, presumably because many tourists exchanged their hard currency on the black market. Direct investment fluctuated but rose markedly from 1978 to 1981. Yet, as of the latter year, only $40 million had come from U.S. firms. In July 1986 General Motors announced plans to build an automobile assembly plant in Egypt. If these plans are realized, more large-scale U.S. investment will probably ensue. And if that happens, Egypt will benefit from its defection from the Arab boycott of Israel and of the firms doing business there—but it will also increase its economic and probably its social dependence on the United States.

Egypt's peace treaty with Israel has made it a ward of the West, whereas before 1979 it had depended on the oil-rich Arab countries. Has this done Egypt more harm than good? On balance, Egypt would serve its own best interests by pursuing policies that win the economic and political support of more than one bloc of states. Egypt has succeeded in restoring ties with Jordan, Iraq, and Saudi Arabia. Although no other Arab government has yet followed Egypt's example, neither have such rejectionist states as Syria been able to stop Israel's invasion of Lebanon or its repression of Palestinian Arabs under its control. Both failures have further divided and frustrated the Arab regimes.

Muslim Militant Opposition

During the last years of Sadat's presidency, the close relationship he had formed with the Egyptian people dissipated. Why? Economic and social conditions may have improved statistically, but most Egyptians did not feel the improvement. Higher income from Western tourism, investment, Suez Canal tolls, oil sales, and emigrant remittances benefited only a few people, thus widening the gap between the haves and the have-nots. Especially menacing was the rising tide of young men and women who graduated from the universities only to find that the jobs guaranteed to them by the government would not be available for several years, that the pay was inadequate, or that they had to work in areas lacking the comforts of Cairo or the amenities of Alexandria. Although they were free to vote for one of the parties opposing Sadat's National Democrats in the periodic elections for the People's Assembly, this freedom did not ease their plight. Many young Egyptians sought more radical cures.

In Nasir's time, the prevalent mood of the university students and recent graduates had been pro-government. During the student uprisings of 1972–1973, they remained mainly Nasirite or Marxist in their views. Hoping to channel the opposition into movements less threatening to his regime, Sadat had freed most of the Muslim Brothers still in jail and let them resume their propaganda. The released Society members tended to be cautious, older men, but their example inspired young Muslims to form more radical groups, thus attracting most of the student activists. One of these groups, *Shabab Muhammad* ("Youth of Muhammad"), tried to take control of the Technical Military Academy in 1974. Its coup was thwarted after many casualties. Three of its leaders were executed and dozens imprisoned. The best-known radical group was one called *Takfir wa al-Hijrah,* a name accurately but inelegantly translated as "Exposing Unbelief and Moving Away." Like *Shabab Muhammad, Takfir wa al-Hijrah* sought to overthrow Sadat's regime and to set up a new government based on Muslim principles. It signaled its existence in 1977 by kidnapping the *waqf*s minister and "executing" him when the government refused to negotiate for his release. Its leaders, too, were captured and executed or imprisoned. It would later draw encouragement from the Khomeini revolution in Iran, but its inspiration came from the fiery agitation of Jamal al-Din al-Afghani, the organizational skills of Hasan al-Banna, who had founded the Society of Muslim Brothers, and the writings of Sayyid Qutb, whom Nasir had hanged. *Shabab Muhammad* and *Takfir wa al-Hijrah* were only two among many such groups that grew up in Cairo and Alexandria, and even in such provincial centers as Asyut.

Western observers have often assumed that Muslim organizations appealed mainly to poor and uneducated city-dwellers, especially newcomers from the countryside, unsettled by the loss of rural family ties and traditional values or angered by the glaring disparities between wealth and poverty. Scholarly studies of these groups show that the members are typically well-educated young men (*Takfir wa al-Hijrah* also included some young women), many of them in colleges of medicine, pharmacy, and engineering, for which admissions standards are the highest in Egypt's universities. They believe that God has created humanity to develop His ideal community on earth, that this community has been described in the Qur'an and the sayings of Muhammad, that the Egyptian government has departed increasingly from this ideal model under the influence of the West, and that good Muslims must work to overthrow this impious regime and replace it with one that will try to reestablish God's community. They try to model their private lives and internal relationships on Qur'anic principles. One outward sign of this observance is the adoption of "Islamic dress" for both sexes: loose robes, sandals, and full beards for the men; enveloping dresses, head coverings, and sometimes face veils and even gloves for women. Reacting to the overcrowding of the universities, some student groups demand segregated classrooms and staircases for men and women. They discourage and even disrupt social gatherings that permit interaction between the sexes. In Sadat's Egypt, once Marxist and Nasirite movements had been banned, joining Islamic groups became the obvious way to oppose the regime. Most Egyptians, having been raised as Muslims, can more easily adapt to a movement that upholds deeply engrained cultural norms than to one introducing alien terms and ideas.

The popularity of Egypt's Muslim movements grew as their co-religionists in Iran ousted the shah and took the American hostages in 1979, not because they hated U.S. citizens but because they resented the United States' political and cultural sway over the Muslim world. They were angry when Sadat publicly backed the shah, condemned the taking of U.S. hostages, and finally invited the shah and his family to take refuge in Egypt (where he died and was given a state funeral in July 1980). The rising militancy of Egypt's 4–6 million Copts both reflected and inspired the growth of revolutionary Muslim societies. Clashes had begun in 1972. More violent ones occurred in a mixed Cairo neighborhood called Zawiyah al-Hamra' in June 1981. The disparities between rich and poor, Westernized and traditional Egyptians, and Sadat's promises and social reality fueled the militancy of the Muslim movements. The Muslims condemned Egypt's peace with Israel, not because they were against Jews (although some were) but because the state of peace freed Begin's government to bomb civilian neighborhoods of Beirut, destroy Iraq's nuclear reactor, increase Jewish settlements on the West Bank, and oppress the Palestinians, in the knowledge that, isolated from other Arab countries, Egypt could not act.

The Assassination of Sadat

Sadat knew that revolutionary societies were plotting to assassinate him and his wife (Jihan had come to symbolize the lifestyle resented by militant Muslims). He took greater precautions to protect himself, often changing his travel plans, using his private helicopter, and wearing a bulletproof vest. In a televised address on 5 September 1981, he lashed out at his opponents and announced that he was jailing more than a thousand of them, including many of the country's most influential religious, political, and intellectual leaders. This act infuriated most politically articulate citizens and made Egypt's atmosphere as oppressive as it had been in the last months of the monarchy or during the darkest days of Nasir's government. Sadat no longer heeded his ministers or his other advisers. He was almost wholly isolated from his own people.

On 6 October, the eighth anniversary of the Egyptian crossing of the Suez Canal, Sadat's government staged a victory parade near the tomb of Egypt's unknown soldier in Nasr City. It was an impressive demonstration of Egypt's military hardware, with long lines of tanks and personnel carriers, as well as fighter planes roaring overhead in formation—all televised and broadcast for the benefit of Egyptians and their neighbors. Sadat sat in a reviewing stand with most of his cabinet ministers, foreign ambassadors, religious dignitaries, and journalists. Just before 1 P.M., one of the trucks in the parade stopped and a lieutenant carrying a Kalachnikov jumped out. Sadat rose to return what he thought was the lieutenant's salute, and the man began firing at the reviewing stand, aided by three other uniformed officers holding rifles and hand grenades. The broadcasting was cut off, the parade ended, and Sadat was rushed to a military hospital—but it was too late to save his life (or the lives of seven other people who had been sitting near him).

Almost immediately, the Egyptian cabinet met and proclaimed a state of emergency in the country, for no one could be sure whether the assassination was part of a wider plot to seize the government. On the following day the People's Assembly met and, following the terms of the constitution, nominated Vice-President Husni Mubarak to succeed the slain leader, subject to a nationwide plebiscite. A state funeral was attended by an impressive array of foreign dignitaries, including former Presidents Nixon, Ford, and Carter, Prime Minister Begin, President Mitterrand, and Prince Charles, but almost no Arab leaders and few Egyptians except high government officials. There were no scenes of public grief, as there had been for Nasir in 1970. The streets of Cairo were almost deserted, except for soldiers on guard everywhere. People stayed home for fear of being arrested or getting caught in a riot. Foreign broadcasting stations reported some fighting in Cairo's poorer neighborhoods. Asyut had a major uprising, which the army put down after killing or wounding hundreds. The government moved swiftly to avert a national uprising, if any were planned.

Sadat had not suppressed the Muslim militants, nor had he solved the political, economic, and social problems that made their message appeal to the Egyptian people. Sadat had died wearing his Pierre Cardin uniform covered with ribbons and medals and viewing a parade, as if he were acting on a political stage. He bequeathed to Mubarak a country at peace with Israel, but not with its Arab neighbors, and certainly not with itself.

CHAPTER TWELVE

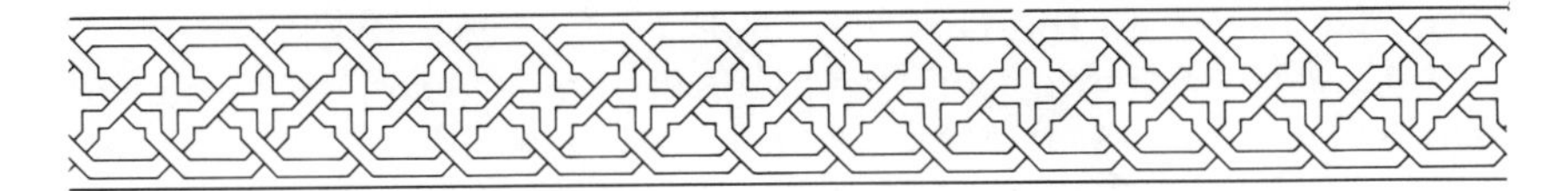

Since Sadat

Husni Mubarak, Sadat's successor, has confronted Egypt's domestic and foreign problems, using a markedly less flamboyant leadership style but making few basic policy changes. In international relations, Egypt remains formally nonaligned, but, in practical terms, its weapons and its support come mainly from the United States. It is still committed to achieving a comprehensive peace settlement with Israel along the lines laid down at the 1978 Camp David Summit and in the 1979 Egyptian-Israeli Peace Treaty, but it has taken some steps to improve its relations with the other Arab countries, most notably Jordan, Saudi Arabia, and Iraq. On the domestic scene, Egypt is evolving toward parliamentary democracy, with a multiparty system, but in practice the National Democratic party remains the dominant legal participatory movement and Mubarak remains the most powerful man in the government, although his methods have been less dictatorial and also somewhat less dramatic than those of his predecessor. Although regime politicians rarely speak critically of earlier leaders, Sadat's passing is no longer a cause for public grieving. Egyptians often criticize him in private. Some nostalgia is expressed for the now rather hazy years of Gamal Abd al-Nasir.

Economic Policy

In economic matters, the Egyptian government still pursues a policy that combines state planning and ownership of basic industries with private enterprise, both domestic and foreign. It has attempted to stanch the outflow of precious foreign exchange on nonessential imports and also to crack down on flagrant cases of corruption. One dramatic episode in the year following Sadat's death was the public destruction of several privately owned villas (including a rest house used by Sadat) in the land close to the Giza Pyramids.

Mubarak seems more dedicated to solving Egypt's economic problems than Sadat ever was. It is not clear, however, whether some of them can ever be solved. The country's population, 50 million in 1988, increases by another million every ten months; at the same time, the amount of arable land has actually declined, owing in part to the demand for housing but also to a legacy of ill-conceived agricultural policies that make it more profitable for some peasants to turn their soil into bricks than to raise the three crops per year made possible by perennial irrigation. Although the Aswan High Dam initially increased the amount of cropped land and now generates more electricity than Egypt can use, it has deprived the land of the silt that formerly came down with the annual flood and, hence, has increased Egypt's need for artificial fertilizers. The water table is also rising dangerously, making it harder to flush away salt accumulations that reduce the productivity of the soil. Egypt now imports more than half the grain consumed by its inhabitants, an ironic situation for a land that was the breadbasket of many ancient and medieval empires.

Egypt has not industrialized as effectively as many East Asian countries; the showcase heavy industries it instituted under Nasir have all lost money. Unemployment is a problem primarily for university graduates; in many skilled trades, even some agricultural ones, the labor supply has been inadequate. The main reason for this scarcity is that 4 million Egyptians have been lured to the oil-exporting Arab countries by wages often ten times the amount that they could earn at home. The decline in oil prices since 1981 has severely cut back employment opportunities abroad. If this trend continues, many expatriate Egyptians will lose their jobs and must then somehow be reabsorbed back home. At a time when Egypt's own oil revenues are falling and when the fear of terrorism has reduced foreign tourism, the earnings sent home by expatriate workers are still a major source of hard currency. If large numbers of people get laid off in the oil-exporting countries and return to Egypt, seeking employment, they are apt to become frustrated by low wages and poor working conditions, even if they succeed in finding jobs. It is not clear how well their families will adjust to lower living standards and to the presence of disgruntled breadwinners.

Falling oil revenues have also reduced the flow of Arab tourism to Egypt and reversed the trend of rising Arab investment in Egyptian real estate and industrial enterprises. Egypt's own oil production and prices have tended to parallel those of the larger oil exporters. Although it has not joined the Organization of Petroleum Exporting Countries,

Egypt tends to set its level of production and prices in tandem with that group. In periods of falling output, Egypt has also suffered revenue shortfalls from the Suez Canal, which since its reopening in 1975 has been heavily used by oil tankers.

Income disparities remain large. Although this was the case before the 1952 Revolution, the egalitarian propaganda of the Nasir era has made Egyptians less willing to accept vast differences between rich and poor. Radios have been ubiquitous since the 1950s and television sets have proliferated since the 1960s; now videocassette recorders are sweeping the land. Each of these media has made the Egyptian people more conscious of others and how they live. Near-universal primary education may get higher marks for quantity than for quality, but it certainly has added to the public's awareness of the difference between the reality with which they are contending and the ideals of either capitalism or socialism. One interesting change has been the degree to which technicians and skilled workers have been able to jack up their wages. Ownership of land and real estate is still the best way to get rich, but rewards have risen for entrepreneurial skill. Under Sadat, this skill often meant milking the public-sector companies, one of Egypt's more interesting forms of corruption; but Mubarak's government has demanded much stricter standards of honesty. The Sadat era spawned at least a thousand new millionaires; since then people have found it harder to climb the economic ladder through graft or corruption. Most Egyptians welcome the new rules; but they are resented, of course, by those people whose ambitions for wealth and power are still unfulfilled.

National Identity

Let us review the problem of "Factor X" that opened Chapter 10. What is the ideological glue holding the Egyptian people together? Short of using his army against his own people, as Sadat did during the 1977 food riots and Mubarak did during the post-assassination uprising in Asyut, what can the president do to gain and retain the obedience of the Egyptian people? This book's subtitle, *The Formation of a Nation-State,* suggests that Egypt is now both a nation (an object of loyalty) and a state (a political and legal system). The concept of the nation-state grew up in early modern times in Western Europe and North America. It did not necessarily apply either to the traditional loyalties of most Middle Eastern peoples or to the behavior patterns of their rulers. Faith and family remained the foci of popular identification. French and British imperialism (and schooling) did spread the spirit of nationalism, but mainly among a small stratum of the educated elite.

Except in the sense of resistance to non-Muslim rulers, nationalism was slow to appear and spread in the Middle East. It has developed in both intensity and extent in Egypt during the twentieth century, especially under Nasir and his successors, because of expanding public education, radio and television broadcasting, and almost universal male military service. Comparisons with other Middle Eastern states are hard to make, but Egyptians have probably developed a clearer sense of nationality than any other Arabic-speaking people, except maybe the Moroccans. They do tend to meander among their Egyptian, Arab, and Muslim identities, responding to current political conditions. Egypt's Arab identity went into eclipse after 1973, but it is now reviving, for the ties of language and culture with other Arabs are strong. Egyptian feeling, deep-seated though it may be, does not exclude other loyalties. Islamic sentiment has been increasing since the June 1967 War and especially since the Iranian Revolution. Sadat's assassins, or at any rate those whom the government managed to capture, belonged to a relatively new secret society called *al-Jihad al-Jadid* ("the New Holy War"). Their feat has actually increased the appeal to the Egyptian people of Islamic revolutionary groups, although they are strictly outlawed.

Egypt and the World

Muslim Egyptians are increasingly critical of the pro-U.S. policies of Mubarak's government and of the peace process with Israel begun by Sadat. They see Israel as intransigent and the United States as indifferent. The Israeli government, a broad coalition since 1984, is divided in its approach to peace with its Arab neighbors and repressive in dealing with the Palestinians under its jurisdiction. The Reagan administration has shifted its attention from Lebanon to the Gulf, effectively shelving the quest for Arab-Israeli peace. Many observers accuse both countries of being shortsighted, particularly after Yasir Arafat's reconciliation with King Husayn and their joint approach to a negotiated peace, strongly backed by Mubarak's government, was allowed to languish in 1985. The fruits of general neglect are evident in the uprisings by the Palestinians in the West Bank and Gaza Strip in late 1987 and early 1988. Mubarak, caught in the middle, played a leading role in working toward a peaceful settlement. Another trend in recent years has been for Egypt to reestablish its ties with the USSR and other Communist countries, in order to reduce its dependence on the West. There is, however, no nostalgia for the dependence on the Soviets that characterized the later Nasir years.

Although most educated Egyptians remain loyal to the ideals of secular nationalism and would not welcome an Iranian-style "Islamic Republic" in their country, they have moved away from Sadat's "liberal socialism." Some, however, are attracted to the extremist groups, and more will join them if economic and social conditions continue to deteriorate. The Muslim extremists do not accord any legitimacy to the present regime and look to Libya and other radical states to help them deliver Egypt from its state of *Jahiliyya* (pre-Islamic ignorance). It was easy for the extremists to exploit the bitter anger among the thousands of young men who serve in the "Security Police" at a monthly wage of six Egyptian pounds—so easy that they exploded into mass demonstrations that destroyed three tourist hotels near the Giza Pyramids in February 1986. Their shouted slogan was "They eat meat, we eat bread." Mubarak's regime is likely to be judged by the degree to which it succeeds in alleviating (if not solving) Egypt's economic problems. Relations with other Arab and Muslim peoples, while certainly relevant, are secondary in importance.

When will Egypt have its next revolution? Foretelling the future is a risky business, but historians do perceive patterns and parallels and sometimes try to lay down odds. Sadat's regime showed ominous parallels with that of Khedive Isma'il, whose deposition preceded by some two years the abortive Urabi Revolution, and with that of King Faruq, whose personal life and political ineptitude contributed to the 1952 Revolution. In all three cases, Western cultural and political influences impinged heavily on Egypt, fueling a reactive Muslim resistance. Egyptians rebel less often than most other Arabic-speaking peoples; their patience is legendary. They defer to autocratic rulers and bureaucrats to a degree that astonishes Syrians and Palestinians. Centuries of dependence on a strong ruler to ensure equitable distribution of Nile waters and protection from foreign invasion have created a political culture that glorifies order, tranquillity, and forbearance. Modernization has sapped this ethos, however, and the danger of a new popular uprising, even against so honest and self-effacing a leader as Husni Mubarak, is never remote.

The United States is spending about $2 billion dollars a year to support the Egyptian government, an aid figure higher than the amount given to any other country except Israel. U.S. aid policy in 1988 is geared more to politics than to need. In the case of Egypt, much of it helps to pay for the subsidies that keep down the prices of bread, rice, cooking oil, and butane gas, thus staving off a popular uprising like the one that occurred in January 1977. Egyptians comprehend this reasoning behind Washington's policy, and the degree of their gratitude depends on whether they want the present government to survive. Many Americans are working in Egypt to try to improve its irrigation system, village sanitation, pest control, family planning, communication networks, and economic conditions generally. Would it be better if they built showcase projects, such as the sports stadium and the concert hall erected by the USSR during the Nasir era? Or should they stand in the streets handing out one-hundred-dollar bills to individual Egyptians? The best projects are the ones that enable Egyptians to solve their own problems, but the greatest drawback to U.S. aid lies in its administration: Washington insists on a degree of supervision far stricter than that imposed on, say, Israel—a stance viewed by the Egyptians as an aspersion against their competence. I believe that Americans could try harder to develop personal relationships with Egyptians, who are generally friendly, hospitable, and eager to learn more about U.S. culture (to which they are heavily exposed by their televisions—a mixed blessing in my opinion).

Foreign governments and foundations should do more to promote scientific, technological, and intellectual development in Egypt, by supporting existing libraries, laboratories, universities, and higher institutes. The brain drain is a serious threat to Egyptian society and culture. It has already cost Egypt much of its traditional leadership within the Arabic-speaking world. Many Egyptian professionals and entrepreneurs have gone to Europe or the United States, where they have made their fortunes or found fame; the time has come for these men and women to start repaying some of the benefits they brought with them from Mother Egypt. The model for such a program could be adapted to Egypt's needs from a movement that nurtured a neighboring state in an earlier era: cultural Zionism.

Egypt is a great and enduring country with a civilization that has lasted for nearly sixty centuries. It has one of the largest and most beneficent rivers in the world, heavily modified by the hand of humanity but capable of further improvement. Its people are diligent and resourceful. The storms of Middle East politics may rumble around and disturb their equanimity. But Egypt has weathered such storms before, and its people are determined to survive.

Glossary of Terms and Places

Abbasid dynasty (ab-BAS-sid): Arab family descended from an uncle of Muhammad named Abbas that ruled from Baghdad over parts of the Muslim world (750–1258)

Abdin Palace (ab-DEEN): Official residence of Egypt's ruler up to 1952, located in central Cairo; later used by Sadat and Mubarak for government offices

Abu-Kir, Battle of (ah-boo-KEER): British victory over Napoleon (1798)

al-Ahram (el-ah-RAHM): Influential Cairo daily newspaper

al-Akhbar (el-akh-BAHR): Popular Cairo daily newspaper

Alexandria: Egypt's major Mediterranean port city

Anglo-Egyptian Sudan: Official name of the Sudan from 1899 to 1956, during the time when it was a condominium of Egypt and Great Britain

Anglo-Egyptian Treaty: 1936 pact defining Britain's military position in Egypt, denounced by Egypt in 1951 and replaced in 1954 by another treaty, which in turn was abrogated following the 1956 Suez Affair

Aqaba, Gulf of (AH-ka-ba): Inlet from the Red Sea, fronted by Egypt, Israel, Jordan, and Saudi Arabia; right of access to this waterway was contested in 1956 and 1967

Arab League: Political association of Arab states, founded in 1945; formerly headquartered in Cairo, it was moved to Tunis, and Egypt was expelled from membership following its 1979 peace treaty with Israel

Arab Legion: Former name of the army of Transjordan or Jordan

Arab nationalism: Movement or ideology that seeks unification of all Arab countries and their independence from non-Arab control; led by Egypt from 1945 until 1974

Arab socialism: Ideology that calls for state control over Arab economies; espoused by Gamal Abd al-Nasir, especially after 1958

Arab Socialist Union: Egypt's sole political party (1962–1978)

al-Arish (el-a-REESH): Abortive peace treaty between France and Britain (1800), providing for evacuation of French forces from Egypt

Armenians: Indo-European Christian people originating in the mountains of eastern Anatolia; later scattered throughout the Middle East

ASU: *See* Arab Socialist Union

Aswan (ass-WAHN): (1) City in Upper Egypt; (2) site of the High Dam, built for Egypt by the USSR (1958–1969)

Attrition, War of: Artillery and air struggle between Egypt and Israel (1969–1970), which ended when both sides accepted the Rogers Peace Plan

Autonomy Talks, Palestinian: Inconclusive negotiations between Egypt and Israel, following the 1979 Treaty, aimed at achieving autonomous status for Gaza Strip and West Bank Palestinians, suspended since 1982

Ayyubid dynasty (eye-YOO-bid): Salah al-Din and his descendants, who ruled in Egypt (1171–1250) and in Syria (1174–1260)

al-Azhar (el-OZ-har): Muslim mosque-university in Cairo, founded in 971

Baghdad Pact: Anti-Communist military alliance formed in 1955, renamed CENTO after Iraq withdrew from membership in 1958

Balfour Declaration: Official statement in 1917 by Britain's foreign secretary supporting the establishment of a Jewish national home in Palestine

Bandung Conference (ban-DOONG): 1955 meeting of Asian and African leaders, including Nasir

Bank Misr: Egyptian bank and holding company founded by Tal'at Harb in 1920

Bar Lev Line: Israel's fortified defense line east of the Suez Canal (1967–1973)

Ba'th (BAHTH): Arab nationalist and socialist party ruling Syria and Iraq since 1963

Bevin-Sidqi Agreement: Abortive pact reached in 1946 between the foreign ministers of Britain and Egypt regarding the Sudan

Black Saturday: The burning and looting of European buildings in central Cairo on 26 January 1952, widely cited as a precursor of the revolution of 23 July

British Agency: Offices and residence of Britain's chief political and diplomatic officer in Cairo to 1914; later called the Residency

Byzantine Empire: Roman Empire of the East (330–1453), having its capital at Constantinople and professing Greek Orthodox Christianity

Cairo: Capital of Egypt, founded by the Fatimids (969)

Cairo University: Egypt's first secular university, founded in 1908 as the "National University"; reorganized in 1925 and set up in Giza

caliph (KAY-lif): Muhammad's successor as head of the Muslim ummah

Camp David: (1) U.S. president's vacation home in northern Maryland; (2) site of intensive peace talks among Begin, Carter, and Sadat in September 1978; (3) adjective applied to the Egyptian-Israeli Peace Treaty or to the subsequent process of negotiations between the two states

Capitulations: System by which Muslim rulers gave extraterritorial immunity from local laws and taxes to subjects of Western countries

centers of power: Cabal of Egyptian leaders at end of Nasir era; term commonly applied to the political enemies of Anwar al-Sadat

CENTO: Central Treaty Organization. *See* Baghdad Pact

Century Storage Scheme: Elaborate system of dams proposed for the tributaries of the Nile, a proposal superseded by the construction of the Aswan High Dam

Charter, National: *See* National Charter

Circassian: Native (or descendant of a native) of the Caucasus region east of the Black Sea; term applied in Egypt to the later Mamluks

Citadel: Fortress built by Salah al-Din (and by later rulers of Egypt) on the Muqattam hills overlooking Cairo

Copt: Egyptian (or Ethiopian) Monophysite Christian, constituting about 10 percent of Egypt's population

Corrective Revolution: Sadat's purge of his political enemies (15 May 1971), purportedly to liberalize Egypt's government

Crusades: European Christian military expeditions against Muslims between the eleventh and fifteenth centuries

Debt Commission: Council representing Egypt's major European creditor nations between 1876 and 1914

Delta: Triangular area of the Nile north of Cairo to the Mediterranean Sea

Dinshaway Incident (den-sha-WYE): British atrocity against Egyptian peasants in 1906

Dual Control: Joint Anglo-French financial administration in Egypt (1878–1882)

Dufferin Commission: Group sent by the British government to study Egypt's government (and to recommend improvements) just after the 1882 occupation

Eisenhower Doctrine: Official U.S. policy statement opposing Communism's spread in the Middle East (1957), interpreted by Egyptians as an attempt to limit Nasir's influence over other Arab countries

Ezbekia Gardens (ez-beh-KEE-ya): Public park in central Cairo, often the site of political rallies or demonstrations

Faluja (fa-LOO-ja): Palestinian village, site of lengthy siege during 1948 War, regarded by the Egyptians as their most heroic stand against the Israeli army

al-Fatah (el-FET-ah): Palestinian guerrilla group founded by Yasir Arafat

Fatimid dynasty (FAW-ti-mid): Arab family of Isma'ili Shi'is claiming descent from Ali and Fatimah, ruling North Africa (909–972) and Egypt (969–1171), and vying with other dynasties for control of Syria, the Hijaz, and Yemen

feddan (fed-DAN): Egyptian unit of land measure, equal to 1.038 acres

Federation of Arab Republics: Abortive combination of Egypt, Libya, and Syria, tentatively accepted by the three countries in 1971

Fertile Crescent: Modern term for the lands extending from the eastern Mediterranean, through Syria and Mesopotamia, to the Gulf

fez: Crimson brimless head-covering worn in the later Ottoman Empire and in some successor-states, including Egypt up to the 1952 Revolution

fida'iyin (fe-DA-ee-yeen): People who sacrifice themselves for a cause; term often applied to Palestinians fighting against Israel, or to militant Shi'is, formerly applied also to Egyptians fighting British in the Suez Canal zone

Four Reserved Points: Britain's limitations on its unilateral declaration of Egypt's independence (1922) and a sticking point in later negotiations

Free Officers: Secret Egyptian army organization, led by Gamal Abd al-Nasir, that conspired successfully to overthrow Faruq in 1952

Fustat (foos-TAWT): Egyptian garrison town in early Islamic times; later an administrative center, south of modern Cairo

Gaza Strip: Small part of southwestern Palestine held by Egyptian forces in 1948 and inhabited wholly by Arabs, administered by Egypt (1948–1956 and 1957–1967), captured by Israel in 1956 and 1967, and administered by Israel since 1967

Geneva Conference: December 1973 meeting of Israel, Egypt, and Jordan, co-chaired by the United States and the USSR; adjourned since then

Gezira Sporting Club (geh-ZEE-ra): Cairo social club that used to exclude Egyptians from membership

Gidi Pass: Strategic point in western Sinai, captured by Israel in 1956 and 1967 and relinquished to UN force in the 1975 Sinai agreement

Golan Heights (go-LAHN): Mountainous area of southwestern Syria, occupied by Israel since 1967 and the scene of intense fighting in October 1973 War

guild: Association of manufacturers or merchants of a particular product, a common social institution in Egypt until the nineteenth century

Gulf, the: The body of water separating Iran from the Arabian Peninsula and connecting the Shatt al-Arab to the Arabian Sea

Hashimite (HA-she-mite): (1) Member of the family descended from Hashim; (2) member of the dynasty ruling the Hijaz (1916–1925), Syria (1918–1920), Iraq (1921–1958), and Jordan (1921–)

Heliopolis: (1) Middle-class suburb of Cairo; (2) site of 1800 battle between Ottoman and French forces in Egypt

High Commissioner: Title of Britain's chief political representative in Egypt (1914–1936)

Hijaz (heh-JAZZ): Mountainous area of western Arabia, ruled by Mehmet Ali in the early nineteenth century

Hilwan (hel-WAHN): Industrial center south of Cairo

Ikhshidid dynasty (ikh-SHEE-did): Egypt's ruling family (934–969)

imam (ee-MAWM): (1) Muslim religious or political leader; (2) one of the succession of Muslim leaders, beginning with Ali, regarded as legitimate by the Shi'is; (3) leader of Muslim congregational worship

infitah (in-fi-TAH): Sadat's policy of free enterprise, a reaction against the Arab socialism of Gamal Abd al-Nasir

Isma'ili (iss-ma-EE-lee): Pertaining to Seven-Imam Shi'ism

Ismailia (iss-ma-ee-LEE-ya): Egyptian city on the Suez Canal; site of Suez Canal Company headquarters

Jeep Case: 1949 court case involving Muslim Brothers in the Egyptian army

al-Jihad al-Jadid (el-jee-HAD el-je-DEED): Muslim revolutionary organization credited with plotting the assassination of Sadat in 1981

jizyah (JIZ-ya): Per capita tax paid by non-Muslim males under Muslim rule

Johnston plan: Proposal for sharing Jordan River waters between Israel and the Arab states, advanced by Eric Johnston in 1955 and partially implemented by Israel (and opposed by Egypt and other Arab states) after 1963

July Laws: Nasir's decrees instituting Arab socialism (1961)

Kafr al-Dawar (KEF-red-da-WAHR): Delta industrial city; site of August 1952 workers' uprising, suppressed by the new revolutionary regime

kharaj (kha-RODGE): Land tax paid on agricultural produce

Khartum (khar-TOOM): (1) Capital of the Sudan; (2) site of August 1967 Arab summit conference, opposing peace negotiations with Israel

khedive (khe-DEEV): "Viceroy," title of Egypt's ruler (1867–1914)

Kilometer 101: Site of Egyptian-Israeli military talks following October 1973 War

Lavon Affair: Israeli political scandal that originated in a botched attempt to undermine Egyptian relations with the United States in 1954

Liberal Constitutionalist party: Largest political rival of the Wafd party from 1922 to 1952

Liberation Rally: First organization created by Nasir to mobilize Egyptians to support his policies

Liberation Square: Major open area in Cairo, east of the Nile

Mamluk (mem-LOOK): (1) Turkish or Circassian slave soldier; (2) member of a military oligarchy that ruled Egypt and Syria (1250–1517) and retained power in some areas until their destruction by Mehmet Ali in 1811

Middle East Supply Center: Cairo-based British organization coordinating manufacturing and distribution in Arab states and Iran during World War II

MiG: Any one of several types of Soviet-made fighter planes

Milner mission: Official British commission sent in 1919 to ascertain Egyptian political aspirations; report indicated strong support for independence

Mitla Pass: Strategic mountain pass in western Sinai, captured by Israel in 1956 and 1967 and relinquished to a UN buffer force in 1975

Mixed Courts: Egyptian tribunals (1876–1949) for civil cases involving foreign nationals protected by the Capitulations

Monophysite (muh-NAW-fiz-zite): Pertaining to Christians (including Copts) who believe that Christ had a single, wholly divine nature in his person, a view condemned by the Council of Chalcedon in 451

Montreux Convention: 1937 agreement to phase out Capitulations and Mixed Court system in Egypt

Muslim Brothers, Society of: Political group, strong in Egypt (1930–1954) and in several other Arab countries, calling for an Islamic political and social system, and opposing Western power and cultural influences; banned in Egypt by Nasir in 1954 but allowed to revive under Sadat

Nasirism: Western term for Nasir's political philosophy and program, including nationalism, neutralism, and Arab socialism

National Assembly: Egypt's parliament under Nasir

National Charter: 1962 Egyptian document describing the goals of Arab socialism

National Congress of Popular Forces: 1962 meeting called by Nasir to debate and to adopt the National Charter

National Democratic party: Egypt's governing party since 1978

National party: Egyptian movement demanding independence from foreign control; also a name applied to followers of Urabi in 1881–1882 and to those of Mustafa Kamil from 1895, though not formally until 1907

National Union: Nasir's organization to mobilize UAR citizens (1958–1962)

Negev (ne-GEV): Desert in southern Israel

Nizam-i-Jedid (ne-ZAWM-e-je-DEED): Ottoman military and political reform program promulgated by Selim III but crushed by the janissaries in 1807; original basis for Mehmet Ali's westernizing reforms in Egypt

October War: War started by Egypt and Syria in 1973 to regain lands occupied by Israel since 1967; also called "Yom Kippur War" or "Ramadan War"

Opera House: Large theater in central Cairo built in 1869 for ceremonies marking Suez Canal opening; destroyed by fire in 1971

Ottoman Empire: A multinational Islamic state (1299–1922) that began in northwestern Anatolia and spread across the Balkans, most of southwest Asia, and the North African coast; ruled over Egypt (1517–1798)

Palestine Liberation Organization: Group formed in 1964 by Arab heads of state; now the umbrella organization for most Palestinian military, political, economic, and social organizations, and led by Yasir Arafat

pan-Arabism: Movement to unite all Arabs in one state, especially popular from 1945 to about 1974

pan-Islam: Movement calling for political unity of all Muslims, promoted by late nineteenth- and early twentieth-century Ottoman governments

Paris Peace Conference: Meeting of the victorious Allies after World War I to restore peace in Europe and the Middle East; Egypt's Wafd (delegation) was formed to attend that conference but was not admitted

Partition Plan for Palestine (UN): Proposed division of the Palestine mandate into Jewish and Arab states, approved by the UN General Assembly in 1947 (the Jewish state was the basis for the State of Israel) but opposed by Egypt and other Arab states

People's Assembly: Sadat's name for Egypt's National Assembly

pharaonic: Pertaining to ancient Egypt or to its rulers, or to anything that distinguishes Egypt from all other Arab countries

PLO: *See* Palestine Liberation Organization

Popular Front for the Liberation of Palestine: Marxist Palestinian group led by George Habash, noted for its extremism

Port Said (sa-EED): Egyptian city at which the Suez Canal meets the Mediterranean; invaded by British and French troops during 1956 Suez War, it became for Egyptians a symbol of popular resistance to Western imperialism

positive neutrality: Nasir's policy of not siding with either the Communist countries or the West, but seeking to reconcile the two blocs

Rafah (RAH-fah): Sinai village near Gaza Strip; now the border town between Egypt and Israel

RCC: *See* Revolutionary Command Council
Residency: *See* British Agency
Revolutionary Command Council: Governing board established by the 1952 junta
Rhodes: Mediterranean island; site of the 1949 "proximity talks" between some Arab states (including Egypt) and Israel, mediated by Ralph Bunche
Rogers Peace Plan: U.S. proposal (1969–1970) to end the War of Attrition, calling on Israel to withdraw from lands occupied since 1967
Sa'dist party: Breakaway faction from the Wafd in 1937, led by Ahmad Mahir and Mahmud Fahmi al-Nuqrashi, and often included in anti-Wafdist coalition governments before 1952
SAM: Any one of several types of Soviet-supplied surface-to-air missiles, used extensively by Egypt in the October 1973 War
Sa'ud dynasty (sa-OOD): Arab family of Najd supporting Wahhabi doctrines since the reign of Muhammad ibn Sa'ud (1746–1765); rulers of most of the Arabian Peninsula during the twentieth century
SCUA: *See* Suez Canal Users Association
Security Council Resolution 242: November 1967 statement of principles for achieving peace between the Arabs and Israel, accepted by both sides (but with differing interpretations) and frequently reaffirmed since then
Security Council Resolution 338: Cease-fire resolution that ended the October 1973 War, calling for direct talks between Israel and the Arab states
Shabab Muhammad (sheh-BAB moo-HOM-mad): Revolutionary Muslim youth movement in the 1970s
Shame, Law of: Authoritarian decree by Sadat (1980), approved by a national plebiscite, that severely limited public criticism of his policies
Sharm al-Shaykh (sharm esh-SHAYKH): Fortified point near the Straits of Tiran used by Egypt from 1949 to 1956 and in 1967 to hamper Israeli passage between Gulf of Aqaba and Red Sea
Shaykh al-Sadat (SHAYKH es-sa-DAT): Highly prestigious Egyptian leader of the descendants of Muhammad
Shepheard's Hotel: Famous Cairo hotel, destroyed by fire on Black Saturday (1952) and later rebuilt in another location
Shi'i (SHEE-ee): Muslim who believes that the leadership of the *ummah* should have gone, after Muhammad's death, to Ali, to whom special legislative powers and spiritual knowledge were vouchsafed
shuttle diplomacy: Kissinger's method of mediating between the Arab countries and Israel (1974–1975), strongly supported by Sadat
Sinai Peninsula: Egyptian territory between the Suez Canal and the Israeli border, invaded by Israel in 1949, 1956, and 1967, then occupied by Israel up to 1982
Students' Day: Annual observance commemorating the students' (and workers') uprising of 21 February 1946 against the British occupation of Egypt
Suez Affair: British, French, and Israeli attack on Egypt (1956), following Nasir's nationalization of the Suez Canal Company

Suez Canal: Human-made channel connecting the Mediterranean and Red Seas, opened in 1869 but closed in 1956–1957 and 1967–1975 due to Egyptian-Israeli fighting; administered by Egypt since July 1956

Suez Canal Users Association: Group proposed by Dulles to run the canal after Nasir had nationalized the Suez Canal Company in 1956

Sufi (SOO-fee): Pertaining to Muslim mystics, or to their beliefs, practices, or organizations

Sunni (SOON-nee): (1) A Muslim who accepts the legitimacy of the caliphs who succeeded Muhammad and adheres to one of the legal rites developed in the early caliphal period; (2) conscientious follower of Muhammad's sunnah

System of Tutelage: Method by which Nasir's government controlled university students' political activities; ended following 1968 protest demonstrations

Taba Affair: 1906 Anglo-Ottoman dispute over possession of the Sinai, resolved by a joint boundary commission; noteworthy because Egypt's nationalists supported Ottoman over Egyptian claims

Takfir wa al-Hijrah (tek-FEER wal-HIJ-ra): Popular Muslim fundamentalist organization, opposed to Egyptian-Israeli Peace Treaty

tax-farming: System of collecting government imposts that allows the collector to keep a share of the proceeds, common in Egypt up to the nineteenth century

Tel-el-Kebir (tel-el-ke-BEER): Site of 1882 battle in which a British expeditionary force decisively defeated the Egyptian army under Ahmad Urabi, leading to the British occupation of Egypt

30 March Program: Egyptian government's promises to restive students (1968)

Tiran (tee-RAHN): Straits linking the Aqaba Gulf to the Red Sea

Treaty of Friendship and Cooperation: 1971 Soviet-Egyptian pact, renounced by Sadat in 1976

Tripartite Aggression: *See* Suez Affair

Tulunid dynasty: Turkish family ruling Egypt (868–905)

Twelve-Imam Shi'i: Any Muslim who believes that the leadership of the *ummah* should have gone to Ali and his descendants, of whom the twelfth is hidden but will someday return to restore righteousness; also known as "Imami," "Ja'fari," or "Twelver"

UAR: *See* United Arab Republic

ulama (OO-le-ma): Collective term for Muslim scholars and jurists

ummah (OOM-ma): (1) The political, social, and spiritual community of Muslims; (2) Egyptian moderate party (1907–1914); (3) Sudanese party opposed to union with Egypt

UNEF: *See* United Nations Emergency Force

United Arab Republic: Union of Egypt and Syria (1958–1961) under Nasir

United Nations Emergency Force: International army stationed between Egypt and Israel (1957–1967 and 1974–)

Wafd (WAHFT): Egypt's unofficial delegation to the Paris Peace Conference; later Egypt's main nationalist party up to 1952, revived in 1978

Wahhabi (wa-HAH-bee): Fundamentalist Muslim sect founded by Muhammad ibn Abd al-Wahhab (d. 1787), now dominant in Saudi Arabia

waqf (WAHKF): Muslim endowment of land or other property; usually intended for a beneficent or pious purpose, but sometimes used in Egypt before 1952 to protect estates from excessive division under Muslim inheritance laws

wazir (wa-ZEER): (1) Egyptian government minister; (2) powerful Fatimid or Ayyubid official

West Bank: Area of Arab Palestine annexed by Jordan in 1948 and captured by Israel in 1967; called "Judea and Samaria" by some Israelis

White Paper: British policy statement (1939) limiting Jewish immigration into and land purchase rights within the Palestine mandate

Yamit (ya-MEET): Israeli industrial town built in occupied Sinai and destroyed before its restoration to Egypt in 1982

Yemen civil war (YEH-men): Struggle (1962–1967) between Saudi-backed royalists and Egypt-supported republican revolutionaries in north Yemen

Young Egypt: Egyptian nationalist movement, popular in the 1930s, having strong Fascist leanings

Young Turks: Group of nationalist students and army officers who took control of the Ottoman government in 1908, restored its constitution, and instituted westernizing reforms

Zionism: Movement to create or to maintain a Jewish state in Palestine/Israel

Biographical Dictionary

Abbas Hilmi I (ab-BASS HEL-mee) (1813–1854): Governor of Egypt (r. 1848–1854)

Abbas Hilmi II (1874–1944): Khedive of Egypt (r. 1892–1914)

Abd al-Hadi, Ibrahim (AB-del-HA-dee) (1898–1981): Prime minister (1949) noted for his repression of Muslim Brothers and other dissidents

Abd al-Halim (AB-del-ha-LEEM) (1830–1894): Unsuccessful claimant to Egyptian throne and possible supporter of the Urabi Revolution

Abd al-Nasir, Gamal: *See* al-Nasir, Gamal Abd

Abduh, Muhammad (AB-doo, moo-HOM-mad) (1849–1905): Muslim reformer

Abdulhamid II (AB-dul-ha-MEET): Ottoman sultan (r. 1876–1909)

Abu al-Dhahab (AH-budh-DHEH-heb) (–1775): Mamluk ruler of Egypt

Adli Yakan: *See* Yakan, Adli

al-Afghani, Jamal al-Din (el-af-GHAW-nee, je-MAWL ed-DEEN) (1838– 1897): Influential pan-Islamic agitator and reformer

Ali Bey "al-Kabir" (1728–1773): Mamluk ruler and early westernizing reformer

Allenby, Edmund (1861–1936): Commander of Egyptian Expeditionary Force in World War I, later high commissioner for Egypt (1919–1925)

Amir, Abd al-Hakim (AH-mur, AB-del-ha-KEEM) (1919–1967): Political leader under Nasir; committed suicide after June War

Arafat, Yasir (ah-rah-FAT, YAH-sir) (1921–): Palestinian Arab nationalist, founder of al-Fatah, and PLO leader since 1968

Arif, Abd al-Salam (AH-ref, AB-des-sa-LAAM) (1921–1966): Arab nationalist leader of Iraq (1958, 1963–1966)

al-Asad, Hafiz (el-ESS-ed, HAW-fez): President of Syria (1970–)

al-Attar, Hasan (el-at-TAWR, HAH-san) (1766–1835): Muslim scholar

Azzam, Abd al-Rahman (az-ZAM, AB-der-rah-MAN) (1893–1976): First secretary general of the Arab League

Badran, Shams al-Din (bed-RAN, SHEM-sed-DEEN): Leading politician under Nasir

al-Banna, Hasan (el-BEN-na, HAS-san) (1906–1949): Founder of the Society of the Muslim Brothers

al-Barudi, Mahmud Sami (el-ba-ROO-dee, mah-MOOD SA-mee) (1839–1904): Egyptian army officer, poet, and nationalist prime minister (1882)

Begin, Menachem (BAY-gin, me-NAH-khem) (1913–): Leader of Israel's right-wing Herut party and Likud coalition, and prime minister (1977–1983)

Ben Gurion, David (1886–1973): Zionist pioneer, politician, and writer; Israel's defense and prime minister (1948–1953 and 1955–1963)

Bonaparte, Napoleon (1769–1821): French general who invaded and conquered Egypt in 1798, escaped in 1799, and later became emperor of France

Cromer, Lord (1841–1917): British consul-general (1883–1907) and a financial and administrative reformer, but resented by Egyptian nationalists

de Lesseps, Ferdinand (1805–1894): French entrepreneur, founder of the Suez Canal project

Dulles, John Foster (1888–1959): U.S. secretary of state under Eisenhower; opposed Britain, France, and Israel during Suez Crisis

Eden, Anthony (1897–1986): British statesman; prime minister during Suez Crisis (1956)

Fahmi, Abd al-Aziz (FEH-mee, AB-del-ah-ZEEZ) (1870–1951): Nationalist and early supporter of Sa'd Zaghlul

Fahmi, Mustafa (1840–1914): Pro-British prime minister (1895–1908)

Farid, Muhammad (fa-REED) (1868–1919): Egyptian nationalist leader

Faruq (fa-ROOK) (1920–1965): King of Egypt (1936–1952)

Faysal (FAY-sul): Son of Abd al-Aziz ibn Saud and king of Saudi Arabia (1964–1975)

Fu'ad I, Ahmad (foo-ODD) (1868–1936): King of Egypt (1917–1936)

Ghali, Butros (GHA-lee, BOOT-ros) (1846–1910): Pro-British prime minister, assassinated by a nationalist

Glubb, John Bagot (1897–1986): British author; former commander of Jordan's Arab Legion, dismissed in 1956 by King Husayn

Gordon, Charles (1833–1885): British general; leader of Anglo-Egyptian force besieged by the mahdi of the Sudan and eventually defeated

Gorst, [John] Eldon (1861–1911): British financial adviser, then agent and consul-general (1907–1911); sympathetic to Khedive Abbas

Harb, Talat (HARB, TULL-ott) (1867–1941): Founder of Bank Misr

Hasanayn, Muhammad Ahmad (HAH-sa-nayn) (1889–1946): Adviser to Kings Fu'ad and Faruq

Haykal, Muhammad Hasanayn (HAY-kal) (1924–): Editor of *al-Ahram* and adviser to Nasir and (initially) to Sadat

Haykal, Muhammad Husayn (1888–1956): Author, editor, and Liberal Constitutionalist party leader

Husayn (hoo-SAYN) (1935–): King of Jordan (1953–)

Husayn, Ahmad (1911–1982): Founder of Young Egypt

Husayn, Ahmad (1902–): Minister of social affairs; Egypt's ambassador to the United States in 1956

Husayn, Taha (1889–1973): Author, editor, and education minister under the last Wafd party government (1950–1952)

Husayn Kamil (1853–1917): Sultan of Egypt (r. 1914–1917); placed in power by British in lieu of Khedive Abbas

Ibn Saud (ibn-sa-OOD) (1880–1953): Arab leader who conquered most of the Arabian Peninsula between 1902 and 1930; also known as Abd al-Aziz

Ibrahim (ib-ra-HEEM) (1789–1848): Son of Mehmet Ali, conqueror and governor of Syria (1832–1840), and briefly governor of Egypt (1848)

Isma'il (iss-ma-EEL) (1830–1895): Khedive of Egypt (1863–1879), noted for his ambitious reforms, which put his government heavily in debt

al-Jabarti, Abd al-Rahman (el-ga-BAR-tee) (1754–1822): Chronicler of Egypt in the era of Napoleon

Jarring, Gunnar (YAR-ring, GUN-nar) (1907–): UN mediator between Israel and the Arab states from 1967 to 1971

Jawhar (GOW-har): Arab general who conquered Egypt for the Fatimids (969)

Jawish, Abd al-Aziz (ga-WEESH or sha-WEESH) (1872–1929): Egyptian nationalist and pan-Islamic writer, editor, and educator

Johnston, Eric (1895–): American businessman sent by Eisenhower in 1953 to negotiate Jordan River development scheme for Israel and Jordan

Kamil, Mustafa (KA-mel, moos-TAH-fa) (1874–1908): Egyptian nationalist leader

Killearn *See* Lampson, Miles

Kitchener, [Horatio] Herbert (1850–1916): Commander of Anglo-Egyptian army that retook the Sudan (1896–1898); later British consul-general in Egypt (1911–1914), best-known for encouraging the "Five Feddan Law"

Kléber, Jean-Baptiste (klay-BAYR) (1753–1800): Napoleon's successor as commander of the French occupying force in Egypt

Lampson, Miles (1880–1964): British high commissioner and ambassador in Egypt (1934–1946) who forced Faruq to appoint an all-Wafdist cabinet in 1942

Lloyd, George Ambrose (1879–1941): British high commissioner (1925–1929)

Lutfi al-Sayyid: *See* al-Sayyid, Ahmad Lutfi

Mahdi (of the Sudan): Muhammad Ahmad (1848–1885), leader of successful Sudanese rebellion against Egyptian rule

Mahir, Ahmad (MA-her) (1885–1945): Sa'dist party leader and prime minister (1944–1945)

Mahir, Ali (1882–1960): Independent politician; first civilian prime minister after 23 July 1952 Revolution

Mahmud, Muhammad (1877–1941): Liberal Constitutionalist party leader and prime minister

Mahmud II (1785–1839): Ottoman sultan (r. 1808–1839) and major westernizing reformer; opposed by Mehmet Ali

al-Maraghi, Mustafa (el-ma-RAH-ghee) (1881–1945): Azharite leader; strong backer of Faruq's bid to become caliph

Mar'i, Sayyid (MAR-ee) (1913–): Influential politician under Faruq, Nasir, and Sadat

McMahon, [Arthur] Henry (1862–1949): British high commissioner (1914–1916), best known for the Husayn-McMahon correspondence

Mehmet Ali (meh-MET a-LEE or moo-HOM-mad AH-lee) (1769–1849): Turkish/Albanian adventurer who gained control of Egypt, then of Syria, and instituted many westernizing reforms (r. 1805–1848)

Meir, Golda (may-EER) (1897–1978): Israel's prime minister (1969–1974)

Menou, Jacques "Abdallah" (meh-NOO) (1750–1810): Last leader of the French occupying force in Egypt (1800–1802)

al-Misri, Aziz Ali (el-MASS-ree) (1879–1965): Popular Arab nationalist general, considered by the RCC for the Egyptian presidency in 1952

Mubarak, Hosni (moo-BAH-rak, HOS-nee) (1929–): Egypt's president (1981–)

Muhyi al-Din, Zakariya (MOH-yed-DEEN, za-ka-REE-ya) (1918–): One of the Free Officers, designated by Nasir (when he resigned) to succeed him

Mukhtar, Mahmud (mookh-TAHR) (1891–1934): Egyptian sculptor

Musa, Salama (MOOS-sa, sa-LA-ma) (1887–1958): Author and editor, well-known advocate of socialism and logical positivism

Nagib, Muhammad (ne-GEEB) (1901–1984): Titular leader of 1952 Egyptian Revolution

al-Nahhas, Mustafa (en-na-HASS, moos-TAH-fa) (1879–1965): Leader of Egypt's Wafd party (1927–1952)

Napoleon III (1808–1873): Emperor of France (r. 1851–1870) and strong backer of De Lesseps' Suez Canal project

al-Nasir, Gamal Abd (en-NAW-ser, ga-MAL abd) (1918–1970): Leader of the 1952 military coup that overthrew Egypt's monarchy; later prime minister, then president (r. 1954–1970) and advocate of reform and Arab unity

Nasser: *See* al-Nasir, Gamal Abd

Nazli (nez-LEE) (–1913): Egyptian princess and backer of Zaghlul

Nelson, Horatio (1758–1805): Commander of British fleet that defeated the French at Battle of Abu Kir (1798)

Nubar, Boghos (noo-BAHR) (1825–1899): Founder of the Mixed Courts and several times prime minister of Egypt

al-Nuqrashi, Mahmud Fahmi (en-nuh-KRAH-shee) (1888–1948): Sa'dist party leader and prime minister, assassinated by the Muslim Brothers

al-Qadhafi, Mu'ammar (el-gad-DOF-fee, moo-AHM-mar) (1942–): Libyan president (1969–) and strong advocate of Arab unity

Qutb, Sayyid (KOTb) (1903–1966): Author and influential spokesman for the Muslim Brothers, executed by the Nasir government

Ramadan, Hafiz (ra-ma-DAWN, HAW-fez) (1879–1955): National party leader

Rifqi, Uthman (RIF-kee, oss-MAHN) (1839–1886): Egyptian war minister (1881)

Riyad, Mustafa (ree-YOD) (1834–1911): Egyptian prime minister (1879–1881 and 1893–1894)

Roosevelt, Kermit: U.S. intelligence agent and friend of the Free Officers

Rushdi, Husayn (ROOSH-dee, hu-SAYN) (1863–1928): Prime minister (1914–1919)

Sabri, Ali (SOB-ree) (1920–): Prime minister (1962–1965), regarded by the United States government as having Communist sympathies

al-Sadat, Anwar (es-sa-DAT, AN-war) (1918–1981): President (r. 1970–1981); relaxed many of Nasir's authoritarian policies, started October 1973 War against Israel, and signed 1979 Egyptian-Israeli Peace Treaty

al-Sadat, Jihan (gee-HAN) (1933–): Wife of Anwar al-Sadat and feminist leader

Sa'id (sa-EED) (1822–1863): Viceroy of Egypt (1854–1863) who signed Suez Canal concession

Saint-Simon, Claude Henri (sa-see-MON): French utopian socialist and advocate of the Suez Canal

Salah al-Din (sa-LAH ed-DEEN): Arabic name for the Kurdish military adventurer who took Egypt from the Fatimids (1171) and Syria from the Zengids (1174), defeated the Crusaders (1187), and regained Jerusalem for Islam (1187)

Sannu', Ya'qub (sa-NOOA, ya-KOOB) (1839–1912): Jewish Egyptian nationalist and satirical journalist

Sa'ud (ibn Abd al-Aziz) (sa-OOD) (1902–1969): King of Saudi Arabia (r. 1953–1964)

al-Sayyid, Ahmad Lutfi (es-SAY-yid, AH-mad LOOT-fee) (1872–1963): Egyptian liberal nationalist and educator

al-Shadhili, Sa'd al-Din (esh-SHAZ-lee, SOD-ed-DEEN) (1922–): General in October 1973 War, later a trenchant critic of Sadat's policies

Sharif, Muhammad (sha-REEF) (1823–1887): Egyptian prime minister (1881–1882) and supporter of first constitution

Sharon, Ariel (sha-ROAN, ah-ri-EL) (1928–): Israeli general and war minister during Israel's invasion of Lebanon (1982)

al-Shuqayri, Ahmad (esh-shoo-KAY-ree) (1907?–1980): First PLO leader (1964–1968)

Siddiq, Isma'il (sed-DEEK) (1821–1876): Powerful politician under Isma'il

Sidqi, Isma'il (SID-kee, iss-ma-EEL) (1875–1950): Egyptian politician, strongly opposed to the Wafd and sometimes regarded as royalist

Sirag al-Din, Fu'ad (se-RAH-ged-DEEN, foo-ODD) (1912–): Wafdist politician

Stack, Lee (1868–1924): Commander of Egypt's army, whose assassination caused a political crisis that ended the first Wafdist government

Tawfiq (tow-FEEK) (1852–1892): Khedive of Egypt (r. 1879–1892)

Thabit, Karim (TA-bet, ka-REEM) (1902–1964): Leading journalist and politician under Faruq, who advocated a major role for Egypt in the 1948 Palestine War

Tharwat, Abd al-Khaliq (SAR-wat, AB-del-KHA-lek) (1873–1928): Liberal Constitutionalist politician, prime minister, and drafter of the 1923 constitution

U Thant (1909-1974): Secretary general of the United Nations who withdrew UNEF from Sinai shortly before the June 1967 War

Ubayd, Makram (oo-BAYD, MEK-rum) (1889–1961): Leading politician, who broke with the Wafd party in 1943 and published an exposé against Nahhas

Urabi, Ahmad (oo-RAH-bee) (1841–1911): Egyptian army officer and nationalist, who led a revolution against Egypt's Dual Control (1881–1882)

Uthman, Uthman Ahmad (oss-MAHN): Leading Egyptian contractor

Wingate, Reginald (1861–1953): British high commissioner (1916–1919)

Yakan, Adli (YEH-ghen, ODD-lee) (1864–1933): Leader of the Liberal Constitutionalist party; prime minister who negotiated for Egypt's independence with British Foreign Secretary Curzon in 1921

Yunus, Mahmud (YOO-nus) (1912–): Director of nationalized Suez Canal Authority

Yusuf, Ali (YOO-sef) (1863–1913): Influential newspaper editor friendly to Khedive Abbas

Zaghlul, Sa'd (zagh-LOOL, SOD) (1860–1927): Egyptian nationalist leader and founder of the Wafd, education and justice minister before World War I, prime minister (1924), and "Father of Egyptian Independence"

Bibliographic Essay

Bibliographic control for the study of modern Egyptian history is almost a contradiction in terms. A reader whose interest in Egypt is that of a new resident should first turn to *Cairo: A Practical Guide* (Cairo: American University in Cairo Press, 1984) and to Kay Showker, *Fodor's Guide to Egypt: 1986* (New York & London: Fodor's Travel Guides, 1985). Young readers can use Shirley Kay, *The Egyptians: How They Live and Work* (New York: Praeger Publishers, 1975), or Zaki Naguib Mahmoud, *The Land and People of Egypt* (Philadelphia: Lippincott, 1972).

Students seeking slightly more specialized guidance may start with Joan Wucher-King, *Historical Dictionary of Egypt* (Metuchen, N.J., and London: Scarecrow Press, 1984), which includes a brief historical introduction, a detailed chronology, an alphabetized glossary of names and terms usually found in writings on modern Egyptian history, and a bibliography classified both by subject and by language. For a current handbook, see *Egypt: A Country Study* (Washington: U.S. Army, 1983), the fourth edition of what used to be called the *Area Handbook for Egypt*; Middle East Research Institute, *MERI Report: Egypt* (London: Croom Helm, 1985); or the Egypt chapter in the latest edition of *The Middle East and North Africa* (London: Europa Publications, annual).

There is no atlas of modern Egyptian history. The Egyptian government's *Atlas of Egypt* (Giza: Egyptian Survey Department, 1928) should be updated. One recent work, William C. Brice, *An Historical Atlas of Islam* (Leiden: Brill, 1981), contains a map showing the Egyptian military (but not naval) campaigns under Mehmet Ali and Isma'il. Francis Robinson, *Atlas of the Islamic World Since 1500* (New York: Facts on File, 1982), and Isma'il R. and Lois Lamya' al-Faruqi, *The Cultural Atlas of Islam* (New York: Macmillan, 1986), cover more Muslim culture than history. I hope one day to produce a biographical dictionary for modern Egypt, more complete than the one appended to this book, but Wucher-King's work is a good reference tool for use in the meantime.

Clio Press is publishing a World Bibliographical Series, but the Egypt volume had not appeared as of January 1988. The best bibliography I know is Rene Maunier, *Bibliographie économique, juridique et sociale de l'Egypte moderne (1798–1916)* (Cairo: Institut Français d'Archéologie Orientale, 1918), to be supplemented by Ida A. Pratt, *Modern Egypt* (New York: New York Public Library, 1929). Nothing more recent is as thorough or as accurate. For a general guide, see Charles L. Geddes, *Analytical Guide to the Bibliographies on*

Modern Egypt and the Sudan (Denver: American Institute of Islamic Studies, 1972). Students may wish to use George N. Atiyeh, *The Contemporary Middle East, 1948–1973* (Boston: G. K. Hall, 1975), for books and articles covering a time span wider than the title indicates; Diana Grimwood-Jones, ed., *The Middle East and Islam: A Bibliographical Introduction* (Zug, Switzerland: Inter Documentation, 1979), for its critical section introductions; David W. Littlefield, *The Islamic Near East and North America* (Littleton, Colo.: Libraries Unlimited, 1977), for its helpful book annotations; and *The Middle East in Conflict* (Santa Barbara, Calif.: ABC-Clio Information Services, 1985), for its summaries of scholarly articles.

General histories include Raymond Flower, *Napoleon to Nasser: The Story of Modern Egypt* (London: Tom Stacey, 1972), for entertainment; Peter M. Holt, *Egypt and the Fertile Crescent, 1516–1922* (Ithaca, N.Y.: Cornell University Press, 1966), for the Arab context; Afaf Lutfi al-Sayyid Marsot, *A Short History of Modern Egypt* (Cambridge and New York: Cambridge University Press, 1985), for a very general survey; and P. J. Vatikiotis, *History of Egypt from Muhammad Ali to Mubarak*, 3rd ed. (Baltimore: Johns Hopkins University Press, 1986), for a detailed one. Collections of scholarly studies include P. M. Holt, ed., *Political and Social Change in Modern Egypt* (London: Oxford University Press, 1968), and Gabriel R. Warburg and Uri M. Kupferschmidt, eds., *Islam, Nationalism, and Radicalism in Egypt and the Sudan* (New York: Praeger Publishers, 1983).

Chapter 1

No satisfactory survey of medieval Egyptian history has been written in almost a century. On the Ottoman period, see Stanford J. Shaw, *The Financial and Adminitrative Organization and Development of Ottoman Egypt, 1517–1798* (Princeton, N.J.: Princeton University Press, 1958), and *Ottoman Egypt in the Age of the French Revolution* (Cambridge: Harvard University Press, 1964); and Andre Raymond, *Artisans et commerçants du Caire au XVIIIe siécle*, 2 vols. (Damascus: Institut français de Damas, 1973–1974). The last half of the eighteenth century is shown in a new light both by Daniel Crecelius, *The Roots of Modern Egypt: A Study of the Regimes of Ali Bey al-Kabir and Muhammad Bey Abu al-Dhahab, 1760–1775* (Minneapolis: Bibliotheca Islamica, 1981), and by Peter Gran, *The Islamic Roots of Capitalism: Egypt, 1760–1840* (Austin and London: University of Texas Press, 1978).

Chapter 2

The pivotal period from 1798 to 1805 is covered, from the European side, by Shafik Ghorbal, *Beginnings of the Egyptian Question and the Rise of Mehemet-Ali* (London: G. Routledge, 1928), and by J. Christopher Herold, *Bonaparte in Egypt* (New York: Harper & Row, 1962). For Egypt's side, see *al-Jabarti's Chronicle of the First Seven Months of the French Occupation of Egypt*, translated by S. Moreh (Leiden: Brill, 1975). The story is carried farther in John Marlowe (pseud.), *Perfidious Albion: The Origins of Anglo-French Rivalry in the Levant* (London: Elek, 1971). On Mehmet Ali's life and reforms, we have Henry Dodwell, *The Founder of Modern Egypt* (Cambridge: Cambridge University Press, 1931); Helen A. B. Rivlin, *The Agricultural Policy of Muhammad Ali in Egypt* (Cambridge, Mass.: Harvard University Press, 1961); and Afaf Lutfi al-Sayyid Marsot, *Egypt in the Reign of Muhammad Ali* (Cambridge and New York: Cambridge University Press, 1984). His conquests are covered by Mordechai Abir, "Modernization, Reaction, and Muhammad Ali's Empire," *Middle Eastern Studies* 13:3 (October 1977), pp. 295–313; Mohammed Sabry, *L'empire égyptien sous Mohamed-Ali et la question d'Orient (1811–1849)* (Paris: Librarie Orientaliste Paul Geuthner, 1930); and John A. P. Sabini, *Armies in the Sand: The Struggle for Mecca and Medina* (New York: Thames & Hudson, 1981). A major theme in economic history is covered by Roger Owen, *Cotton and the Egyptian Economy, 1820–1914* (Oxford: Clarendon Press, 1969), and an equally important social one, by Judith Tucker, *Women in Nineteenth Century Egypt* (Cambridge and New York: Cambridge University Press, 1985). For a study of Egypt's sufi orders, see Fred de Jong, *Turuq and Turuq-Linked Institutions in Nineteenth Century Egypt* (Leiden: Brill, 1978). On educational reforms, see J. Heyworth-Dunne, *An Introduction to the History of Education in Modern Egypt* (London: Luzac, 1938). For an analysis of ideological changes in Egypt from Mehmet Ali to 1952, see Nadav Safran, *Egypt in Search of Political Community* (Cambridge: Harvard University Press, 1961). On a related subject, a fine recent study is Jack A. Crabbs, Jr., *The Writing of History in Nineteenth-Century Egypt* (Detroit: Wayne State University Press, 1984). Papers presented to a meeting sponsored by the Centre Nationale de la Recherche Scientifique (CNRS) at Aix-en-Provence in June 1979 were published as *L'Egypte au XIXe siécle* (Paris: CNRS, 1982). A thorough treatment of social change in this period is Gabriel Baer's *Studies in the Social History of Modern Egypt* (Chicago: University of Chicago Press, 1969). See also his *History of Landownership in Modern Egypt, 1800–1950* (London: Oxford University Press, 1962). Some of his findings have been corrected by Kenneth M. Cuno, "Egypt's Wealthy Peasantry, 1740–1820: A Study of the Region of al-Mansura," and by Abd al-Rahim A. Abd al-Rahim, "Land Tenure in Egypt and Its Social Effects on Egyptian Society: 1798–1813," both in Tarif Khalidi (ed.), *Land Tenure and Social Transformation in the Middle East* (Beirut: American University of Beirut, 1984). A related work is Alan Richards, *Egypt's Agricultural Development, 1800–1950* (Boulder, Colo.: Westview Press, 1982). The classic study of Egyptian folklife is Edward Lane, *Manners and Customs of the Modern Egyptians,* 3rd ed. (London: C. Knight & Co., 1842), which has been reprinted often.

Chapter 3

A good introduction to the period between Mehmet Ali's reforms and the British occupation is John Marlowe, *Spoiling the Egyptians* (New York: St. Martin's Press, 1975). The building of the Suez Canal is covered by John

Marlowe, *The Making of the Suez Canal*, (London: Cresset, 1964), and by Sir Arnold T. Wilson, *The Suez Canal* (London: Oxford University Press, 1933). On its chief organizer, see Charles Beatty, *Ferdinand de Lesseps: A Biographical Study* (London: Eyre & Spottiswoode, 1956). For some interesting travelers' accounts from this period, see Francis Steegmuller, *Flaubert in Egypt: A Sensibility on Tour* (Boston: Little, Brown, 1972), and Lady Lucie Duff-Gordon, *Letters from Egypt (1862–1869)*, reedited with additional letters by Gordon Waterfield (New York: Praeger Publishers, 1969). Changes in Egypt's bureaucracy are detailed in F. Robert Hunter, *Egypt Under the Khedives, 1805–1879* (Pittsburgh: University of Pittsburgh Press, 1984). A sympathetic portrait of Ismail is given by Pierre Crabites, *Ismail, the Maligned Khedive* (London: Routledge, 1933); on his expansionist policies, see Mohammed Sabry, *L'empire égyptien sous Ismail et l'ingérence anglo-française (1863–1879)* (Paris: Librairie Orientaliste Paul Geuthner, 1933), and for details of his financial undoing, see David S. Landes, *Bankers and Pashas: International Finance and Economic Imperialism in Egypt* (Cambridge: Harvard University Press, 1958). New light on this period is shed by the *Mémoires de Nubar Pacha,* edited by Mirrit Boutros Ghali (Beirut: Librairie du Liban, 1983). His greatest achievement is the subject of Jasper Y. Brinton, *The Mixed Courts of Egypt,* rev. ed. (New Haven, Conn.: Yale University Press, 1968).

Chapter 4

The era of Egypt's history popularly called the Urabi Revolution is treated masterfully by Alexander Schölch, *Egypt for the Egyptians! The Socio-Political Crisis in Egypt, 1878–1882* (London: Ithaca Press, 1981), although the reader who knows German should check the original, *Ägypten den Ägyptern!* (Zurich: Atlantis-Verlag, 1972) for its footnotes. The motives for Britain's occupation of Egypt are analyzed in Ronald Robinson and John Gallagher, *Africa and the Victorians* (New York: St. Martin's Press, 1961). Of the books treating British rule in Egypt generally, a good starter is Peter Mansfield, *The British in Egypt* (New York: Holt, Rinehart & Winston, 1971), but more advanced students should read Jacques Berque, *Egypt: Imperialism and Revolution*, translated by Jean Stewart (London: Faber & Faber, 1972). Opponents of British rule draw heavily on Wilfrid S. Blunt, *Secret History of the English Occupation of Egypt* (New York: Knopf, 1922), while apologists cite Alfred Milner, *England in Egypt* (London: Arnold, 1892), and Lord Cromer, *Modern Egypt* (London and New York: Macmillan, 1908). Cromer has been the subject of two recent scholarly studies: Afaf Lutfi al-Sayyid [Marsot], *Egypt and Cromer: A Study in Anglo-Egyptian Relations* (New York: Praeger Publishers, 1968), and John Marlowe, *Cromer in Egypt* (London: Elek, 1971). For a general analysis of the British occupation, see Robert L. Tignor, *Modernization and British Colonial Rule in Egypt, 1882–1914* (Princeton, N.J.: Princeton University Press, 1966).

Chapter 5

The rise of Egyptian nationalism is treated, somewhat superficially, by Jamal M. Ahmed, *The Intellectual Origins of Egyptian Nationalism* (London: Oxford University Press, 1960), which should be read together with Albert Hourani, *Arabic Thought in the Liberal Age, 1789–1939,* 3rd ed. (New York: Cambridge University Press, 1983), and Ibrahim Amine Ghali, *L'Egypte nationaliste et libérale, de Moustapha Kamel à Saad Zaghloul (1892–1927)* (Hague: Nijhoff, 1969). Lord Cromer's successors are studied by Lord Lloyd, *Egypt Since Cromer,* 2 vols. (London: Macmillan, 1933); Peter Mellini, *Sir Eldon Gorst: The Overshadowed Proconsul* (Stanford, Calif.: Hoover Institution, 1977); and Sir Philip Magnus, *Kitchener: Portrait of an Imperialist* (New York: E. P. Dutton, 1959). Egypt's Muslim reformers are studied in C. C. Adams, *Islam and Modernism in Egypt,* reprinted (New York: Russell & Russell, 1968); Malcolm H. Kerr, *Islamic Reform: The Political and Legal Theories of Muhammad Abduh and Rashid Rida* (Berkeley and Los Angeles: University of California Press, 1966); Nikki R. Keddie, *Sayyid Jamal al-Din "al-Afghani"* (Berkeley: University of California Press, 1972); and Zaki Badawi, *The Reformers of Egypt: A Critique of al-Afghani, Abduh, and Rida* (Slough, England: Open Press, 1976). Reactions to Qasim Amin's call to women's liberation are analyzed in Juan Cole, "Feminism, Class, and Islam in Turn-of-the-Century Egypt," *International Journal of Middle East Studies* 13 (1981), pp. 387–407. Mounah A. Khouri, *Poetry and the Making of Modern Egypt* (Leiden: Brill, 1971), depicts poetic expressions of nationalism. P. G. Elgood, *Egypt and the Army* (London: Oxford University Press, 1924), remains the best work on Egypt during World War I. On the social background to the 1919 Revolution, see Marius Deeb, "The 1919 Popular Uprising: A Genesis of Egyptian Nationalism," *Canadian Review of Studies in Nationalism* 1 (1973), pp. 106–119.

Chapter 6

Great Britain and Egypt, 1914–1951 (London: Royal Institute of International Affairs, 1951), and John Marlowe, *Anglo-Egyptian Relations, 1800–1953* (London: Cresset Press, 1954), are older studies of Egypt's ties with Britain during this period. For a more recent treatment, see John Darwin, *Britain, Egypt, and the Middle East* (New York: St. Martin's, 1981), and "Sa'd Zaghlul and the British," in Elie Kedourie, *The Chatham House Version and Other Middle-Eastern Studies,* reprinted (Hanover, N.H.: University Press of New England, 1984), pp. 82–159. Ronald Wingate wrote a biography of his father, *Wingate of the Sudan* (London: John Murray, 1955), which sympathetically treats his role as high commissioner in Egypt. For a more scholarly study, see Gabriel Warburg, *The Sudan Under Wingate* (London: Cass, 1971). On his successor, see Brian Gardner, *Allenby of Arabia* (New York: Coward McCann, 1966). Egypt's national identity during this era is extensively treated in Israel Gershoni and James Jankowski,

Egypt, Islam, and the Arabs: The Search for Egyptian Nationhood, 1900–1930 (New York: Oxford University Press, 1986). The role of the Wafd is covered by Marius Deeb, *Party Politics in Egypt: The Wafd and Its Rivals* (London: Ithaca Press, 1979), and by Janice Joles Terry, *Cornerstone of Egyptian Political Power: The Wafd, 1919–1952* (London: Third World Center, 1979). The classic study of the constitutional period is Marcel Colombe, *L'évolution de l'Egypte, 1924–1950* (Paris: G. P. Maisonneuve, 1951). It should be supplemented by Afaf Lutfi al-Sayyid Marsot, *Egypt's Liberal Experiment: 1922–1936* (Berkeley: University of California Press, 1977). A recently published study fills a gaping void: B. L. Carter, *The Copts in Egyptian Politics* (London: Croom Helm, 1986). Its complement for Jews is Gudrun Krämer, *Minderheit, Millet, Nation?: die Juden in Ägypten, 1914–1952* (Wiesbaden: Harrassowitz, 1982). This era was preeminently one for lawyers, about whom see Enid Hill, *Mahkama! Studies in the Egyptian Legal System* (London: Ithaca Press, 1979); Donald M. Reid, *Lawyers and Politics in the Arab World, 1880–1960* (Minneapolis: Bibliotheca Islamica, 1981); and Farhat J. Ziadeh, *Lawyers, the Rule of Law, and Liberalism in Modern Egypt* (Stanford, Calif.: Hoover Institution, 1968). One of Egypt's best-known lawyers, author of an oft-cited life of Muhammad, is the subject of a study by Charles D. Smith, *Islam and the Search for Social Order in Modern Egypt: A Biography of Muhammad Husayn Haykal* (Albany: SUNY Press, 1983). On economic changes, see Robert L. Tignor, *State, Private Enterprise, and Economic Change in Egypt, 1918–1952* (Princeton, N.J.: Princeton University Press, 1984), and Eric Davis, *Challenging Colonialism: Bank Misr and Egyptian Industrialization, 1920–1941* (Princeton, N.J.: Princeton University Press, 1983). For an English view of the times, read Laurence Grafftey-Smith, *Bright Levant* (London: John Murray, 1970); for an Egyptian view, see *The Education of Salama Musa*, translated by L. O. Schuman (Leiden: Brill, 1961). The same writer is analyzed in Vernon Egger, *A Fabian in Egypt: Salamah Musa and the Rise of the Professional Classes in Egypt, 1909–1939* (Lanham, Md.: University Press of America, 1986).

Chapter 7

The last years of the Mehmet Ali dynasty centered on the tragic figure of King Faruq, whose life is treated by Barrie St. Clair McBride, *Farouk of Egypt* (London: Robert Hale, 1967), and Hugh McLeave, *The Last Pharaoh: Farouk of Egypt* (New York: McCall, 1969). Less sympathetic to Farouk and to Egyptian nationalism, but essential to studies of this era, are Miles Lampson's diaries, edited by Trefor Evans as *The Killearn Diaries, 1934–1946: The Diplomatic and Personal Record of Lord Killearn* (London: Sidgwick & Jackson, 1972). Radical groups were becoming central in Egypt's political history. On the Muslim Brothers, the standard work is by Richard Mitchell, *The Society of the Muslim Brothers* (Princeton, N.J.: Princeton University Press, 1969). It may be read in conjunction with *Five Tracts of Hasan al-Banna'*, edited by Charles Wendell (Berkeley: University of California Press, 1978), and Sayyid Kotb's *Social Justice in Islam,* translated by John B. Hardie (Washington, D.C.: American Council of Learned Societies, 1953). James P. Jankowski's *Egypt's Young Rebels* (Stanford, Calif.: Hoover Institution, 1975) deals with Young Egypt. For this group's influence on the leaders of the 1952 Revolution, see P. J. Vatikiotis, *Nasser and His Generation* (New York: St. Martin's Press, 1978). On World War II in Egypt, read George Kirk, *The Middle East in the War* (London: Oxford University Press, 1952), and Martin W. Wilmington, *The Middle East Supply Centre* (Albany: SUNY Press, 1971). Gabriel Warburg, "The 'Three-Legged Stool': Lampson, Faruq, and Nahhas, 1936–1944," in his *Egypt and the Sudan* (London: Cass, 1985), deals with British policy during this period. See also Charles Smith, "4 February 1942: Its Causes and Its Influences on Egyptian Politics," *International Journal of Middle East Studies* 10:4 (November 1979), pp. 453–479. Postwar British policy is ably covered by W. Roger Louis, *The British Empire in the Middle East, 1945–1951* (New York: Oxford University Press, 1984). See also Howard M. Sachar, *Europe Leaves the Middle East, 1936–1954* (New York: Knopf, 1972). Egypt's decision to enter the Palestine War is best understood in terms of its growing involvement in Arab nationalism, on which see Israel Gershoni, *The Emergence of Pan-Arabism in Egypt* (Tel Aviv: Shiloah Center for Middle Eastern and African Studies, 1981); Ahmed M. Gomaa, *The Foundation of the League of Arab States* (London: Longman Group Ltd., 1977); James Jankowski, "Egyptian Responses to the Palestine Problem in the Interwar Period," *International Journal of Middle East Studies* 12:1 (August 1980), pp. 1–38; Thomas Mayer, *Egypt and the Palestine Question, 1936–1945* (Berlin: Schwarz, 1983); Yehoshua Porath, *In Search of Arab Unity, 1930–1945* (London: Cass, 1986); Barry Rubin, *The Arab States and the Palestine Conflict* (Syracuse, N.Y.: Syracuse University Press, 1981); and several articles in Amnon Cohen and Gabriel Baer, eds., *Egypt and Palestine: A Millennium of Association* (New York: St. Martin's Press, 1984). On the political culture of Egyptian workers during this era, see Ellis Goldberg, *Tinker, Tailor, and Textile Worker: Class and Politics in Egypt, 1930–1952* (Berkeley and Los Angeles: University of California Press, 1986).

Chapter 8

An excellent general book on modern Egypt is Derek Hopwood, *Egypt: Politics and Society 1945–1984*, 2nd ed. (London: Allen & Unwin, 1985). The background to the 1952 Revolution has generated more myth than history. The standard Egyptian accounts are Mohammed Neguib, *Egypt's Destiny: A Personal Statement* (Garden City, N.Y.: Doubleday, 1955); Gamal Abdul Nasser, *Egypt's Liberation: The Philosophy of the Revolution* (Washington, D.C.: Public Affairs Press, 1955); and Anwar al-Sadat, *Revolt on the Nile* (London: Allan Wingate, 1957). The U.S. role is discussed in Miles Copeland (pseud.), *The Game of Nations* (New York: Simon & Schuster, 1969); Wilbur Eveland, *Ropes of Sand: America's Failure in the Middle East* (New York: Norton, 1980); and Gail E. Meyer, *Egypt and the United States: The Formative Years* (Rutherford, N.J.: Fairleigh Dickinson University Press, 1980). Economic conditions during this time are covered in Charles Issawi, *Egypt at Mid-Century: An Economic Survey* (London: Oxford

University Press, 1954). For discussions of educational issues in their social context, see Abu al-Futouh Radwan, *Old and New Forces in Egyptian Education* (New York: Columbia University Teachers College, 1951); Lois Aroian, *The Nationalization of Arabic and Islamic Education in Egypt: Dar al-'Ulum and al-Azhar* (Cairo: American University in Cairo Press, 1983); and A. Chris Eccel, *Egypt, Islam, and Social Change: al-Azhar in Conflict and Accommodation* (Berlin: Schwarz, 1984). A good general description of this period is Jean and Simonne Lacouture, *Egypt in Transition*, translated by Francis Scarfe (New York: Criterion, 1958).

Chapters 9–10

Many biographies of Gamal Abd al-Nasir have been written. My favorite general one is *Nasser: A Biography*, by Jean Lacouture (New York: Knopf, 1973). It should be supplemented by *Nasser and His Generation*, which was cited earlier. On his leadership, see R. Hrair Dekmejian, *Egypt Under Nasir: A Study in Political Dynamics* (Albany: SUNY Press, 1971). Early studies of his regime include Keith Wheelock, *Nasser's New Egypt: A Critical Analysis* (New York: Praeger Publishers, 1960); P. J. Vatikiotis, *The Egyptian Army in Politics: Pattern for New Nations?* (Bloomington: Indiana University Press, 1961); and Anouar Abdel-Malek, *Egypt: Military Society*, translated by Charles Lam Markmann (New York: Random House, 1968). On his relations with world leaders, see Mohamed Heikal, *The Cairo Documents* (Garden City, N.Y.: Doubleday, 1973). The 1956 Suez crisis is covered by Hugh Thomas, *Suez* (New York: Harper & Row, 1967); Kennett Love, *Suez—The Twice-Fought War: A History* (New York: McGraw-Hill, 1969); Chester L. Cooper, *The Lion's Last Roar: Suez, 1956* (New York: Harper & Row, 1978); and Mohamed H. Heikal, *Cutting the Lion's Tail: Suez Through Egyptian Eyes* (London: Andre Deutsch, 1986). Nasir's relations with the other Arab states are treated by A. Dawisha, *Egypt in the Arab World: The Elements of Foreign Policy* (New York: Wiley, 1976), and by Tawfig Y. Hasou, *The Struggle for the Arab World: Egypt's Nasser and the Arab League* (London and Boston: Routledge, Kegan Paul, 1985). Nasir's detractors included foreigners, such as Ivor Powell, *Disillusion by the Nile* (London: Solstice Publications, 1967); Egyptian Marxists using pseudonyms, such as Hasan Riyad, *L'Egypte nassérienne* (Paris: Editions de minuit, 1964); and Egyptians who wrote after his death, such as Tawfiq al-Hakim, *The Return of Consciousness*, translated by R. Bayly Winder (New York: NYU Press, 1985). Another Egyptian Marxist, Mahmoud Hussein, wrote a thought-provoking study in French, translated as *Class Conflict in Egypt* (New York: Monthly Review Press, 1973). Although many authors deny or disregard U.S. military aid to Israel during the June 1967 War, Stephen Green, *Taking Sides: America's Secret Relations with a Militant Israel* (New York: William Morrow, 1984), describes the secret activities of U.S. aerial photographers based in the Negev.

Chapter 11

There has been much soul-searching among Egyptian and foreign scholars over the aborted promises of the 1952 Revolution. Even before his death, Nasir was starting to change direction. Sadat carried the process further. See Raymond William Baker, *Egypt's Uncertain Revolution Under Nasser and Sadat* (Cambridge: Harvard University Press, 1978); Mark N. Cooper, *The Transformation of Egypt* (Baltimore: Johns Hopkins University Press, 1982); Khalid Ikram, *Egypt: Economic Management in a Period of Transition* (Baltimore: Johns Hopkins University Press, 1980); and John Waterbury, *The Egypt of Nasser and Sadat: The Political Economy of Two Regimes* (Princeton, N.J.: Princeton University Press, 1983). The loss of Soviet influence is described by Mohamed Heikal, *The Sphinx and the Commissar* (New York: Harper & Row, 1978), and by Pedro Ramet, *Sadat and the Kremlin* (Santa Monica: California Seminar on Arms Control and Foreign Policy, 1980). On the corresponding rise of the Americans, see William J. Burns, *Economic Aid and American Policy Toward Egypt, 1955–1981* (Albany: SUNY Press, 1985), and relevant sections in Henry Kissinger, *Years of Upheaval* (Boston: Little, Brown, 1982), and in Jimmy Carter, *Keeping Faith: Memoirs of a President* (New York: Bantam, 1982); but any tendency toward self-congratulation is corrected by Marvin Weinbaum, *U.S. Aid to Egypt* (Boulder, Colo.: Westview Press, 1986).

The continuing leadership of the rural gentry is evident in Leonard Binder, *In a Moment of Enthusiasm: Political Power and the Second Stratum in Egypt* (Chicago: University of Chicago Press, 1978); Robert Springborg, *Family, Power, and Politics in Egypt* (Philadelphia: University of Pennsylvania Press, 1982); and Hamied Ansari, *Egypt: The Stalled Society* (Albany: SUNY Press, 1986). Sadat discusses his life and policies in a well-written but self-serving autobiography, *In Search of Identity* (New York: Harper & Row, 1978). Raphael Israeli examines his patrimonial tendencies in *"I, Egypt": Aspects of President Anwar al-Sadat's Political Thought* (Jerusalem: Magnes Press, 1981). He has also edited *The Public Diary of President Sadat,* 3 vols. (Leiden: Brill, 1979) and written what is thus far Sadat's most balanced biography in English, *Man of Defiance: A Political Biography of Anwar Sadat* (London: Weidenfeld & Nicolson, 1985). Polemics against him include David Hirst and Irene Beeson, *Sadat* (London: Faber & Faber, 1981), and Mohamed Heikal, *Autumn of Fury: The Assassination of Sadat* (New York: Random House, 1983). For a more balanced assessment, see Raymond A. Hinnebusch, Jr., *Egyptian Politics Under Sadat* (New York: Cambridge University Press, 1985). Sadat's role in the 1973 war is criticized in Saad El Shazly, *The Crossing of the Suez* (San Francisco: American Mideast Research, 1980).

A good general description of Egypt in the Sadat era is John Waterbury, *Egypt: Burdens of the Past, Options for the Future* (Hanover, N.H.: American Universities Field Staff, 1976). One by a perceptive Israeli journalist is Amos Elon, *Flight into Egypt,* rev. ed. (New York: Pinnacle Books, 1981). Richard Critchfield, *Shahhat: An Egyptian* (Syracuse: Syracuse University Press, 1978), is evocative of Egyptian village life. On urban conditions, see Unni Wikan, *Life Among the Poor in Cairo,* translated by Ann Henning (London: Tavistock Publications, 1980). Egyptian women have begun to get their share of attention; recent books include Nayra Atiya, *Khul-Khaal: Five Egyptian Women Tell Their Stories* (Syracuse, N.Y.: Syracuse University Press, 1982); Nawal El Saadawi, *The Hidden Face of Eve* (Boston: Beacon Press, 1980); and Earl Sullivan, "Women and Work in Egypt," *Cairo Papers in Social Science* 4 (December 1981). Egypt's bureaucracy is studied in Nazih N. M. Ayyubi, *Bureaucracy and Politics in Contemporary Egypt* (London: Ithaca Press, 1980). Egyptian students under Nasir and Sadat are covered in Ahmed Abdallah, *Student Movement and National Politics in Egypt* (London: Saqi Books, 1985). The best account of the religious opposition is Gilles Kepel, *Muslim Extremism in Egypt: The Prophet and Pharaoh,* translated by Jan Rothschild, with an Afterword (Berkeley and Los Angeles: University of California Press, 1986). See also Robin Wright, *Sacred Rage: The Wrath of Militant Islam* (New York: Simon & Schuster, 1986), especially Chapter 7. An Egyptian writer has linked the rise in Islamic militant groups during the 1970s with a corresponding rise in Coptic political activism, especially among expatriate Egyptian Christians. See Nadia Ramses Farah, *Religious Strife in Egypt: Crisis and Ideological Conflict in the Seventies* (New York: Gordon and Breach Science Publishers, 1986).

Index

Abbas Hilmi I (governor of Egypt), 22, 24, 26
Abbas Hilmi II (khedive of Egypt), 41, 42, 43, 44, 45, 46–47, 49, 50, 51, 53, 56
Abbasid caliphate, 1, 6–7, 8
Abd al-Aziz. *See* Ibn Sa'ud
Abd al-Hadi, Hasan, 85
Abd al-Hadi, Ibrahim, 89, 96
Abd al-Halim (son of Mehmet Ali), 28
Abdallah (amir of Transjordan/king of Jordan), 79, 82
Abdin Palace (Cairo), 34, 35, 73, 151
Abduh, Muhammad, 1, 27, 30, 56
Abdulhamid (sultan), 45, 46, 49
Abraham, 2
Abu al-Dhahab, Muhammad Bey, 11, 13, 16
Abu Kir Bay, 15, 80(fig.)
Acre (Palestine), 15, 21
Adam, Juliette, 45
Afghani, al-, Jamal al-Din, 30, 33, 56, 158
Agriculture, 2, 17–18, 55, 62, 74, 112, 147, 164
  cash crops, 18, 25, 67
  crops, 4, 5, 13, 63
  production, 39, 48, 104, 105
  wages, 68, 149
Agriculture, Ministry of, 52
Ahmad, Muhammad, 37
Ahram, al- (Cairo), 46, 47, 151
Aida (opera), 28
Air force officers' sentences (1968), 131
Akhbar, al- (Cairo), 123
Al-Alamain, 2(fig.), 74
Alawites, 125
Albanians, 17, 19
Alcohol, 74
Alexander I (tsar of Russia), 20
Alexander the Great (king of Macedon), 1, 4, 11
Alexandretta (Turkey), 124
Alexandria, 1, 2(fig.), 5, 6, 15, 19, 24, 29, 48, 68, 80(fig.), 148
  British occupation of (1882), 36
  Europeans in, 27, 36
  riots (1882, 1954, 1977), 36, 38, 102, 151
Alexandria University, 131
Algeria, 46, 104, 106, 108, 113
  independence (1962), 120
Ali (Muhammad's cousin and son-in-law), 7
Ali Bey "al-Kabir," 11, 13, 16
Allenby, Edmund, 57, 58, 59, 60, 61, 63
Al-Samu' (Jordan), 125
American University (Cairo), 60
Amin, Mustafa, 123
Amir, Abd al-Hakim, 89, 98, 118, 128
Amman (Jordan), 126(fig.), 133
Amr ibn al-As, 6
Anatolia, 20, 36
Ancient Egypt, 4–5

Anglo-Egyptian Treaty
1936, 64, 67, 69, 73, 76, 77, 87, 88, 92, 101
1954, 100, 101, 107, 109, 110
Anglo-Iranian Oil Company, 87
Anglo-Ottoman commercial treaty (1838), 21
Anti-imperialism, 103, 110
Aqaba, Gulf of, 2(fig.), 49, 108, 109, 126, 127, 130
Aqsa, al-, Mosque (Jerusalem), 152
Arab creation legend, 4–5
Arab East, 1
Arabia, 1, 5, 7, 19, 20, 23, 113, 120, 124. *See also* Saudi Arabia
Arabian Nights, 7
Arabic (language), 13, 48, 64
Arabism. *See* Arab nationalism
Arab League (1944), 75, 82, 100, 103, 104, 119, 120, 121, 156
Arab Legion (Transjordan/Jordan), 83, 106
Arab nationalism, 71, 72, 103, 111, 112–113, 117, 119, 121, 122, 146, 147, 149. *See also* Pan-Arabism
Arabs, 1, 6–8, 11, 18, 57, 60, 70, 71, 75, 113, 166
Palestinian, 70, 71, 76, 83, 111, 121, 128, 130, 132, 133, 140, 142, 143, 144, 152, 153, 154, 155, 156, 159, 166. *See also* *Fida'iyin*
Arab socialism, 115, 117–118, 119, 120, 121, 123, 135, 140, 146, 147
Arab Socialist party. *See* National Democratic party
Arab Socialist Union (ASU), 119, 121, 123, 131, 134, 151, 153
Arab states, 102, 122, 129, 155, 156–157, 163. *See also under* Nasir, al-, Gamal Abd; Sadat, al-, Anwar
Arab West, 1
Arafat, Yasir, 130, 133, 149, 157, 166
Archaic Period, 4
Arif, Abd al-Salam, 120, 124
Arius (theologian), 1, 5
Armaments, 18
Armenians, 8, 11, 27, 29, 57, 85
Arms purchases, 84, 102, 103, 106, 138, 139, 140, 142, 145, 150, 156, 163
Art, 60, 104
Asad, al-, Hafiz, 134, 142
Ashiqqa party (Sudan), 86
Assembly, 30, 31, 35. *See also* General Assembly; Legislative Assembly; National Assembly; Parliament; People's Assembly
Assyrians, 4, 11
ASU. *See* Arab Socialist Union
Aswan, 2(fig.), 3, 41
High Dam, 2(fig.), 104, 105–107, 113, 114, 119, 122, 138, 147, 164
Asyut, 158, 160, 165
Ataturk, Kemal, 69
Athanasius (patriarch of Alexandria), 1, 5
Atlantic Charter (1941), 76
Atlantic Monthly, 115
Atlantic Ocean, 9
Attar, al-, Hasan, 11, 13
Austerity measures, 130
Austria, 14, 20, 36, 45, 72, 143
Authoritarianism, 154
Awqaf, 17
Ayyubid dynasty, 8, 9
Azhar, al-. *See* University of Al-Azhar
Azharites, 30, 46, 51, 69
Azzam, Abd al-Rahman, 75, 82, 83

Badeau, John, 120
Badr, 143
Badran, Shams, 98, 128
Baghdad Pact (1955), 102, 103, 106, 113
Bahri Mamluks, 9
Balance of payments, 123

Balfour, Arthur, 57
Balfour Declaration (1917), 70
Balkans, 36
Bandung Conference (1955), 103, 116
Bangladesh, 139
Bank Misr, 60, 68, 116
Banks, 52, 60, 117, 148
Banna, al-, Shaykh Hasan, 85, 88, 158
Baring, Evelyn. *See* Cromer, Lord
Bar-Lev Line, 133, 143
Barley, 4
Barrages, 18, 39, 104
Barudi, al-, Mahmud Sami, 34, 35
Ba'th party
  Iraq, 120, 121, 156
  Syria, 111, 112, 113, 117, 120, 124, 125
Battle, Lucius, 122
Bedouin Arabs, 18
Begin, Menachem, 151, 152, 153, 154, 156, 159, 160
Belgium, 20, 60, 113
Belly-dancers, 114
Ben Bella, Ahmad, 120, 124
Ben Gurion, David, 102, 108, 109
Beni Murr, 2(fig.), 99
Berque, Jacques, 60
Bevin, Ernest, 77
Bilharzia, 68
Black, Eugene, 105
Black Book (Ubayd), 80, 84
Black Death, 9, 13
Black Saturday (1952), 87–88, 89
Blue Nile, 105
Bonaparte, Napoleon (emperor of the French), 2, 10, 11, 14, 15, 16, 17, 24
Book publishing, 60
Bosnia, 19, 36
Bosporus, 21, 23
Bourgeoisie, 118, 147, 148
Brain drain, 168
Bridges, 28
Brigandage, 38, 40
British Commonwealth, 109
Brzezinski, Zbigniew, 155
Building materials, 68
Bulganin, Nicolai, 109
Bunche, Ralph, 83
Bureaucracy, 22, 31, 38, 48, 53, 60, 112, 118, 149
Burji Mamluks, 9
Buyids, 8
Byzantine empire, 2, 5, 6, 9, 11

Cairo (al-Qahirah), 1, 2(fig.), 3, 7, 9, 11, 13, 24, 28, 29, 68, 80(fig.), 104, 148
  British occupation of (1882), 37
  Europeans in, 27
  French occupation of, 15
  riot (1952), 87, 88
  riot (1954, 1964), 102, 122
  riot (1972, 1973), 141
  riot (1977), 151
  riot (1981), 159
Cairo Tower, 99
Cairo University, 87, 104, 131
Caliphate, 69
Camp David talks (1978), 154–155, 163
Canada, 14, 109
Canals, 18, 23, 24, 27, 28, 39, 104
Cape of Good Hope, 10, 24
Capitalism, 116, 120, 135, 147
Capitulations, 27, 48, 52, 60, 64
  abolished (1937), 67
Caradon, Lord, 129
Caribbean, 10
Carter, Jimmy, 150, 152, 154, 155, 160
Castro, Fidel, 124
Cataracts, 3
Cattle, 4
Caucasus, 8, 19, 46
Cement, 74
Censorship, 96, 114, 142
Centers of power, 134, 135, 138, 139–140
Central Asia, 8, 19, 46
Central Intelligence Agency (CIA), 90, 99, 111, 124

"Century Storage Scheme," 105
Cereal grain imports, 149, 151, 164. *See also* Wheat
Chalcedon, Council of (451), 6
Charles (prince of Wales), 160
China, People's Republic of, 106
Cholera epidemic (1883), 38
Chou En-lai, 103
Christianity, 1, 5–6, 8
CIA. *See* Central Intelligence Agency
Cigarettes, 74
Circassians, 8, 11, 34, 37, 48, 59
Citadel (Cairo), 15, 19, 141
Civil liberties, 93, 95, 96, 138
Class struggle, 146
Cleopatra (queen of Egypt), 5
Climate, 3
Cloth, 10
Coffee, 10
Cohen, Lilianne, 82
Columbus, Christopher, 10
Communism, 91, 100, 111, 112, 140, 146
Communist party, 75, 79, 85
Communists, 89, 90, 97, 99, 100, 101, 106, 113, 122, 123, 139
Condominium, 77
Congo (Zaire), 113, 122
Constantinople (Turkey), 6, 9
Constitution, 31, 33, 58, 59
  1876, 51
  1881, 35
  1923, 60, 62, 63, 64, 69, 77, 93, 95–96
  1930, 63
  1956, 110, 116
  1964, 121, 134, 160
Constitutional Reform party, 50
Consultative Assembly (1956), 110
Consumer cooperatives, 51
Convention of al-Arish, 15
Coptic Orthodox church, 6
Copts, 51, 54, 57, 71, 85, 130, 159
Corn, 74
Corrective Revolution of 15 May 1971, 134–135, 138
Corruption, 84, 97, 141, 163, 165
Cotton, 13, 18, 22, 25, 28, 29, 48, 61, 62, 63, 68, 74, 103, 106, 130
Court system. *See* Mixed Courts; National Tribunals; Revolutionary court
Crete, 19
Crimean War (1854–1856), 25
Cromer, Lord, 39, 40, 41, 42, 44, 45, 47, 48, 50, 56
Crusades, 8
Curzon, George, 58, 59
Cyprus, 36, 126(fig.)
Czechoslovakia, 83, 103, 106

Dams, 18, 39, 104–105
Danzig (Poland), 72
Dardanelles, 21, 23, 31
Dar'iyah (Arabia), 19
Dates, 4
Dayan, Moshe, 109, 127
Day of Atonement, 143
Dayr Yasin massacre (1948), 152
Debt Commission. *See* Foreign debt, nineteenth century
De Lesseps, Ferdinand, 24, 25, 26, 36
Democracy, 69, 75, 79, 84, 95, 96, 112, 116, 163
Democratic socialism, 60
Depression (1930s), 68
Description de l'Egypte, 14
Deserts, 1, 2(fig.), 3, 112
Dhofar rebels (Oman), 150
Dictatorship, 95, 99, 137
Diem, Ngo Dinh, 124
Dinshaway, 49–50, 51
Disease, 19, 38, 68, 80
Donkeys, 4
Drug smugglers, 114
Dual Financial Control (1878), 29, 30, 31, 33, 35, 106
  abolished (1882), 38
Dufferin, Frederick, 38
Dufferin Commission, 38, 40

Dulles, John Foster, 102, 106, 107, 108

Eastern Desert, 2(fig.), 3
East Germany, 122
Economic Development Organization (1957), 116
Eden, Anthony, 67, 109
Education, 63, 68, 80, 114, 118, 156, 157, 165
  under British, 48
Educational institutions, 1, 18, 22, 27, 28, 30, 38, 51, 60, 168
  fees abolished, 86
Edward VII (king of England), 47
Egyptian Delegation. *See* Wafd
Egyptian-Israeli Peace Treaty (1979), 155, 157, 159, 163
Egyptian Military Academy, 88, 89, 100
Egyptian Museum, 28, 104
"Egypt's Reawakening" (statue), 104
Eilat (Elat) (Israel), 2(fig.), 126
Eilat (Israeli destroyer), 129
Eisenhower, Dwight D., 103, 108, 109, 121, 131
Eisenhower Doctrine (1957), 111
Elections, 35, 56, 61, 62, 63, 64, 69, 81, 86, 93, 96, 121, 158
Electricity, 164
Elite, 4
  educated, 30, 37, 44, 81, 96, 153, 157–158, 159, 166
  See also Land, ownership
Emigration, 164, 168. *See also* Remittances
Emmer, 4
Endowments. *See Awqaf*
English (language), 48
Entente cordiale, 47
Eshkol, Levi, 127
Ethiopia, 1, 64, 72, 126(fig.)
Euphrates River, 20
Europe, 2, 9–10, 13, 19, 23
European Common Market, 145
European settlers, 27, 30, 32, 36, 42, 48, 60, 72, 110, 116
Ezbekia Gardens (Cairo), 28, 141

Fahmi, Abd al-Aziz, 56
Fahmi, Mustafa, 41, 56
Faluja (Israel), 83
Family planning, 119
Famine, 13
Farid, Muhammad, 51, 53, 62, 153
Farida (wife of King Faruq), 81
Faruq (king of Egypt), 34, 64, 69, 73, 74, 75, 77, 79, 80, 81, 82, 83, 85, 87, 88, 89, 124, 127, 138, 167
  deposed (1952), 90
Fascists, 64, 72
Fatah, al-, 125, 130
Fatimah (Muhammad's daughter), 7
Fatimids, 7–8, 11
Fawzi, Muhammad, 134
Faysal (king of Saudi Arabia), 120, 123, 124, 139, 142, 149
Feddan, 86
Federation of Arab Republics proposal, 134, 135, 140
Fertile Crescent, 8, 10, 74, 124
Fezzes, 91
Fida'iyin, 87, 102, 103, 107, 108, 130, 133, 142
Figs, 4
Film companies, 60
Firearms, 9, 10
First five-year economic plan (1959), 113, 117
Fish, 4
Flax, 4, 13
Food processing, 68
Food riots (1977), 151, 165
Forced labor, 25–26, 39, 48
Ford, Gerald, 160
Foreign debt
  19th century, 27, 28, 29, 31, 34, 36, 37, 38
  1970s, 148, 150, 151
Foreign exchange, 123, 163
Foreign policy, 72, 77, 92, 142, 163. *See also individual countries*, and

Egypt; *under* Nasir, al-, Gamal Abd; Sadat, al-, Anwar
Foreign residents, 67, 93, 96. *See also* European settlers
Foreign rule, 4, 5, 6, 7–9, 17. *See also* France, and Egypt; Great Britain, and Egypt, occupation of; Ottoman Empire
Four Reserved Points (1922), 59, 62
France, 14, 20, 21, 23, 25, 36, 38, 42, 43, 47, 70, 107, 110
  and Africa, 36, 45, 46, 106
  Directory government, 14, 15, 24
  and Egypt, 10–11, 14–16, 17, 19, 20, 21, 24, 25, 29, 30, 31, 32, 36, 37, 40, 41, 45, 47, 102, 103–104, 108, 109, 110, 111–112, 120, 132
  and Germany, 31, 72
  and Israel, 103, 108, 109
  mandates, 70, 71, 124
  and World War II, 73
"Freedom, Socialism, Unity" slogan, 117
Free Officers, 88–91, 93, 95, 96, 97, 98, 105, 116, 121, 122, 134
French (language), 48
French and Indian War. *See* Seven Years' War
French Law School, 45
French Revolution (1789), 14
Fu'ad (sultan/king of Egypt), 55, 58, 60, 61, 62, 63, 64, 69
Fu'ad II (king of Egypt), 90, 97
Furniture, 74
Fustat, 7, 80(fig.)

Gas lights, 27, 30
Gaza, 2(fig.), 82, 83, 102, 104, 109, 125
Gaza Strip, 127, 154, 155, 156, 166
General Assembly, 40, 51, 52
General Motors (U.S. firm), 157
Genoa (Italy), 8
Geographical Society, 28
George III (king of England), 14
Germany, 31, 45
  Nazi, 70, 71, 72, 73, 85
  and Ottoman Empire, 46, 53
Gezira region (Sudan), 61
Ghali, Butros, 52
Ghana, 124
Gibb, Hamilton, 115
Gidi Pass, 2(fig.), 143, 149
Giza, 80(fig.), 167
Gladstone, William, 36, 37, 41, 45
Glass, 74
Glubb, John Bagot, 83, 106
Goats, 4, 39
Golan Heights, 127, 143, 144
Gold, 10, 13, 19
Gordon, Charles, 38
Gorst, Eldon, 50–51, 52, 56
Goshen, 2
Grain, 11, 18, 39. *See also* Cereal grain imports
Grapes, 4
Great Bitter Lake, 2(fig.), 144
Great Britain, 14, 15, 16, 20, 23, 25, 36, 46, 47, 61, 70, 85, 102, 129, 132
  and Egypt, 17, 19–20, 21, 24, 25, 29, 30, 31, 32, 35–36, 62, 63, 64, 67, 68, 72, 73, 74, 75, 76–77, 86, 87, 88, 92, 93, 97, 100, 101, 105, 106, 107, 108, 109, 110, 111–112, 113
  and Egypt, occupation of (1882–1922), 37–42, 43, 44, 45, 47, 48, 49–51, 52, 53–54, 55, 58–59, 116
  and Germany, 72
  and Iraq, 70, 72
  and Jordan, 111
  and Ottoman Empire, 20, 21, 31, 36, 41, 43, 49, 58, 101
  and Palestine, 70, 71, 72, 76
  and Southern Arabia, 120
  and Suez Canal, 29, 76–77, 83, 86, 87, 92, 97, 100, 102, 107, 108, 109, 110
  textile mills, 28
Greece, 86

Greek Orthodox, 6
Greeks, 19, 20, 23, 27, 85
Green, Stephen, 129
Gromyko, Andrei, 144
Gross domestic product, 141
Guatemala, 124
Gulf Organization for the Development of Egypt, 148
Gum'ah, Sha'rawi, 134
Gumhuriyya, al- (Cairo), 138

Harb, Salih, 88
Harb, Tal'at, 60, 68
Hasan II (king of Morocco), 120, 152
Hasanayn, Ahmad, 69, 81
Hashimite kings, 83, 103, 120, 124
Haykal, Muhammad Hasanayn, 90, 143, 150
Haykal, Muhammad Husayn, 60, 84
Head tax, 6
Heliopolis, 16, 80(fig.), 133, 148
High Commissioners, 57, 63
Hijacking, 133
Hijaz, 20, 49, 71
Hilwan, 80(fig.), 112, 131
Hitler, Adolf, 72
Hizb al-ummah. See Ummah party
Holland, 145
Holy Alliance, 20
Horse nomads. *See* Hyksos
Housing, 68, 114, 118, 164
Hudaybi, al-, Hasan, 86
Hudson, Michael, 101
Humphrey, Hubert, 127
Hungary, 109
Husayn (king of Jordan), 106, 111, 127, 129, 133, 142, 154, 157, 166
Husayn, Ahmad, 86, 106
Husayn, Taha, 60, 86
Hydroelectric power, 105
Hyksos, 4, 11

Ibn Khaldun, 1
Ibn Sa'ud (king of Saudi Arabia), 70
Ibn Tulun, Ahmad, 7
Ibrahim (son of Mehmet Ali), 19, 20, 21, 23, 24
Identity, 3, 5, 11, 166
Ikhshidids, 7
Illiteracy, 121
Imam, 1, 7, 120
Imbaba, 15, 80(fig.)
IMF. *See* International Monetary Fund
Income, 117, 149
  gap, 68, 81, 157, 165
  See also Remittances
Independence
  1922, 59
  1936. *See* Anglo-Egyptian Treaty
  1952, 2, 74, 79, 90–93
India, 14, 20, 23, 24, 42, 107, 108, 109, 125
  independence (1947), 77
Indigo, 18
Indonesia, 124
Indo-Pakistan War (1971), 139
Industrialization, 63, 68, 156
Industry, 18, 20, 22, 26, 28, 68, 74, 117, 118, 163, 164
  Egyptian-owned, 60, 116
  foreign control, 60, 68
Infitah, al-, 146, 148–149, 151
Inflation, 149, 150
Inheritance laws, 92
In Search of Identity (Sadat), 95
Inshas Palace, 77
Intellectuals, 27, 30, 60, 62, 153
International Bank for Reconstruction and Development. *See* World Bank
International line, 49
International Monetary Fund (IMF), 124, 150, 151
Invasions, 4, 11. *See also* Foreign rule
Investment, 68, 91, 112, 116, 135, 148, 150, 156, 157
Iran, 9, 87, 99, 102, 124, 126, 145, 148, 156, 158, 159, 167
Iran-Iraq war (1980–), 156

Iraq, 70, 74, 75, 83, 102, 103, 109, 112, 120, 121, 124, 126(fig.), 155, 156, 157, 163
  oil, 107, 112, 119
  revolution (1958), 111, 113
  See also under Great Britain
Irrigation, 18, 38, 39, 48, 62, 67, 104, 116, 164, 168
Ishaq, Adib, 30
Islam, 1, 6, 7–8, 71, 72, 124
  converts to, 8, 11, 16
  as egalitarian, 117
  and nationalism, 43
  See also Pan-Islam
Islamic Congress, 138
Islamic law. *See* Shari'ah
Islamic scholars, 13–14
Islamic Socialist party, 75, 85, 96
Islamic solidarity, 115
Islamische Welt, Die (pan-Islamic monthly), 53
Isma'il (khedive of Egypt), 22, 27–31, 33, 34, 37, 44, 61, 116, 167
Isma'il (son of Ja'far), 7
Ismailia, 2(fig.), 29, 36, 68, 72, 87, 129, 147
Isma'ilis, 7
Israel (1948), 79, 82, 83, 111, 124, 126(fig.), 128–129, 130, 142, 143, 151
  and Africa, 145
  Defense Force, 127, 144
  and Egypt, 82–83, 86, 92, 102, 103, 104, 106, 107, 108–109, 113, 125, 127, 129, 131, 132, 133, 134, 141–144, 146, 149, 152, 153, 155, 156, 161, 163, 166
  and Jordan, 125
  and Lebanon, 157, 159
  recession, 125
  terrorism in, 149
  water supply, 121
  and West Germany, 122
  See also under France; Nasir, al-, Gamal Abd; Soviet Union; Syria; United States
Istanbul. *See* Constantinople
Italian city states, 8
Italians, 27
Italy, 53, 64, 72, 73
Ivory, 10, 19

Jabarti, al-, Abd al-Rahman, 11, 13
Ja'far (sixth imam), 7
Jaffa (Israel), 83
Janissary soldiers, 20
Jaridah, al- (newspaper), 50
Jarring, Gunnar, 130, 132, 133
Jawish, Abd al-Aziz, 51, 53
"Jeep Case," 85
Jerusalem, 2(fig.), 8, 127, 152
Jewish Agency, 143
Jews, 8, 27, 30, 57, 85, 110, 125, 130
  and Palestine, 70, 71, 72, 75. *See also* Israel
Jiddah (Arabia), 11, 126(fig.)
Jihad, 53
Jihad, al-, al-Jadid, 166
Jizyah. See Head tax
Johnson, Lyndon, 122, 126, 127, 131, 132
Johnston, Eric, 121
Jordan, 79, 102, 106, 109, 111, 118, 120, 121, 125, 126(fig.), 127, 129, 130, 132, 133, 142, 152, 155, 157, 163
Jordan River valley development, 121
Joseph, 2
Judaism, 2
July Laws (1961), 117–118, 119
June 1967 War, 127–128, 131

Kafr al-Dawar, 80(fig.), 91
Kamil, Husayn (sultan of Egypt), 53
Kamil, Mustafa, 44, 45, 46, 47, 49, 50, 51, 62, 153
Karameh (Jordan), 130
Keith, Thomas, 20
Kennedy, John F., 119, 122
Khan al-Khalili bazaar, 30

Kharaj. See Land, tax
Khartum, 38, 86, 135
Khedival Law School, 45
Khedive, 28, 31, 32, 33, 45
Khomeini, Ruhollah (ayatollah), 158
Khrushchev, Nikita, 122
Killearn, Lord. *See* Lampson, Miles
Kilometer 101, 146
Kissinger, Henry, 144, 145–146, 147, 149, 150
Kitchner, Herbert, 41, 52–53, 56
Kléber, Jean-Baptiste, 15, 16
Knights of Malta, 15
Kreisky, Bruno, 143
Kurds, 8, 11
Kush, 4
Kushites, 4, 11
Kuwait, 107, 126(fig.), 130, 135, 148

Labor unions, 51, 75, 96, 97, 99, 118
Lampson, Miles, 63, 69, 73, 81, 88
Land
  distribution, 9, 86, 92, 114, 116, 117, 118, 148
  ownership, 26, 62, 67, 81, 82, 93, 96, 118, 147, 165
  reform (1952), 91–92, 97
  rents, 68
  state control of, 17, 26
  tax, 6, 10, 27, 29
Lane, Edward, 29
Language, 5, 13, 48
Lavon Affair (Israel), 102
Law of Shame, 154
League of Nations, 64, 67, 70
Lebanon, 70, 74, 75, 111, 112, 120, 121, 124, 126(fig.), 132, 149, 156. *See also under* Israel
Legislative Assembly, 53, 56
Legislative Council, 40, 51
Legitimacy, 101, 104
"Lesseps" (code name), 107
Levant campaign (1831–1833), 20
Liberal Constitutionalists, 62, 63, 69, 84
Liberals, 153
Liberation Province, 2(fig.), 112
Liberation Rally, 98, 99, 110, 130–131
Liberty (U.S. intelligence ship), 129
Libres chez nous, hospitaliers pour tous, 44
Libya, 53, 64, 72, 73, 139, 142, 156
  and Egypt, 120, 134, 135, 140, 142, 150, 152, 167
Libyan Desert. *See* Western Desert
Libyans, 4, 11
Limestone, 3
Literature, 60
Liwa, al- (newspaper), 47, 50, 51
Lloyd, George, 63
London Convention (1841), 21
Loraine, Percy, 63
Louis Philippe (king of France), 20
Louis XVI (king of France), 14
Lydda (Israel), 83

Ma'adi, 80(fig.), 132
Macedonian empire, 2, 11
Madrasah, al- (student monthly), 45
Maghrib, al-. *See* Arab West
Mahdi, 37, 38, 39
Mahir, Ahmad, 69, 84
Mahir, Ali, 73, 84, 88, 91, 138
Mahmud, Muhammad, 56, 84
Mahmud II (sultan), 20, 21
Malta, 15
Mamluks, 8–9, 10, 11, 13, 15, 16, 17, 18–19, 20, 26
Manager class, 147
Manners and Customs of the Modern Egyptians (Lane), 29
Maoists, 123
Maps, 2, 80, 126
Maraghi, al-, Mustafa, 69
Mar'i, Sayyid, 91
Maronite Christians, 111
Marxists, 152, 158, 159
Mashriq, al-. *See* Arab East
Masonic lodges, 30

Mecca (Arabia), 11, 19, 126(fig.)
Medical care, 68, 86, 114, 116, 118
Medieval Egypt, 6–8
Medina (Arabia), 19
Mediterranean Sea, 1, 2(fig.), 3, 9, 20, 21
Mehmet Ali, 17–22, 23–24, 25, 26, 28, 29, 31, 37, 39, 44, 116
Meir, Golda, 143, 144, 146
Menou, Jacques Abdallah, 16
Merchant guilds, 15, 17
Metternich, Clemens, 20
Middle class, 93, 153
Middle East Supply Center, 74
Middle Kingdom, 4
Military, 19, 28, 30–31, 34–35, 79, 102, 141, 160
  academies, 26, 88, 158
  under British, 38, 41, 47, 48, 59, 61
  under Mehmet Ali, 19–20, 21, 22, 23
  officers, 26, 30, 34, 35, 37, 38, 47, 59, 98, 115, 128, 131, 141. *See also* Free Officers
  professionalism, 139
  and Russo-Turkish War, 29
  and Suez crisis (1956), 107, 109
  See also June 1967 War; October War; Palestine, War; War of Attrition
Millet, 4
Milner, Alfred, 58, 59
Minimum wage, 118
Minorities, 27, 59, 85, 96
Misri, al-, Aziz Ali, 73, 88, 89, 137
Misr party, 153
Mitla Pass, 2(fig.), 109, 143, 149
Mitterrand, François, 160
Mixed Courts, 30, 40, 67
Modernization, 11, 27, 119, 123, 167
Monarchy ended (1953), 97
Monasticism, 1
Mongols, 9
Monophysitism, 6
Montreux Convention (1937), 67
Morea, 23
Morocco, 19, 104, 120, 152
  independence (1956), 106
Mortality rates, 68
Moses, 2
Mosque Gamal Abd al-Masir, 133
Mosque of al-Husayn, 141
Mu'ayyad, al- (newspaper), 46, 47, 50
Mubarak, Husni, 160, 161, 164, 165, 166, 167
Muhammad (prophet), 7, 60, 143, 158
Muhyi al-Din, Zakariya, 89, 122, 123, 127, 128
Mukhtar, Mahmud, 60, 104
Munich Olympics, 140
Muqattam, al- (newspaper), 45, 46
Murjan oil fields, 130
Musa, Salama, 60
Musaddiq, Mohammed, 87, 99, 124
Muslim Brothers, Society of the, 72, 75–76, 77, 82, 84, 85–86, 87, 89, 90, 91, 96, 97, 98, 101, 115, 123, 137, 158
  youth movement. *See* Rovers
Muslim calendar, 41
Muslims, 1, 2, 6, 9, 11, 24, 27, 44, 54, 69, 71, 130, 152, 166, 167
  reformers, 27, 30
  and socialism, 116
  societies, 158–159, 161
  See also Shi'is; Sunnis; Ulama
Muslim Sisters, 85
Mussolini, Benito, 72

Nagib, Muhammad, 74, 82, 83, 89, 92, 93, 95, 96, 97, 98, 99, 100
Nahhas, al-, Mustafa, 63, 64, 69, 73, 75, 80, 81, 84, 86, 87, 91, 92, 98
Napoleonic Law Code, 40, 45
Napoleon III (emperor of the French), 26
Nasir, al-, Gamal Abd, 74, 76, 82, 117, 128, 131, 134, 137–138, 163

and Arab states, 103, 106, 107, 110–112, 113, 114, 120–121, 123–124, 125, 127, 133, 135, 150
assassination attempt (1954), 101
death (1969), 133
as dictator, 99, 110, 114
and economy, 117–118
education of, 99–100
foreign policy, 103, 104, 106, 114, 119–124, 127, 129, 130
and Free Officers, 89, 90, 100
and Israel, 92, 100, 102, 104, 111, 131, 132
opposition to, 98, 101, 121, 123
and RCC, 95, 97, 98, 99
and Suez Canal, 107, 109
See also Arab socialism
Nasirism, 111, 139, 147, 148
Nasirites, 112, 120, 121, 124, 134, 158, 159
Nasser, Gamal Abd. *See* Nasir, al-, Gamal Abd
National Assembly, 121, 128, 134, 138. *See also* People's Assembly
National Committee of Workers and Students, 85
National Congress of Popular Forces (1961), 119
National Democratic party, 153, 158, 163
Nationalism, 26, 30, 31, 32, 33, 35, 37, 42, 43, 44, 45–50, 53, 56, 72, 74, 85, 112, 115, 116, 135, 140, 166, 167. *See also* Arab nationalism; National party; Revolutionary movement; Wafd
Nationalizations, 107, 110, 113, 117
National Library, 28
National party, 50, 51–52, 54, 55, 62, 67, 84, 153
National Tribunals, 40
National Union, 110, 113, 117, 119, 131
National university (Giza), 60
National Water Carrier Project (Israel), 121
Nation-state, 5, 44, 165
Navy, 19, 26, 28, 107
Nazli (khedivial princess), 56
Negev, 2(fig.), 102
Nehru, Jawaharlal, 103, 124
Nelson, Horatio, 15
New Kingdom, 4
New Order. *See Nizam-i-Jedid*
Newspapers, 30, 33, 45, 46–47, 50, 52, 60, 96, 117, 138
Newsweek, 140
Nicaea, Council of (325), 5
Night schools, 51
Nile, River, 1, 3–4, 61
Delta, 3, 15, 16, 17, 18, 39, 79, 80(fig.)
flooding, 4, 13, 39, 105
Upper, 19, 28
Valley, 4, 6, 17, 18, 47, 79, 105
Nile Corniche, 104, 148
Nile Hilton Hotel (Cairo), 104, 121
Nixon, Richard M., 131, 132, 142, 145, 146, 160
Nizam-i-Jedid, 16
Nkrumah, Kwame, 124
Noble Rescript of the Rose Chamber (1839), 21
Nomads, 10, 13. *See also* Hyksos
Nonaligned countries, 142
North Africa, 7, 11, 73
Nouvelle revue, La (French weekly), 45
Nubar, Boghos, 29, 40
Numayri, al-, Ja'far, 139
Nuqrashi, al-, Mahmud Fahmi, 69, 77, 84, 85
Nur al-Din, 8

October Paper, 147
October War (1973), 141–143, 145–146, 147, 149
peace conferences, 153, 154–155
Oil, 102, 107, 108, 113, 117, 130, 144, 147, 148, 164–165
embargo (1973), 145, 147
Old Kingdom, 4

Oman, 20, 126(fig.), 150, 152, 156
Opera House (Cairo), 28, 141
Organization of African Unity, 142
Organization of Petroleum
 Exporting Countries, 164
Ottoman Empire, 1, 9–10, 11, 13,
 15, 16, 17, 18, 19, 20–21, 23,
 25, 27, 28, 31, 33, 36, 40, 41,
 43, 45, 46, 49, 51, 53, 58, 70,
 71
Ottoman Land Law (1858), 26

Pakistan, 77, 100, 102, 109
Palestine, 8, 11, 15, 57, 65, 74, 113,
 124
 and Egypt, 71, 77, 79, 82, 86
 partition (1947), 76, 82, 83
 War (1948–1949), 82–83, 85, 127
 See also Arabs, Palestinian; Israel;
 under Great Britain; Jews
Palestine Liberation Organization
 (PLO) (1964), 121, 133, 146,
 149, 154
Palestinian refugees, 83, 102, 130,
 133. *See also* Arabs, Palestinian;
 Fida'iyin
Palmerston, Henry, 20, 21, 25
Pan-Arabism, 112–113, 124, 125
Pan-Islam, 46, 47, 49, 51, 112
Paper, 18
Paris Peace Conference (1919), 57
Parliament, 35, 40, 47, 61, 62, 63,
 64, 68
 dissolved (1952), 96
Party of the nation. *See* Ummah
 party
Peasants, 5, 10, 13, 18, 19, 26, 27,
 30, 38, 39, 48, 62, 63, 68–69,
 86, 92, 93, 116, 118, 148–149,
 164. *See also* Forced labor
Peninsular and Oriental Shipping
 Line, 24
People's Assembly, 141, 152, 158,
 160
People's party, 62, 84
Peres, Shimon, 151
Persians, 4, 11
Pharaonism, 71, 72
Philosophy of the Revolution, The
 (Nasir), 90
Pigs, 4
PLO. *See* Palestine Liberation
 Organization
Poetry, 60
Poland, 72
Police, 87, 122, 134, 167
Political parties, 50, 61, 62, 69, 75,
 84–85, 90, 110, 119, 153, 163
 banned (1952, 156), 96, 110
 opposition, 152, 158
Popular Front for Liberation of
 Palestine, 133
Population, 1, 10, 13, 18, 25, 62,
 105, 112, 119
 1977, 148
 1988, 164
Port cities, 1, 2(fig.), 28, 29, 60,
 148
Port Said, 1, 2(fig.), 29, 68, 109,
 129, 147
Portugal, 10
"Positive Neutrality," 114
Poverty, 38, 63, 68, 80
Private enterprise, 147, 148, 149,
 163, 165
Private property, 116, 164
Protectorate, 58, 59
Ptolemies, 5

Qadhafi, Mu'ammar, 134, 139, 140,
 142, 150
Qasim, Abd al-Karim, 120, 124
Qasr al-Nil Bridge (Cairo), 104
Qur'an, 91, 158, 159
Qusayr, 1, 2(fig.)
Qutb, Sayyid, 123, 158

Radio, 82, 165
Radio Cairo, 103, 106, 107, 138
Railroads, 24, 25, 27, 28, 67
Rainfall, 3
Ramadan, Hafiz, 84

Ramadan, 143
Ramleh (Israel), 83
Ramses auto assembly plant, 112
Ramses Hilton, 148
Ramses II statue (Cairo), 104
Rashid, al-, Harun, 7
Rayon, 63
RCC. *See* Revolutionary Command Council
Reconstruction, 147, 148
Recording studio (Cairo), 60
Red Sea, 1, 2(fig.), 9, 20
Remittances, 123, 147, 149, 156, 164
Repression, 131, 134–135
Republican Decrees, 121
Reshid, Mustafa, 21
Revolutionary Command Council (RCC), 91, 95, 96, 97, 98, 99, 101, 116, 138. *See also* Liberation Rally
Revolutionary court, 96
Revolutionary movement
  1919, 54, 55, 57, 58
  1928, 72
  1952, 74, 79, 90–93, 167
  1971, 134
  See also Urabi Revolution
Rhineland, 72
Rhodes, 83
Rice, 10, 13, 25, 74, 130, 141
Rifqi, Uthman, 34
Riyad, Mustafa, 33, 34, 35, 41, 46
Roads, 18, 29
Rogers, William, 132, 134
Rogers Peace Plan (1969–1970), 132–133, 135, 139
Roman empire, 2, 5, 11
Rommel, Erwin, 73, 137
Roosevelt, Franklin, 146
Roosevelt, Kermit, 99
Rovers, 85
Rural cooperatives, 52, 118, 148
Rushdi, Husayn, 53, 55, 57
Russia, 19, 20–21, 25, 31, 36, 40, 41, 45, 46, 70. *See also* Soviet Union
Russo-Turkish War (1877–1878), 29, 36, 46

Sabri, Ali, 122, 123, 134, 139
Sadat, al-, Anwar, 73, 74, 76, 88, 95, 133–134, 135, 137–138, 139, 140, 149, 151, 154, 157, 159–160, 161, 165, 167
  and Arab states, 142, 145, 147, 148, 149, 150, 152, 155, 156
  assassination (1981), 160
  as dictator, 137, 154
  and foreign policy, 145, 146, 150, 151, 153, 159
  and Free Officers, 89, 90, 96, 137
  and Nasir, 137, 138
  and Nasirism, 147–148
  and Nazis, 137
  nickname, 138
  opposition to, 158–159, 160
  visit to Israel, 152
  See also Corrective Revolution of 15 May 1971; October War
Sadat, al-, Jihan, 139, 151, 159
Sadat, al-, Shaykh, 47
Sa'dist party, 69, 82, 84
Safavids, 9
Sa'id (viceroy of Egypt), 22, 24, 25, 26, 27, 31, 39
Sa'id, al-, Nuri, 75, 120
Sailing ship, 24
St. Mark, 1
Saint-Simon, Claude Henri, 20, 24
Salah al-Din, 8
Salinization, 63, 164
Sallal, al-, Abdallah, 120
Salt tax, 39
Sandstone, 3
Sannu', Ya'qub, 30, 33
Sanusi rebels (Libya), 53
Sa'ud (king of Saudi Arabia), 112, 123
Saudi Arabia, 70, 75, 120, 126(fig.), 149, 155

and Egypt, 112, 120, 123, 125, 130, 132, 135, 142, 148, 157, 163
oil, 102, 107, 113, 117, 144
See also under United States
Sayyid, al-, Ahmad Lutfi, 27, 50, 101
Schönau Castle (Austria), 143
Scientific socialism, 122
Scranton, William, 131
SCUA. *See* Suez Canal Users Association
Scuplture, 60, 104
Secret police, 134, 138
Secret societies, 33, 44, 50, 52, 61, 88, 166
Selim I (sultan), 9
Senegal, 46
Service sector, 68
Seven Years' War (1756–1763), 14
Sewage disposal, 68
Shabab Muhammad, 158
Shadhili, al-, Sa'id al-Din, 143, 144
Shafi'i (imam), 1
Sharaf, Sami, 134
Sha'rawi, Huda, 60
Shari'ah, 43, 44, 47, 69, 72
Sharif, Muhammad, 31, 33, 35, 39
Sharm al-Shaykh, 2(fig.), 109
Sharon, Ariel, 144
Sheep, 4, 39
Shi'is, 7, 8
Shoes, 74
Shuqayri, Ahmad, 121
Shuttle diplomacy, 146, 149
Siddiq, Isma'il, 27
Sidqi, Isma'il, 62, 63, 77, 84
Sinai, 2(fig.), 3, 20, 41, 49, 82, 109, 125, 127, 128, 129, 131, 132, 139, 142, 143, 144, 145, 153, 154, 155
Sirag al-Din, Fu'ad, 153
Sixth imam, 7
Skilled workers, 149, 164, 165
Slaves, 10, 19, 25, 48. *See also* Mamluks; Turkish slave warriors
Soap, 18, 74
Social clubs (British), 49
Social insurance program, 86, 116, 118
Socialism, 113, 116, 117, 120, 139, 167. *See also* Arab socialism; Scientific socialism
Socialist Labor party, 153
Socialist Vanguard, 131
Socialist Youth Organization, 131
Social justice, 116
South America, 10
South Vietnam, 124
Soviet Union, 86, 108, 109, 145
and Egypt, 3, 75, 100, 103, 109, 113, 114, 119, 122, 125–126, 128, 131, 132, 135, 138, 139, 140, 142, 144, 145, 150, 152, 166–167, 168
and Israel, 85, 127
and Middle East, 104, 110, 111, 116, 129, 132
and U.S., 139, 144, 145, 150
See also under Syria
Spain, 10
Spices, 10, 13
Stack, Lee, 61, 77
Stagecoach line, 24
State audit department, 117
State ownership and control, 116, 117, 118, 146, 147, 163
State planning agencies, 116, 163
State security department, 91, 98
Steadfastness and Rejection Front, 153
Steamship, 24
Strikes, 51, 57, 59
Student political activities, 52, 53, 57, 76, 85, 96, 130–131, 141, 158
Students' Day (Feb. 21), 131
Student Union, 131
Subsidies, 116, 118, 150, 151, 167
Sudan, 3, 4, 19, 47, 59, 61, 64, 71, 72, 75, 77, 84, 86, 104, 105, 106, 126(fig.), 152, 156
Anglo-Egyptian, 77, 86, 92

coup (1971), 139, 140
independence (1956), 106
rebellion (1880s), 37–38, 39, 42
Sudanese, 34
Sudetenland, 72
Suez, 1, 2(fig.), 13, 24, 68, 129, 144, 147
Suez, Gulf of, 2(fig.), 149
Suez, Isthmus of, 10, 23, 24, 25
Suez Canal (1869), 1, 25–26, 28, 32, 36, 42, 49, 64, 76–77, 102, 108, 110, 113, 128, 129, 130, 131, 132, 139, 141, 143, 144, 148, 149
crisis (1956), 108–110
reopened (1975), 165
See also under Great Britain
Suez Canal Authority, 108
Suez Canal Company, 29, 36, 52, 60, 106, 108
nationalized (1956), 107
Suez Canal Users Association (SCUA), 108
Sufi brotherhoods, 15, 17
Sugar, 9, 13, 18, 25, 28, 74
Sukarno, 103, 124
Sunnis, 7, 8, 46
Syria, 4, 7, 8, 9, 19, 20, 21, 23, 49, 71, 74, 75, 106, 121, 124–125, 126(fig.), 155, 156
Communists, 113
and Egypt, 111, 112, 118–119, 120, 121, 125, 133, 134, 135, 140, 142, 143, 144
and France, 70
and Israel, 125, 141, 143, 144, 146
and Jordan, 133
and June 1967 War, 127
and October War, 146
revolution (1949), 79
and Soviet Union, 111, 144
Syrian Protestant College (Beirut), 46

Taba, 2(fig.), 49
Taba Affair (1906), 49, 50
Taj al-'arus (Zabidi), 13
Takfir wa al-Hijrah, 158
Taking Sides (Green), 129
Tamerlane. *See* Timur
Tariffs, 68, 116
Tawfiq (khedive of Egypt), 31, 33, 34, 35, 36, 37, 40, 41, 43, 46, 93
Taxes, 6, 10, 11, 13, 17, 30, 31, 39, 48, 68, 117
Tax-farming, 10, 17, 21
Technical Military Academy, 158
Technocrats, 93, 122
Tel Aviv (Israel), 82
Telegraph lines, 24, 28, 30
Tel-el-Kebir, 36–37
Telephones, 30
Television, 165, 168
Terrorism, 149, 164
Textiles, 9, 10, 13, 18, 68
Textile workers riot (1952), 91
Thabit, Karim, 82, 83, 127
Thant, U, 125, 130
Tharwat, Abdal-Khaliq, 59, 62, 84
30 March Program (1968), 131
This Is Your Uncle Gamal (Sadat), 138
Tiberias, Lake, 121
Timur, 9
Tiran, Straits of, 2(fig.), 108, 126
Tobacco, 18
Topography, 3
Toulon (France), 15
Tourism, 48, 114, 141, 148, 156, 157, 164
Trachoma, 68
Trade, 9–10, 13, 21, 28
Transjordan, 74, 75, 82, 83
Transportation, 18, 24, 25, 67, 68, 148
Tripartite Aggression, 109
Tripoli, 19
Tulunids, 7
Tunis (Tunisia), 7
Tunisia, 36, 46, 104
and Egypt, 120

independence (1956), 106
Turco-Egyptian fleet, 19
Turkey, 1, 100, 102, 111, 124, 126(fig.)
Turkish (language), 17
Turkish slave warriors, 6, 11
Turkish titles abolished, 91
Turks, 8, 9, 34, 37, 48, 59
Tutelage system, 131
Twelfth imam, 7
Twelvers, 7

UAR. *See* United Arab Republic
Ubayd, Makram, 75, 80, 84
Ulama, 10, 11, 15, 16, 17, 30, 72, 88
Ummah, 72
Ummah party, 50, 51, 53, 56
Sudanese, 77, 86
Underemployment, 63
UNEF. *See* United Nations Emergency Force
Unemployment, 63, 164
Union party, 62
United Arab Airlines, 125
United Arab Republic (UAR) (1958–1961), 111, 112, 114, 117, 118–119, 120
United Nations, 76, 77, 83, 87, 101, 108, 110, 126, 127, 129, 144
Resolution 242 (1967), 129–130, 131, 132, 135, 139
United Nations Emergency Force (UNEF), 125
United States, 28, 46, 70, 107, 139
and Arab states, 102
and communism, 111, 139
and Egypt, 3, 58, 81, 90, 92, 99, 100, 101, 103, 104, 105, 106–107, 108, 111–112, 113, 114, 119–120, 122, 124, 127, 129, 132, 138–139, 142, 144, 146, 147, 150, 151, 156, 157, 163, 166, 167–168
and Israel, 102, 109, 129, 131, 132, 139, 142, 144, 146, 147, 150, 155, 167
and Lebanon, 111, 112
and Middle East, 110, 111, 121, 132, 139
and Saudi Arabia, 124, 139, 145
Zionists, 122
See also under Soviet Union
Universal male suffrage, 96
University of al-Azhar (Cairo), 1, 7, 11, 13, 30, 56, 69
Unkiar-Iskelesi treaty (1833), 21
Upper Egypt, 99, 104
Urabi, Ahmad, 26, 34, 35, 36, 37, 38, 43, 45, 46, 110
Urabi Revolution (1879–1882), 34, 50, 56, 167
Urban areas, 13, 29–30. *See also* Port cities
Uthman, Uthman Amin, 138, 147

Vance, Cyrus, 155
Venice (Italy), 8
Victoria (queen of England), 47
Virgin Mary, 130
"Voice of the Arabs" broadcasts, 103

Wafd, 55, 57, 58, 59, 60, 61, 64, 75, 77, 79, 81, 85, 86, 87, 91, 96, 97
neo-, 153
opposition to, 62, 63, 69, 74, 80, 84, 88, 92
reforms, 86, 100
Wafdist bloc, 84
Wahhabis, 19, 23
Waqfs, 92, 116, 158
War Ministry, 34
War of Attrition (1969), 132–133, 139
Warships, 18
Water, 27, 30, 68
Waterfowl, 4
Wazir, 8
Weirs, 18
West Bank, 83, 127, 154, 155, 156, 159, 166

Western Desert, 2(fig.), 3, 80(fig.)
Westernization, 16, 18, 22, 23, 24, 29–30, 31, 32, 37, 44, 115, 116, 159, 167
West Germany, 119, 122
West Indies, 10
Wheat, 10, 13, 74, 119, 122, 141, 151
White Nile, 105
White Paper (1939), 72
Wilson, Woodrow, 58
Wingate, Reginald, 57
Women, 57, 60, 85, 110, 119, 159
Woolen cloth, 10, 13
World Bank, 105, 148
World War I (1914–1918), 53–54, 55, 71
World War II (1939–1945), 72–75, 137
Writers, 30, 60, 86, 142

Xenophobia, 44

Yakan, Adli, 58, 59, 62, 84
Yamit (Israel), 2(fig.), 142, 153
Yemen, 1, 10, 13, 75, 106, 126(fig.)
  revolution (1948), 79
  and UAR, 114, 120, 123, 130, 150
Young Egypt, 75, 79, 84–85, 87, 89, 96, 97
Young Turk Revolution (1908), 51
Yugoslavia, 125
Yunis, Mahmud, 108
Yusuf, Shaykh Ali, 46, 47, 50

Zabidi, al-, Murtada, 13
Zaghlul, Sa'id, 26, 50, 54, 56–58, 59, 60, 61, 63, 84
Zakat, 117
Zebu cattle, 4
Zionism, 71, 74, 91, 100, 103, 107, 110, 168